Commun

Also by Henry Tam

Punishment, Excuses and Moral Development
The Citizens' Agenda
Marketing, Competition and the Public Sector
Serving the Public
Responsibility and Personal Interactions: A Philosophical Study of the Criteria for Responsibility Ascriptions

Communitarianism

A New Agenda for Politics and Citizenship

Henry Tam

First published 1998 by
MACMILLAN PRESS LTD
Houndmills, Basingstoke, Hampshire RG21 6XS
and London
Companies and representatives
throughout the world

ISBN 0–333–67482–0 hardcover
ISBN 0–333–67483–9 paperback

A catalogue record for this book is available
from the British Library.

10   9   8   7   6   5   4   3   2   1
07   06   05   04   03   02   01   00   99   98

Copy-edited and typeset by Povey–Edmondson
Tavistock and Rochdale, England

Printed in Hong Kong

Contents

Preface

It is not uncommon in political discourse for a new set of ideas to gain wider currency and lose clarity of meaning at the same time. Some may even suggest that the two are inextricably linked. Such is the fate which has befallen the theory of communitarianism. Just when communitarian ideas are beginning to secure widespread recognition and political influence, they have also become frequently distorted and misunderstood. This is partly due to the fact that, although a number of thinkers have written about particular aspects of communitarianism, there is no single text which draws the different elements into a critical synthesis. In the absence of such a reference point, communitarianism has been attacked for whatever its opponents take it to mean, regardless of what it may actually imply.

My aim in writing this book is to bring together the different strands of communitarian ideas which have been developing in Europe and America and formulate a unified theory which carries clear implications for practical reforms. Central to my exposition is the ideal of 'inclusive communities', based on the three communitarian principles of co-operative enquiry, mutual responsibility, and citizen participation. I want to argue that we should move beyond the outmoded Left–Right divide, and recognize that the real challenge before us is to find a viable alternative to both individualist and authoritarian approaches to social and political problems. The politics of building inclusive communities is put forward to meet this challenge.

The book sets out what communitarianism is about at three interrelated levels. First, there is the theoretical level where the key communitarian principles and their implications for the evaluation of conflicting claims, the identification of common values, and the reform of power structures, are examined. Second, at the policy level, those principles are applied to questions concerning the education, work opportunities and protection which should be secured for all members of inclusive communities as the basic condition of citizenship. Third, at the organization level, I turn to what citizens involved with institutions in the state sector, the business sector, and the third sector of voluntary and community groups can do to bring about the necessary reforms.

One of the difficulties in presenting any social and political theory is maintaining a good balance between breadth and depth. Without adequate breadth, a theory could be mistaken as only applicable to a small sub-set of issues. This has been one of the problems with many books on communitarian ideas, which give the impression that these ideas are just about the decline of community spirit in American cities in recent years. In fact, a rich tradition of communitarian ideas can be found in Europe, especially amongst British and French thinkers, and they have long provided inspiration to people who reject the pseudo-freedom preached by individualists as much as the oppressive conformity glorified by authoritarians. Accordingly, I have brought a much wider range of communitarian ideas to bear on my arguments, and have drawn examples from a variety of countries, many of which have developed communitarian practices independently from America. The result, I hope, is a comprehensive picture of communitarian reforms and their applications to, not just community and voluntary action, but action by government and commercial organizations. Furthermore, it should establish that it is not just families and schools in neighbourhood communities which should be measured against the yardstick of 'inclusive community', but also employers, unions, protective agencies, multinational corporations, and any organization which can impact on the physical, moral, or intellectual development of citizens across the world.

Lack of sufficient depth can pose a different kind of problem. Books on communitarian philosophy tend to provide intricate conceptual analyses, but seldom penetrate beyond that to real life problems, and it is difficult for students of politics to discern their practical relevance. On the other hand, populist books and think-tank pamphlets focus sharply on specific issues such as moral education, parenting skills or corporate responsibility, and they have been criticized for offering quick and simplistic solutions with little intellectual substance. By contrast, I have attempted to articulate and defend the key communitarian principles, and then apply them to tackling an interrelated set of practical problems. What I want to show is that there is a unified worldview which can be deployed against individualist and authoritarian arguments, and guide us in reforming current social and political practices for the better. Of course, the depth in holistic exposition I strive for is different from the depth of the single discipline specialist. Inevitably, there are detailed arguments and case studies which I could not address at length in a book with the intended scope. However, the bibliographical references should provide a useful guide to where much more extensive treatment is given to particular topics.

In writing this book, I am conscious of the considerable intellectual debt I owe to the forerunners of communitarian ideas. I would mention in particular L. T. Hobhouse, Emile Durkheim and John Dewey for their contributions to the development of a communitarian form of liberalism in opposition to the individualistic liberalism which is so destructive of all that is good about community life. I am also grateful to the many contemporary theorists and practitioners who helped me set up the Communitarian Forum in 1995 which has enabled a wide range of issues concerning the development of inclusive communities to be discussed under conditions of co-operative enquiry. As Chair of the Forum, I have been fortunate in being able to draw on the ideas and support of the members of our Advisory Council, particularly Professor Peter Atteslander (Swiss Academy for Development), Professor Ferdinand Kinsky (Centre International de Formation Européenne, France), Andrew Phillips (Citizenship Foundation, UK), Professor Benjamin Barber (Walt Whitman Center for Democracy, USA), and Professor Amitai Etzioni (Center for Communitarian Policy Studies, USA).

Many other people helped me turn the ideas I have been discussing in the Communitarian Forum into the present work. I would like to thank my publisher Steven Kennedy for his advice on the style and structure to adopt for writing this book; Charles Handy, Robert E. Goodin and David Marquand for their encouraging remarks upon reading early drafts of the book; Terry McLaughlin, Jonathan Boswell, Tony Skillen, John Stewart, Chris Ormell and Antony Duff for the discussions we had on particular communitarian arguments; Carole Ulanowsky, Kevin Healy, Jonathan Pinkney-Baird and Chris Thorpe for their support in furthering communitarian debates; and the students from the Universities of Oxford and Cambridge who participated actively in a number of seminars convened to discuss communitarianism.

Finally, and most importantly, this book could not have been written without the support of my family. Celia's encouragement and the understanding of our young daughters, Jessica and Antonia, have been vital for me in keeping up with the tight schedule. To them, and Celia's parents, Alan and Gwenda, who have always been there for us, a big thank you.

HENRY TAM

1
What is Communitarianism?

The subjection of human beings to oppressive power structures is an evil from which we are supposed to have been delivered by the gospel of market forces. By cutting back collective constraints and encouraging individuals to pursue their own interests in the marketplace, we were told, the freedom of all would expand more than ever before. In the aftermath of the 1989 revolutions and the collapse of totalitarian regimes in Eastern Europe and the Soviet Union, the ascendancy of market individualism as the supreme global ideology did momentarily offer the promise of liberation across the world. Yet when the dust of the crumbling Berlin Wall settled, the spectre of oppression remained depressingly clear for all to see.

Under the new world order of market individualism, social and political power is concentrated even more in those in command of material wealth. Those lacking the skills or motivation to secure increasing economic resources are marginalized, and their needs are viewed as being parasitic on the welfare support made available by the economically powerful. To justify the disintegration of community life that follows from such stark economic polarization, market individualists insist it is their approach that has helped to achieve an unprecedented growth in the production and consumption of material wealth, and warn that any attempt to replace this approach would necessitate the imposition of values and systems on individuals, leading inevitably to authoritarianism (Hayek, 1944; Friedman, 1962; Nozick, 1974; Bosanquet, 1989).

The idea that politics can only be carried out in line with either individualism or authoritarianism has increasingly come to be accepted, on the one hand, by conventional political parties, drifting towards the individualist 'give-the-customers-whatever-they-want' 'centre ground' and, on the other hand, by extremist groups

1

determined to secure their fundamentalist objectives without the slightest concern for working towards a wider consensus. However, since the late 1980s, this false dichotomy has come under concerted attack from a range of political theorists who share what is now generally described as the 'communitarian' perspective (Marquand, 1988; Miller, 1990; Galston, 1991; Walzer, 1992; Boswell, 1994; Tam, 1995a; Etzioni, 1995b; Barber, 1995). In rejecting both authoritarian practices and individualist ideas, communitarians point to the need for a new agenda for politics and citizenship. They set out the ways in which a much more inclusive form of community should be developed, socially and politically, to overcome the corrosive effects of individualism, and protect all citizens from authoritarian threats.

In Europe and America communitarian networks have been set up to promote ideas and practices across party political boundaries. Commentators have observed that politicians engaging with communitarian themes come from all parts of the traditional Left–Right spectrum (Steinfels, 1992; Phillips, 1993; Winkler, 1994; Cohen, 1995). In Germany, for example, Rudolf Scharping of the Social Democrats, Kurt Biedenkopf of the Christian Democratic Party, and Joschka Fischer of the Green Party, have all made pro-communitarian statements (Etzioni, 1995b, p. ix; Scharping, 1996). In the United Kingdom, not only are the Labour Prime Minister Tony Blair, and the Leader of the Liberal Democrats, Paddy Ashdown, enthusiastic about communitarian ideas, but supporters of those ideas can also be found in the Conservative Party (Baxter, 1995; Walker, 1995; Etzioni, 1997, ch. 3, n. 72). In America, support for the communitarian movement has been voiced by Democrats such as Vice President Al Gore and Senator Daniel Patrick Moynihan, and Republicans such as Senator Alan Simpson and Jack Kemp, who served as Secretary of Housing and Urban Development under President Bush (Barnes, 1991; *Responsive Community*, 1991/2, pp. 21–6). In the former Soviet Union, Mikhail Gorbachev, who led the way in dismantling authoritarian rule in his country and its Eastern European neighbours, maintains that the world must now look beyond individualism for a sustainable alternative to authoritarianism:

It is vital that we develop a common global policy for the new era . . . While we must calmly analyse the dangers of collectivism, we must do the same for the individualism of the West. Changes in the world must affect and alter the consumerist direction of Western culture. . . . The crisis of modern civilisation has done immense damage to mankind. It has undermined social instinct, family values, moral principles. This trend is evil as it tends towards the self-destruction of mankind. (Gorbachev, 1993, p. 14)

The call to refocus on the importance of community life needs, of course, to be backed by an analysis of the prevailing problems, and a programme of reforms, or the rhetorical embrace of communitarian ideas by politicians would merely mask the absence of action to change society for the better. The purpose of this book is to explain why the hegemony of market individualism must now be brought to an end, and why communitarianism offers a viable alternative that avoids authoritarian pitfalls. It aims to bring together communitarian ideas developed by a wide range of thinkers; formulate a critical synthesis about the kind of inclusive community we should strive for, with its implications for the education, work opportunities, and protection to be secured for all citizens; and suggest how the agenda for change can be advanced through action in the state, business and third sectors.

Central Communitarian Concerns

What lies at the heart of the communitarian objection to market individualism is the latter's cancerous effects on community life. Human beings who are in control of more economic resources than others are able to set the agenda for everyone from a privileged bargaining position. They can make substantial private 'donations' to those in government; they can distort public opinion by buying control of the media; and they can subdue all those who are dependent on the employment, investment or purchases they offer, by threatening to withdraw them. Others have to conform to their demands, or risk losing the income they need to look after themselves and their families. So out of fear and insecurity, people work under greater stress and for longer hours, which in turn leads to the neglect of children by overtired parents, to family breakdowns, and to a dwindling sense of responsibility for the well-being of others (Etzioni, 1995b; Young and Halsey, 1995). Selfishness becomes a moral creed. Individuals are encouraged at every turn to put their own interests first, and to demand the freedom to make their own choices regardless of the implications for the civic order. Like an infected cell, the ethos of putting the needs of oneself above the needs of others spreads to every aspect of social life, and the ability of communities to rely on their members' readiness to give support to each other is gradually destroyed from within (Marquand, 1988; Selbourne, 1994).

The trade-off between economic prosperity and community neglect has become untenable, not just because of increasing doubts about the system's ability to deliver sustainable economic growth, but because even with the growth that has been achieved, the harm to community life through the marginalization of those with job insecurity, low pay – or no job at all – has reached a point where it can no longer be tolerated (Dahrendorf, 1995; Gray, 1995a). For those who feel that they can barely keep up with the relentless demands of market competition, a variety of anti-community dispositions are manifesting themselves. There is growing apathy about established political mechanisms, the readiness to vote or participate in civic deliberation is in decline, and the numbers engaged in communal activities have fallen steadily (Putnam, 1995; Knight and Stokes, 1996). The sense of futility, of not being able to contribute anything to the prevailing social order, or to change the oppressive distribution of power, breeds a drop-out culture. More and more people turn to alcohol and drugs to shut out of their consciousness a reality that alienates them. They do not see any hope for the future, and refuse to share any responsiblity for the way it develops. Related to this withdrawl from engagement in collective obligations is the rise in disrepect for the law. From petty theft to business frauds, from vandalism to violent attacks against the vulnerable, the criminal code itself is coming to be viewed as just another set of state-imposed regulations which interfere with what individuals can get away with in pursuit of their own interests. Not surprisingly, the fear of crime has risen despite increased expenditure on law and order, and has spread extensively to rural as well as urban areas.

Although individualist defenders of the dominant socioeconomic system may suggest that the trade-off will, in time, become more favourable when economic growth is fuelled by even greater marketization of the public domain, it is precisely their dismissal of civic discourse that prevents them from seeing why the trade-off is in fact structured in an inherently unacceptable way. By denigrating all attempts to articulate the public good as authoritarian intervention, by removing decisions from civic forums and reducing them to private bargains between individuals, and by evaluating the trade-off solely in terms of what can be quantified economically, the individualist outlook systematically denies that there can be a public perspective by which the outcomes of individual transactions can be criticized. Yet what individuals want for themselves in isolation from others can in fact seriously undermine what they need as fellow members of a community. Even if a majority of individuals get what they want superficially, the negative impact on others remains a moral problem for which they must take responsibility. What is needed is a reconstruction of our political processes so that citizens are no longer trapped in the unequal bargaining positions they have as individuals, but are enabled to participate as members of an inclusive community in determining what constitutes the common good, and how it is to be pursued (Barber, 1984; Habermas, 1984; Giddens, 1994).

The claim that, by establishing am economic 'level playing field', everyone would have equal freedom, playing by the same rules, to pursue their own interests distorts social reality on two counts. First, the rules are not neutral. They are geared to benefit those good at the economic game of market transactions. Those who might otherwise score highly in non-economic terms are simply told that their game does not count any longer. It is analogous to a federation of basketball players imposing the rules of their game on the players of all other sports, on the grounds that it would be unfair, for example, for football players to have larger teams and be able to use their feet, and so on. When players of other sports demand that, in return, basketball players should play to *their* rules, they are told that, for the sake of fairness and efficiency, there should be just one set of rules for everyone. Second, being forced to play a game for which one has not developed the necessary skills means, in the real world, being relegated to the lower social divisions. This is not so much a matter of comparative competitiveness as a question of how power is structured to the permanent disadvantage of those whose abilities are not readily translatable into material wealth. No amount of pseudo-scientific economic modelling can legitimise such structures (Ormerod, 1994).

The crude value system of the individualist world order also measures human progress in the most blinkered terms, focusing on 'growth' in material production and consumption but neglecting the vital environmental and social factors that are the common concerns of all communities (Doyal and Gough, 1991; Twine, 1994). The economic growth so dear to market individualists is already, among other things, helping to double the level of carbon dioxide in the atmosphere. It is anticipated that the resulting climate change and rise in water levels will threaten the homes of around 100 million of the world's poorest people. This economic growth has been achieved by a global market system which forces economically weak countries to concentrate on cash crops such as coffee and cotton, which are useless to the millions who are starving. It is also a system that promotes the military capability of conflicting groups and nations. The number of international refugees has gone up from 1 million in 1963 to 27 million in 1995. In fact, despite the much trumpeted removal of the Soviet threat to world peace, the arms business worldwide at US$80 million a year shows no sign of declining (Vidal and Harvey, 1996).

Business dealings with oppressive regimes demonstrate that market individualists' opposition to authoritarianism is confined to areas where authoritarian action may threaten to harm the interests of the economically powerful. Where this does not apply, the expanding market system has little interest in tackling authoritarianism in, for example, the tortures of political dissenters, the cultural oppression of women, or the abuse of children. Indeed, if certain economically powerful groups were to benefit from the authoritarian practices in question – hardline repression of those who speak out against pro-market regimes, discrimination against women to achieve greater labour flexibility, and forcing children to work for low wages in inhumane working conditions – the economic elites might even lend their support, quite legitimately on individualist grounds, to those implementing the practices. Far from providing the best safeguard against authoritarian oppression, the individualist world order provides selective sanctuary to any oppressor with whom the economic elites can do profitable business. Thus the triumph of market individualism will not turn the world into one big, peaceful marketplace (Fukuyama, 1992); instead, its commercially motivated coexistence with all forms of oppressive power strucutres would drive more and more people to violence and extremism to break out of their predicament, unless communities are able to pursue their common values through truly democratic interactions (see Giddens, 1994, ch. 9).

The Communitarian Alternative

In order to provide an alternative to both individualism and authoritarianism, communitarianism sets out the ways in which social and political practices are to be reformed in relation to their contributions to the development of sustainable forms of community life. It is based on three central principles. First, any claim about what is to be accepted as true can only be validated under conditions of co-operative enquiry. Second, common values validated by communities of co-operative enquirers should form the basis of mutual responsibilities to be undertaken by all members of those communities. Third, power relations at every level in society must be reformed so that all those affected by them can participate as equal citizens in determining how the power in question is to be exercised.

What communitarians advocate is the transformation of prevailing attitudes and conditions in society in order to build *inclusive communities* which respect all three principles. This means that questions about what collective action is to be taken for the common good are not to be left either to political elites who are rarely answerable to their fellow citizens (perhaps once every four or five years), or to individuals in the marketplace, but are considered through informed community discussions. Questions about values are not allowed to be hijacked by authoritarians who want to impose their views on others, or to be ignored in the name of liberal neutrality, but are dealt with by citizens themselves deliberating over what values and responsibilities they share. It also means that power relations are not to be protected or altered for the exclusive benefit of any particular religious, racial, gender, or socioeconomic group, but they are to be continuously revised to approximate the conditions wherein all citizens can play a constructive part in applying collective power in pursuit of common values.

People live in overlapping communities, with varying degrees of emotive ties and subject to different power relations. These communities may range from an extended family, a school, a neighbourhood, a research society, a professional group, a co-operative or a business enterprise, to a region, a country, an international association or a global network. The memberships of some of these groupings are voluntary, but others are largely determined by external circumstances. In both cases, it is operative power relations that shape the interactions of community members. Those who find themselves in oppressive power relations will suffer either moral degradations as oppressors, or ill-treatment as the oppressed. This may occur in an authoritarian state where those in control dictate to the rest how they should live; in an anarchic labour market, where individuals with little bargaining power have to bow to the demands of employers; in hierarchical organizations, where directives from above are not to be questioned; or in a family, where a woman can be beaten for disagreeing with her husband. Oppression can take diverse forms, and the pain and alienation it causes may vary in different cases. But oppression is unavoidable if the potential for community life is not safeguarded by communitarian principles.

Although community life is essential for human fulfilment, not all communities enable their members to attain that fulfilment. Inclusive communities are to be distinguished from other forms of community by their operative power relations, which enable all their members to participate in collective processes affecting their lives. Any community that requires or allows some of its members to be excluded from participating in its deliberations, in effect cuts off the flow of communications without which the potential for mutual enrichment of ideas and feelings cannot be realized. Human beings need to relate to others on a sustained basis to develop their experience of love, collaborate in the discovery of truths, establish justice, and expand on their opportunities for genuine fulfilment. Only inclusive communities which respect their members as having equal shares of the overall power for determining collective action, and welcome their exercise of that power, can ensure that what people need from community life will be attained in practice.

In order to build inclusive communities in every sphere, and at every level of social existence, communitarian politics requires the development of citizens who can take part in co-operative enquiries determining a wide range of issues; who recognize that they share a respect for common values and accept the responsibilities these values imply; and who actively support the transformation of power relations for the common good. Such development must involve changes to the way citizens are educated, engaged in productive work for their communities, and enabled to protect themselves from the threats to their common values.

Let us first look at education. Inclusive communities can only be sustained by citizens who have been brought up with the abilities and motivation to carry out their responsibilities. Since the nature of co-operative enquiry is incompatible with indoctrination, each new generation must be educated in a way that encourages them to develop their understanding of how they should live, through responding constructively as well as critically to ideas put forward by others. This involves parents, schools, employers and government bodies adopting the most effective practices for developing the moral and rational faculties of the young.

Parents must recognize that to have children is to take on a major social responsibility. Whatever they might wish to do has to be considered in relation to the possible effects on their children. Unless one parent is abusive towards the other or the children, or is incapable of behaving responsibly – which may necessitate separation for the sake of the abused spouse or neglected children – parents should weigh their children's need for a stable family environment against their own lifestyle preferences. It is in families where loving care, clear expectations of responsible behaviour, open discussions, co-operative approaches to problem solving, and shared enjoyments are present that children can develop their appreciation of shared values and respect for others.

All educational institutions, from playgroups and nurseries to schools and universities, need to accept that they have a vital responsibility for the character formation of the young. Those who step back from this responsibility in the name of liberal neutrality expose young people to every kind of influence except for that of their educators. The myth that the teaching of common values must involve authoritarian assumptions can be discarded once methods of co-operative enquiry are adopted by teachers. Of course, there are disagreements over specific moral issues, but there is also substantial common ground on which shared values can be built. No teacher should feel hesitant about taking on the commitment to teach young people the values of love and compassion for others, the critical quest for truth, the pursuit of fairness, and personal fulfilment. The real challenge is to enable pupils to develop the skills and confidence in exploring how these are best realized in practice.

Parents and schools should in turn receive support from employers and state bodies to carry out their educative responsibilities. Employers should acknowledge that where the demands of work conflict with the responsibilities of parenthood, they must play their part in changing economic conditions and workplace practices that currently require all too many parents to work long hours because they cannot otherwise survive financially. Governments should help employers work together to improve conditions so that the endeavours of caring employers are not undermined by irresponsible ones. They should also play a leading role in ensuring that parenting and education standards are raised through the setting of evolving standards and the extensive dissemination of best practices. The nature of communitarian education will be looked at in detail in Chapter 3.

Turning to the issue of work opportunities for citizens, the distribution of productive work poses a problem that must be tackled. Work is needed to convert resources into goods and services sought by communities, to provide a source of income, and to give people a means of fulfilling their potential in applying their talents. When some community members have little prospect of securing work opportunities, they become increasingly excluded from community life. They are marginalized not just because they lack the financial resources to gain access to a wide range of activities, but rather because they are perceived as being deficient in not making a fair contribution to the well-being of their fellow citizens.

The conditions that deprive millions of people of the opportunity to engage in productive work cannot be overturned by individuals on their own. Neither can they be dealt with by a few large business corporations or government departments operating in isolation from those affected by these conditions. The task demands the embodiment of communitarian principles in the working of every organization in the economy, in the private as well as the public sector. Companies must learn to treat their workers, suppliers and customers, as well as their senior management and shareholders, as members of a shared community. Strategies to improve and sustain the well being of all members should be developed through co-operative enquiry carried out by those members, so that the experience, insight and interests of every member can be drawn into the deliberative process.

Governments, for their part, would need to support the development of participatory mechanisms for businesses, financial institutions, trade associations, worker representatives and professional groups, to co-operate at a local, regional, national and global level. Co-operation in this context does not mean bargaining to secure the best advantages for one's own group with minimal concessions to others, but to developing shared values and long-term goals so that each is ready to contribute to the well-being of the whole enterprise.

Crucially, the interpretation of what is for the good of the business is not to be left to an inner core with no accountability to others, but is to be determined with the help of all those affected by the practical consequences of such deliberations. Communitarian reforms of economic relationships are considered in Chapter 4.

In addition to providing appropriate educative support and work opportunities, communitarian citizenship is concerned with enabling citizens to protect themselves without having to rely on some group or agency that might usurp their power. All members of inclusive communities are to be informed not only of their entitlements in terms of the level of personal and environmental protection they can rightly expect, but they are also to be made aware of their responsibility to protect their fellow citizens from harm, to meet the basic needs of those who cannot provide for themselves, and to safeguard opportunities for co-operative enquiries among themselves.

Citizens need to have much more involvement in shaping protective policies and practices. Instead of allowing professional politicians to alarm voters by claiming that too much, or too little, is being spent on tackling different kinds of threat to their well-being, citizens should be encouraged to participate in non-party political deliberations about the nature of these threats, the resources being deployed, and where improvements are needed. Through such deliberations, citizens should also become more active in community-based initiatives to detect dangers and alert those with specific authority to deal with them. Far from leaving protective duties completely to state agencies, citizens should be reminded of their own role in keeping their communities safe from prejudices, discrimination, violence, poverty, diseases and pollution. They must behave responsibly themselves, if the resources they pool together are to be most cost-effectively targeted at problems beyond their immediate control.

Preventative measures are particularly needed to stop the spread of diseases, tensions giving rise to violent conflicts, environmental degradations, and poverty leading to social alienation. Citizens should not just take appropriate measures to deal with these; they should also learn to see the connections between these threats to their common values, and develop holistic approaches to dealing with them. One of the most important connections is to be found at the global level. Marginalizing poor communities, instead of helping them to become active members of the global community, leads to problems for all citizens.

The weak and the vulnerable, wherever they are, must be helped to cope with the particular difficulties they face. Those with the potential for recovery, in terms of their health or economic circumstances, should be assisted to do so. Charities which merely alleviate the symptoms are no substitute for developmental support which can restore to citizens the capacity to participate as full members of their communities. Those who cannot recover should not only be supported in coping with their physical or economic disadvantages, but also be empowered to develop their views and to continue to participate in discussions on matters affecting them and their fellow citizens.

Inclusive communities do not turn away from their responsibilities towards their members. This commitment is to apply even to those who pose a threat to their community through behaviour that undermines common values. Violence, discrimination, theft, deception, negligence or recklessness, for example, can in different ways deprive people of opportunities to secure loving relationships, adequate understanding, fair treatment, and fulfilling experiences in life. Those guilty of antisocial behaviour should be made to see the harm they do to others, and learn to change their attitudes and inclinations as part of the process of becoming reintegrated into the wider community. In extreme cases, some individuals may have to be detained indefinitely to prevent further harm to others; in most cases, however, the objective must be to minimize the numbers in any community who are branded 'criminals', through effective preventative and reformative measures. This can only be achieved in conjunction with the development of communitarian educational and work opportunities for all citizens. The communitarian approach to the protection of citizens will be looked at further in Chapter 5.

The Three Communitarian Principles

In order to build inclusive communities, reforms of educational, economic and protective arrangements in society should be guided by the three communitarian principles which deal, respectively, with co-operative enquiry, mutual responsibility, and citizen participation. These three principles apply the ideas developed by communitarian thinkers to the three interrelated problems of how claims about what should be believed are to be judged, what common values should shape the responsibilities to be undertaken by all citizens, and how existing power relations are to be transformed.

Co-operative Enquiry

The communitarian principle of co-operative enquiry requires that any claim to truth may be judged to be valid only if informed participants deliberating together under conditions of co-operative enquiry would accept that claim. No individual can, in isolation from the independent cross-checking of evidence and reasoning which can only be carried out by other people, legitimately declare any claim to be indisputably true. The objectivity of claims to the truth can only be secured through open communication between people engaged in a common enquiry. The provisional consensus reached by one group of individuals must be open to possible revision resulting from input by other groups. The ultimate strength of any claim to the truth thus rests, not with the confidence of individuals or with their social status, but with the likelihood of that claim surviving the critical deliberations of ever-expanding circles of co-operative enquirers.

Although, in practice, many claims can legitimately be accepted without having to go through a long process of re-examination by different groups, the validity of acceptance still depends on the probability of the consensus in support of the claim being backed by further enquiries. This is why, when a particular claim is challenged, the likelihood of new evidence or reasoning being introduced is a key factor in judging whether a new enquiry is worth conducting. This applies as much to a verdict pronouncing someone guilty of murder, as to a policy declaring certain levels of radiation to be safe. Under conditions of co-operative enquiry, all those who participate in the enquiry should have access to relevant information, be able to put forward their views without intimidation, be allowed to question what others have suggested, and learn from their common deliberations to formulate an agreed judgement on the validity of the claims in question.

In the past, too many communities have been ruled by elites who proclaim their claims to the truth as being beyond all criticism. By invoking 'knowledge' derived from family connections, divine transmission, or their unique understanding of some indisputable text, they would forbid others from discussing their ideas, let alone suggesting alternatives. Across the world, such communities still exist. They demand the unquestioning acceptance of the norms imposed by the elite, and any indication of a possible challenge is met with stigmatization, if not direct persecution. The imposed cohesion of such communities is utterly incompatible with the requirement for open community deliberations. However, for some people, such imposed cohesion is the only way to secure strong community life. Francis Fukuyama, for example, writing of the American political experience, claims that:

in an intellectual climate that weakens the possibility of belief in any *one* doctrine because of an overriding commitment to be open to *all* the world's beliefs and 'value systems', it should not be surprising that the strength of community life has declined in America . . . This suggests that no fundamental strengthening of community life will be possible unless individuals give back certain of their rights to communities, and accept the return of certain historical forms of intolerance. (Fukuyama, 1992, p. 326)

Such a view is a direct consequence of the common failure among social commentators to recognize that authoritarianism is not the only alternative to the 'anything goes' relativist attitude born out of misguided individualist neutrality. It has led people such as Fukuyama to think that attempts to strengthen community life must involve resurrecting some traditional forms of community with in-built dogmas and intolerance. It is neither dogmatic intolerance nor blind tolerance of all claims being equally valid, but the critical selection of true claims by means of open exchange, which holds the key to identifying specific beliefs and values on which to anchor a strong community life.

Common Values and Mutual Responsibility

The communitarian principle of mutual responsibility requires all members of any community to take responsibility for enabling each other to pursue common values. Unlike relativists, who think that people's values are so different that there is no sense in talking about common values, communitarians believe that certain types of value have stood the test of time across different cultural variations. Where conditions of co-operative enquiry have prevailed, a consistent consensus has been maintained over four types of deeply valued human experience.

First, there are the experiences of loving and being loved, caring for others, passion, tenderness, friendship, sympathy, kindness, compassion and devotion. These can be grouped together as the *value of love*. Second, there are the experiences of understanding, clarity of thought, being able to think for oneself, to weigh evidence, and to make good judgements. These constitute the *value of wisdom*. Third, there are the experiences of being fairly treated by others, of being able to relate to others without any sense of discrimination or subjugation, and of knowing that reciprocal relationships are respected. These values are encapsulated in the golden rule 'do as you would be done by', to be found in the core moral code of every advanced culture. It is the *value of justice*. Finally, there are the experiences of developing and realizing one's potential, being able to enjoy oneself, to feel satisfied, and to take pride in one's actions and achievements. These can be viewed together as the *value of fulfilment*.

While these four types of value do not cover all possible values, they are so well established that they provide a clear basis for defining our mutual responsibilities to each other. If an individual values something that goes against these common values – for example, the persecution of a minority in society – then there would be a *prima facie* case to take action against any attempt to pursue that value. It follows from the recognition of such values that our range of mutual responsibilities would cover looking after our dependents, extending help to those who would otherwise be neglected, respecting evidence and coherent reasoning, treating fairly all whom we deal with, developing our own potential, and ensuring the pursuit of our personal goals does not undermine the common values of society.

Common values not only enable individuals within a community to come together to support each other, they also provide the moral bonds that bring diverse communities together in the context of a global community. By contrast, individuals or groups who place their distinctive values above the common values they share with others, run the risk of cutting themselves off from harmonious interactions with others. The wall of exclusion may be erected at the level of a neighbourhood, a tribe, or a country, but in all such cases there is the assumption that the values accepted inside cannot be compared with, nor revised in the light of, values accepted outside. At their best, such groups pursue their own activities and ignore the needs and potential contributions of others. At their worst, they damage the well-being of other communities because, to them only their own well-being is of any significance. Yet such insularity, far from being a sustainable source of values, creates problems that will be destructive of community life. As we approach the twenty-first century, no community on Earth can pretend that what other communities believe and do will have no bearing on its well-being. It can either try in vain to shut out all interactions with 'outsiders', or to work out how best to interact with other communities.

It could be argued, however, that without a shield of insularity, no values can take hold within any given community, not to mention an inclusive community of communities. This would be because values can only be derived from living traditions that have been carried on by particular communities, and the values of different traditions cannot be compared one with another. However, in practice, traditions evolve through what people think and do through the ages. Traditions which fail to sustain vibrant community life because they rely on dogmas and outmoded hierarchies will become discredited. Whether or not more appropriate traditions take root and new means of determining common values emerge will depend on the extent to which communities adopt co-operative enquiry in their collective deliberations.

As for the idea that a moral tradition can only be cultivated within an insular community, historical evidence points unequivocally in the opposite direction. The common values cited above can be traced back thousands of years and across different cultures. Indeed, values such as universal compassion and justice have long been an important part of human history. Their development has in successive ages replaced suspicion and hostility between disparate communities by mutual understanding, respect and collaboration. These values have underpinned healing processes for former enemies, and facilitated exchanges of ideas and practices between strangers. On the basis of such values, every community should behave towards other communities as individuals within them should be encouraged to behave – namely, to bring their beliefs and experiences together in a co-operative spirit to develop and fulfil their mutual responsibilities for the common good.

Communitarian Power Relations

The communitarian principle of citizen participation requires that all those affected by any given power structure are able to participate as equal citizens in determining how the power in question is to be exercised. The power structure could be a neighbourhood community, a school to which one's children are sent, a local authority, a government department, or a multinational corporation. In all cases, power relations should become more democratic.

Communitarian democratization goes far beyond the multiparty electoral competition that characterizes the process of 'democracy' in the Western world. Electoral democracy has been described by Joseph Schumpeter as the 'institutional arrangement for arriving at political decisions in which individuals acquire the power to decide by means of a competitive struggle for the people's vote' (Schumpeter, 1976, p. 269). In this view, democracy has nothing to do with enabling citizens to pursue their common values more effectively, by means of reforming the many overlapping power structures under which they live. It is merely concerned with the periodic allocation of power to a minority of people who seek to rule others. For fear of power being handed to authoritarians who would claim to have exclusive political knowledge of what is to be done for all, electoral democrats place their faith in rules and procedures that prevent the issue of political knowledge being raised at all. There is no question about what is to be done for the good of all, but only what individuals think they can get out of the electoral bargains promised by politicians. Far from developing their understanding of how their shared communities are to be improved, citizens are reduced to being political shoppers who only wonder whether they can secure a few more items for themselves regardless of the implications for others.

In rejecting the attempt to bypass the problem of political knowledge, communitarianism holds that there are non-authoritarian processes through which claims regarding what should be done for the good of all can be evaluated openly and effectively. Such processes would enable all citizens to appreciate the dangers and opportunities they share, and come to a considered view that reflects their common deliberations. Politics would no longer be confined to citizens casting the occasional vote to give power to people to run their public policies and services for four or five years. Instead, it would involve citizens learning about, reviewing, and determining how to reform decision-making processes, in relation to not only government institutions but also businesses and community organizations which may affect their lives.

Barriers must be removed that prevent citizens from having an equal say in the ongoing development of the decision-making processes that affect their lives. It follows that power relations should not retain structural barriers that prevent people from accessing information, putting forward their suggestions, questioning proposals, or sharing in the decision-making processes. The same also applies to cultural barriers which undermine the confidence of certain categories of citizen who seek to participate. Those who lament the loss of deference in society, when what they really object to is the refusal of previously submissive citizens to accept everything done by those in authority, should be reminded that blind deference merely feeds the growth of dictatorships.

In order to democratize power relations, citizens have to engage in action which will alter the political arrangements that govern them. They cannot just retreat into a utopian community of their own making, however benign that may be to its members. A strong ethos of sharing and volunteering may be a positive community feature, but no community that attempts to ignore the political system or disengage itself from the world of business can give its members the moral, intellectual and active development they are capable of attaining. If it is lucky, it may be tolerated as a quirky exception. If not, it will be confronted by government or business action that will undermine its very existence.

The Evolution of Communitarian Ideas

The communitarian principles considered here point clearly to active engagement to bring about change in prevailing social and political practices. The direction of the required change is towards a much more inclusive form of community life than has hitherto been realized. There may be useful lessons to be learnt from the history of human development, but the objective is certainly not to re-create some idealized community of the past. Although communitarianism does connect with past traditions, these are traditions that have consistently championed progressive evolution as the approach to reforming society. They are traditions which look, not backwards to a golden age, but forward to improved conditions of life made possible by the co-operative efforts of citizens. These traditions have evolved in four key phases.

The first phase began in the fourth century BC with Aristotle, who is rightly often cited as a major source of communitarian thinking (Aristotle, 1966, 1987). While recognizing that allowing individuals to exercise power without developing their capabilities to do so could cause serious problems, Aristotle rejected as untenable the claim by his tutor, Plato, that there are objects of higher knowledge beyond the reach of ordinary people (Plato, 1975). The cornerstone of Aristotle's philosophy is that in all discussions about the world and our place in it, we must begin with the world as we experience it. Universal claims can only be accepted if they are backed by evidence concerning the particular. Aristotle's insights also suggest that there are no special realms of knowledge only accessible to a certain class of people who can in some way transcend the empirical limitations of all other classes of people. Knowledge relevant to political matters, like knowledge in general, is to be obtained through co-operative enquiries. Individual findings about particular cases are to be pulled together in the formulation of generalized theories. While what an individual believes to be the case in a single instance may in itself have little value, in conjunction with the perceptions and ideas of others, a wider body of knowledge can be developed (Guthrie, 1990, ch. 10).

It follows from the Aristotelian conception of knowledge that all citizens can learn to behave morally and make political judgements. The virtues to cultivate and the duties to fulfil in any community would not be matters to be left to a special minority. Humans are all inherently social beings: we need others and have strong natural tendencies to reciprocate affection and respect. Except in pathological cases, we see ourselves, our worth, and the meaning of our lives in the context of how others see us. To be encouraged to think only of oneself would be destructive of our nature to care for and share with others. In working out how best to live our own lives, we should at the same time arrive at conclusions about how best we should live together in a political community.

The second phase began in the seventeenth century with Francis Bacon's proposals for research communities, and was taken forward by the progressive thinkers of the eighteenth century, who applied Bacon's ideas to all institutions that claimed to have knowledge beyond the scope of ordinary people. Bacon's theory of how the knowledge of what would improve human lives is to be advanced by co-operation over data collection, experimentation and critical analysis led to the development of research communities such as the Royal Society (Urbach, 1987). These communities, in turn, served as practical models for others about how epistemological disputes are to be settled, not by dogmatic assertions or sceptical withdrawls, but by the exchange of information and ideas, and by critical experimentation and open discussion (Purver, 1967).

Bacon argued that knowledge claims based on ancient authorities or individual assertions are worthless unless their accuracy can be validated by positive results when subjected to practical experimentation. He warned against factors that can distort our common quest for knowledge, and maintained that such distortions can be minimized and rectified only through organized research enterprise, which will bring people together who will conduct experiments, develop axioms, check for confirmations or rejections, and gradually expand the range of knowledge on which humankind can rely to improve their quality of life. He envisaged the process as one that will draw all people into a co-operative venture benefiting them all far more than if each were to try to come up with new knowledge in isolation (Bacon, 1905, p. 293).

In the hands of eighteenth century thinkers such as Voltaire and Denis Diderot, Bacon's ideas became a powerful tool with which to challenge the 'knowledge establishment', from the Church to state guardians of what was to be regarded by all as the truth (Gay, 1970). They insisted that no pronouncement on what should or should not be done could be validated if people who could make a useful contribution to these matters were excluded from the process of considering them. Pronouncements without the needed validation, even if they were made by people in powerful positions, should then be subject to ridicule, or simply superseded by findings derived from the work of communities of co-operative enquirers.

With the third phase, which took place during the middle part of the nineteenth century, the communitarian links between the way that truth claims are to be evaluated and the structure for participatory decision-making were gradually brought together. In fact, when the term 'communitarian' first gained currency in the nineteenth century, it was used to characterize the community-based transformation of society advocated by Robert Owen, Charles Fourier and Pierre Joseph Proudhon (see Bestor, 1950; and Bowle, 1954, chs 6 and 7). These thinkers all condemned the consequences of a greed-driven market system, and rejected the notion that the problem could be solved by the establishment of a single absolute authority. They believed that better education for all citizens, more autonomy for local groups, and greater encouragement for people to develop co-operative communities which respect and care for all their members were the ingredients for social improvement.

The gradualist approach put forward by these early communitarian thinkers was endorsed by John Stuart Mill (Mill, 1987, pp. 115–16), who added the further ingredient of reorientating political institutions towards the developmental needs of citizens. Mill recognized that even where there were willing citizens to experiment with co-operative arrangements, the lack of political support could prevent them from making much progress. On the basis that 'the most important point of excellence which any form of government can possess is to promote the virtue and intelligence of the people themselves' (Mill, 1972, p. 193), Mill insisted that the machinery of representative government must be supplemented by wider participatory democracy. It is through participation in their own governance that citizens can acquire the understanding and motivation to work together for improvements as members of a shared community. As he observed:

> Still more salutary is the moral part of the instruction afforded by participation of the private citizen, if even rarely, in public functions. He is called upon . . . to apply, at every turn, principles and maxims which have for their reason of existence the common good . . . Where this school of public spirit does not exist . . . the utmost aspirations of the lawgiver or the moralist could only stretch to make the bulk of the community a flock of sheep innocently nibbling the grass side by side. (Mill, 1972, p. 217)

Mill believed that the example of participatory development would spread not only to the active involvement of citizens in local representative bodies (Mill, 1972, pp. 346–59), but also to the equal participation of women and men in economic and political processes, and to the association of workers on terms of equality, collectively owning the capital with which they carry on their operations, and working under managers elected and removable by themselves (Mill, 1994, IV, pp. 138–9 and pp. 147–56).

The fourth phase, which foreshadowed the emergence of contemporary communitarian movements, took place during the late nineteenth and early twentieth centuries. Representative figures of this phase included the Oxford philosophers, Thomas Hill Green and Leonard Trelawney Hobhouse; the French sociologist, Emile Durkheim; and the American educationalist, John Dewey. They shared a deep commitment to develop liberal ideals, and to combat the distortion of those ideals into free market slogans in praise of the 'everyone-for-themselves' brand of individualism. They wanted to stop liberal concerns for toleration from being used as a justification for moral neutrality, and to prevent the powerful from exploiting the language of 'rights'. It was Hobhouse who challenged the claim that individuals can have rights in isolation from their relationships with other people in their communities. He asked:

> What, for example, is my right? On the face of it, it is something that I claim . . . If my claim is of right it is because it is sound, well grounded, in the judgement of an impartial observer. But an impartial observer will not consider me alone. He will equally weigh the opposed claims of others. He will take us in relation to one another, that is to say, as individuals involved in a social relationship . . . An individual right, then, cannot conflict with the common good, nor could any right exist apart from the common good. (Hobhouse, 1994, p. 61)

Similarly, Durkheim's concern with reinforcing social cohesion in the face of greed and market forces was not derived from any interest in preserving oppressive communities, but rather from his belief in the need for inclusive communities in which social bonds of mutual respect and care were safeguarded. For him, the common good emerges from 'the deliberation, reflection, and critical spirit of a democratic society', and it is the common good that 'resists authoritarian regimes which threaten the autonomy of the individual, and . . . blocks secondary groups (unions, families, professional organizations, and so on) from "swallowing up their members", placing them under "immediate domination"' (Cladis, 1992, p. 137).

Dewey, too, regarded the true mission of liberalism as freeing individuals from barriers that would otherwise prevent them from coming together as fellow members of an inclusive community. The problem is the diversion of liberalism from this course in the name of protecting the rights of those individuals who had themselves been liberated and gone on to acquire positions of power. Dewey's assessment of this problem reveals not only that any interpretation of communitarian ideas as being basically anti-liberal is misconceived, but that the process of liberation needs to be driven by communitarian expectations if it is not to be suspended arbitrarily by the powerful in society. Arguing against the exploitation of the notion of 'liberty' by vested interests, he wrote:

Soon after liberal tenets were formulated as eternal truths, [liberty] became an instrument of vested interests in opposition to further social change, [by contrast] . . . Liberty in the concrete signifies release from the impact of *particular* oppressive forces . . . The direct impact of liberty always has to do with some class or group that is suffering in a special way from some form of constraint exercised by the distribution of powers that exist in contemporary society. (Dewey, 1939, pp. 450–1)

For communitarians, liberty is a mode of power relationship which must be progressively extended to all citizens if society is to attain the status of a truly inclusive community. With democratized power relations, citizens would be able to develop a shared understanding of the common good through open communication and co-operative enquiry, and this understanding then provides the moral framework that guides their common endeavours. It follows that social and political problems can only be solved by the introduction of communitarian practices which enable people to learn, question and deliberate together, without intimidation, in relation to how they should live under the conditions they face.

The Emergence of Communitarian Movements

As the end of the twentieth century approaches, and after both state-dominant and market-led attempts to solve society's problems have been found to be inadequate, the hitherto diverse strands of communitarian ideas have begun to converge towards a unified theory of social and political reforms. In Britain, for example, debates on how the notion of 'social democracy' can be developed to overcome the shortcomings of authoritarian forms of socialism provided a springboard for reconsidering how state and society should interact to develop community life (Tam, 1981; Marquand, 1988; Miller, 1990; Hirst, 1994; and Boswell, 1994). In America, the inadequacies of the individualist conception of liberalism in underpinning social justice stimulated a strong communitarian response (Sandel, 1982; Walzer, 1983, 1987, 1992; Barber, 1984; Taylor, 1990, 1993; and Etzioni, 1995b).

Suspicions about authoritarian approaches to government, coupled with disillusionment with the individualism that pervades free market thinking, pave the way for the emergence of communitarian movements. Although some commentators have mistaken such movements as seeking to revive traditional forms of small-scale self-contained communities, any serious attempt to examine what the leading communitarian figures have to say would confirm that the central focus of these movements is to build inclusive communities that are mutually supportive in the context of an overarching global community. By providing consistent advocacy for the merits of inclusive communities, raising citizens' awareness of the barriers to sustainable community life, and pointing to reform opportunities which citizens can actively support, communitarian movements are establishing a new agenda for politics and citizenship.

Amitai Etzioni pointed out that the goal is to 'provide the social bonds that sustain the moral voice, but at the same time avoid tight networks that suppress pluralism and dissent' (Etzioni, 1995b, p. 122). To achieve this, Michael Walzer has called for a multiplicity of interrelated communities each operating on a democratic and inclusive basis. He urged all citizens to engage actively in organizations and processes that affect their common well-being. But he also indicated that he was acutely aware of the difficulties that must be overcome:

> [A] growing number of people seem to be radically disengaged – passive clients of the state, market drop-outs, resentful and posturing nationalists . . . [Hence we need] (1) to decentralize the state, so that there are more opportunities for citizens to take responsibility for (some of) its activities; (2) to socialize the economy so that there is a greater diversity of market agents, communal as well as private; and (3) to pluralize and domesticate nationalism, on the religious mode, so that there are different ways to realize and sustain historical identities. (Walzer, 1992, p. 106)

The theme of decentralization through a network of communities was echoed by Charles Taylor, who regarded it not as an issue about the efficiency of political machinery, but rather as a means to facilitate the meaningful empowerment of citizens. He warned that:

> [W]e have seen that fragmentation grows to the extent that people no longer identify with their political community, that their sense of corporate belonging is transferred elsewhere or atrophies

altogether . . . [But] successful common action can bring a sense of empowerment and also strengthen identification with the political community . . . [Also] devolution, or a division of power, as in a federal system, particularly based on the principle of subsidiarity, can be good for democratic empowerment. (Taylor, 1993, pp. 29–30)

Communitarian remedies for the fragmentation of communities have nothing to do with imposing past traditions; they are concerned with realizing the full potential of community life. Jonathan Boswell, for example, applied communitarian ideas to the functioning of economies, and confronted the myth that prosperity is most reliably generated by individualistic conflicts and competition (Boswell, 1990). At a time when the success of East Asian economies are leading some Western observers to suggest erroneously that market forces should be balanced by a measure of authoritarian control of society to attain the best economic results, Boswell's diagnosis provides an essential corrective in arguing for co-operation for the common good as the real key to a stronger economy.

The question of power distribution has to be addressed not only at the macro, but also at the micro, level of the economy. At the beginning of the twentieth century, Durkheim looked to organizations to provide a new arena for community life when economic forces are undermining communal existence elsewhere, but towards the end of the twentieth century organizations themselves are finding it difficult to give their members any real sense of stability. One solution is the federal organization – big enough at the corporate level to achieve economies of scale and enhance competitiveness, but small enough at the divisional level to retain and develop the personal dimension of work relationships (Handy, 1994, p. 102). However, as Carole Pateman has pointed out, management's friendly relationships with staff are no substitute for changes to power structures that would make participation genuinely possible (Pateman, 1970, p. 106).

The temptation to bring in authoritarian elements to redress the weaknesses of free market practices is one which communitarian movements aim to eradicate. It is not the lack of absolute certainty that prevents citizens from acknowledging their common values and shared responsibilities: it is the cultural marginalization of co-operative enquiry as the method of resolving social and political differences. Looking to the future, instead of conceding to Fukuyama's trade-off of more authoritarian intolerance for less individualist fragmentation, we should turn to what David Marquand has called:

> [A] notion of politics as mutual education: of the political domain as a public realm, where the members of a political community listen to, argue with and persuade each other as equal citizens, so as to find solutions to their common problems . . . Above all, politics as mutual education implies some notion of a common good transcending private goods: of membership of a political community as partnership in a common enterprise. (Marquand, 1988, pp. 231–2)

This epistemological shift from an individualist to a communitarian framework of political enquiry has important consequences for the related debates about values and power relations. From the communitarian position, that there are objective ways to discover the common values by which citizens should live, it follows that any political system which insists that only individuals' self-interested calculations matter in public decisions must be impoverished. Such a system would exclude references to values from policy deliberations. It would push politicians to appeal to individuals' narrow concerns for themselves, even at the expense of their wider concerns for their fellow citizens. Worst of all, it risks engendering a self-fulfilling prophecy in diminishing the willingness of successive generations to support the common good (see Marquand, 1988, pp. 219–20; and Ormell, 1996).

The ultimate goal of all communitarian movements is to transform social and political aspects of community life so that everyone can participate responsibly as equal citizens in shaping decisions that affect them. In place of the superficial form of democracy which, in the name of protecting rights, allows individuals in positions of power to deny their responsibilities to others, there is to be a strong, communitarian form of democracy which, in the words of Benjamin Barber, 'relies on participation in an evolving problem-solving community that creates public ends where there were none before by means of its own activity and of its own existence as a focal point of the quest for mutual solutions' (Barber, 1984, pp. 150–2).

By anchoring politics to the pursuit of common values through co-operative enquiries, communitarian movements pose a challenge to all power structures which deny citizens a real role in shaping their communities. This applies not just to the superficial democracy favoured by individualist advocates of the free market, but also to every anti-democratic variant advocated by authoritarians. In fact, the options represented by these two groups are rejected as a false dichotomy which has dominated political thinking for too long. While authoritarianism maintains that the power to govern should rest with those who can demonstrate their absolute authority (by force; by invoking some abstract principle or holy text; or by lineage), market individualism insists instead on a conditional selection process that gives power to those who have enough resources to attract more votes than their nearest competitor for any given election. In both cases, the ruling elite claims total sovereignty over the domain it governs. Citizens, in whom the sovereignty to rule truly rests, are denied any real influence over the wide-ranging decisions made by politicians and their officials.

So long as the authoritarian option appeared to be a serious rival in the form of the Soviet regime, the citizens of Western market democracies could be told that their own system gave them greater economic prosperity, and communitarian reforms were not to be considered. It would not be worth rocking the boat, especially when any attempt to do so might also be branded as giving tacit support to the totalitarian rival. C. B. Macpherson had long maintained that the market model of democracy would:

> continue to be accepted as an adequate justificatory model, as long as we in Western societies continue to prefer affluence to community (and to believe that market society can provide affluence indefinitely), and as long as we continue to accept the cold-war view that the only alternative . . . is a wholly non-liberal totalitarian state. (Macpherson, 1977, pp. 91–2)

However, with the collapse of the Soviet regime, it was no longer possible to point to an inadequate rival to demonstrate the strength of superficial democracy. One of the most important legacies of the 1989 anti-Communist revolutions has turned out to be the urgent call for a critical reappraisal of the politics of individualism (see Macpherson, 1962). Apathy of voters, particularly among the young; emergence of single issue pressure groups; distrust of politicians; and disdain for petty party-political gestures are all symptoms of political systems that have so alienated their citizens they are no longer willing to accept being kept on the sidelines while the ruling elites make all the important decisions. Furthermore, an increasing number of citizens believe that the electoral mechanism for changing the ruling elite periodically is not sufficiently efficacious, when the underlying power structures remain the same. The pattern of citizens' frustration has been confirmed by Russell J. Dalton in a detailed study of changing political trends in Western democracies during the 1970s and 1980s. He observed that:

> Because the political process in most democracies presumes a passive and deferential public, there are insufficient opportunities for citizens to increase their participation in political decision making. Especially in Western Europe, democratic institutions were designed to limit and channel citizen participation, not to maximize popular control of elites . . . This situation has been described as the governability crisis of Western democracies. (Dalton, 1988, p. 226)

From a communitarian point of view, both individualism and authoritarianism make untenable assumptions about the nature of political knowledge, and have undesirable implications for political power distribution. Mixing the two wrongs – for example, be it the neo-conservative mix of economic individualism with social authoritarianism, or the state socialist combination of social individualism with economic authoritarianism – would not create a good solution either. The politics of building inclusive communities, however, does not bring with it a prescriptive ideology of what policies are to be implemented by governments. In focusing on how citizens must become the driving force in developing what is to become a global community of inclusive communities, communitarian movements are pressing for new ways to think about and practise politics, which draw on community deliberations on what would constitute the common values of citizens, and what action may strengthen or damage them. And since community deliberations need to take place under conditions of effective citizen participation, we cannot simply rely on prevailing community structures, past or present, to provide a framework for political reforms. Community structures themselves need to be re-examined critically.

Communitarian politics will therefore be radically different from the party politics that prevails in most developed countries. Party politics relies on citizens entrusting the power to govern to political elites who organize themselves for the sole purpose of competing for an electoral mandate. Rather than challenging existing power relations to facilitate the development of inclusive communities, it focuses the attention of political groups on presenting a distinct package of benefits that would attract more voters than do the packages of rival parties. In refusing to take a stand on what kinds of attitude and expectations are more worthy of cultivation, it has become increasingly vulnerable to attack, both from those who maintain that collective action should give way to individual choice in the face of market forces, and those who want to impose their views on others regardless of what these others think. Individualists would like to reduce party politics entirely to a marketplace for votes, even if voters were making their choices on the basis of wrong information or immoral values. Authoritarians, on the other hand, would like to hijack political parties and through them translate their own dogmas into laws and regulations for everyone else.

In the next chapter, we shall look at how ideas on politics and society are currently mapped out, and explain why a new agenda for politics and citizenship is needed. It will be seen that a proper understanding of the communitarian approach requires a displacement of the Left–Right divide. Communitarianism is not to be located alongside conservatism, liberalism and socialism as a rival ideology. Instead, it challenges all those attracted to elements of conservative, liberal or socialist ideas to avoid making the assumption that such ideas can only be pursued within a framework which mixes varying degrees of individualist and authoritarian practices.

Conservatives, liberals and socialists who approach politics in a communitarian manner will share a very important common agenda, distinguishing them from their colleagues who are steeped in the dichotomous practice of dividing problems into two groups: those that are to be left to individuals to sort out on their own, and those that are to be left to government institutions to sort out, with minimum involvement from citizens in general. For communitarians, whatever their party political differences, the development and involvement of citizens in the governance of their own communities is a fundamental objective of politics.

Chapters 3 to 5, as we have seen, will consider, respectively the educative, economic and protective elements of communitarian citizenship. They will be followed by an examination of what levers of change are available and how they can be used to break down barriers and facilitate reforms. Chapter 6 looks at how citizens should direct government institutions in opening themselves up to citizen participation. Chapter 7 focuses on action through the business sector, where considerable reforms should and could be carried out if citizens, in their capacity as managers, workers, investors and consumers, work to a common agenda for change. In addition to what can be done through the state and business sectors, Chapter 8 examines how the politics of building inclusive communities is also to be carried forward in the third sector of voluntary and community action.

Chapter 9 will deal with criticisms of communitarianism as a general theory, and its strengths and weaknesses as a social and political theory will be assessed. The book concludes in Chapter 10 with a look at the prospects for a genuine renewal of community life, and the impact to be expected from applications of the communitarian approach. By its very nature, communitarianism cannot accept that leaving individuals to their own enlightened self-interest, or handing power to a vanguard of revolutionary leaders, would bring about the development of inclusive communities. Yet gradual, progressive reforms take time, against strong opposition from those who do not wish to see their power base weakened. In the end, communitarianism will have to be judged by its contributions to the deliberations of citizens in heralding a new era of social and political reform.

2

Re-mapping the Ideological Battleground

The communitarian agenda for social and political action aims to repair the damage caused by the individualist world order by developing inclusive communities which:

(a) At the epistemological level, accept knowledge claims only to the extent that their validity could be established under conditions of co-operative enquiry, which requires that all those with a contribution to make are able to deliberate together to consider the merits of any given claim honestly, without intimidation, bribery, or any other form of pyschological pressure.

(b) At the moral level, ensure that values such as love, justice, wisdom and fulfilment which meet the tests of co-operative enquiry, form the basis of the responsibilities of all members towards each other. All community members would be expected to apply the resources and influence at their disposal to protect and enhance their common values.

(c) At the political level, structure power relations so that all members can participate as equal citizens in influencing the way that the power which affects them is exercised in practice. All community members would be able to participate directly, or entrust others whose judgement they respect and whose integrity they have no reason to doubt, to participate in making key decisions that apply to everyone.

Such inclusive communities are to be built upon the structures involving human interactions – not just in families and neighbourhood areas, but also in schools, business organizations, state institutions, professional and community groups, voluntary associations, and international networks. In all cases, reforms need to facilitate the development of citizens' attitudes and abilities as effective participants of inclusive communities, with the help of education, work opportunities, and collective protection. Reforms also need to improve the power relations and practices of state, business and third-sector organizations so that citizens can interact with each other without undue hindrance, epistemologically, morally or politically.

To establish this new agenda, it would be necessary to challenge a number of assumptions that currently distort social and political debate. First, there is the outmoded Left–Right divide, which still purports to locate political ideas along a meaningful continuum when it has become conceptually confused, and quite inadequate for exposing the false and dangerous authoritarian–individualist dichotomy. Second, there is the belief that while the adoption of individualist ideas may have unfortunate side effects, individualism is an inherently sound system of thought which should not be dislodged unless a rival theory can deliver better results. This assumes that the process of validation put forward by individualists – namely, asking individuals to judge for themselves what is best without providing any structure to enable them to reflect on their common needs as a community, is acceptable. In reality, individualism is not an adequate theory for evaluating what ought to be pursued in society, let alone guiding us how to pursue it. Third, there is the assumption that, because authoritarian approaches to politics currently lack the intellectual respectability secured by individualist thinkers, it is an element which can be ignored. Sadly, authoritarianism is on the rise, through the emergence of fundamentalist campaign groups and the resurgence of Fascist movements. They may not be led by anyone as obvious as an Adolf Hitler or a Benito Mussolini, but their strengths are growing (Swift, 1990; Eco, 1995). Resentment against the individualist world order can fuel authoritarian reaction, and communitarian critics of individualism have a responsibility to warn against the adoption of authoritarian practices. Indeed, the notion of 'community' can itself be hijacked by fundamentalists who want to create highly insular communities within which members have to submit to the absolute rule of the elite, and which is intolerant towards outsiders. Some commentators have even suggested that any movement founded on concern for community life would inevitably degenerate into some form of Fascist authoritarianism

(Stone, 1994; *Economist*, 1995). Instead of condemning blindly any departure from individualism as a move towards authoritarianism, we should put a spotlight on the real dangers posed by authoritarian power distribution. Finally, there is the assumption that with the large-scale and rapid changes taking place all over the world, uncertainty prevails over every aspect of life, and we should abandon all attempts at rational planning to deal with our common future. This is the 'post-everything syndrome', a call to surrender to amoral relativism in theory and practice. If the communitarian agenda is to advance, the untenability of such a position must be exposed.

Beyond the Left–Right Divide

Let us begin with the Left–Right divide. Since the mid-1980s, citizens in the Western world have become increasingly disillusioned with conventional party politics. They have discovered that, behind the superficial labels of 'Left' and 'Right', political parties have generally abandoned all attempts to articulate, let alone strive to realize, any long-term vision. The commercialized promotion of political parties has displaced the development of morally coherent political programmes. Instead of being brought together to deliberate over their common good, citizens are encouraged to behave as self-centred consumerists, deciding what personal gains to purchase with their votes. What is on offer is constantly repackaged to suit what the largest number of voters seems to favour, however prejudiced or ill-informed those views might be. Instead of pointing to any kind of meaningful demarcation, the Left–Right divide merely masks the moral vacuum created by politicians' abdication of their responsibility to ensure that we live in communities greater than the sums of the individual parts.

The danger is that the vacuum could come to be filled by authoritarians, who want to impose their moral dogmas on everyone. Sensing the revulsion against the petty, unprincipled manifestations of party politics, extremist groups will try to step in with their uncompromising plan to solve every problem in society. Exploiting the dissatisfaction with the political marketplace, they will promise all kinds of moral regeneration in return for the exercise of total power. By focusing hatred against vulnerable minority groups, and tapping into the desire among the gullible for simplistic solutions, they could end up replacing the politics of individualism by new forms of Fascist and fundamentalist oppression. The best safeguard against the authoritarian threat is not to pretend that the individualism embodied in contemporary party politics is the only alternative. To force people to choose from this false dichotomy could push many of them into the arms of authoritarians. What should be done is to raise citizens' awareness of the communitarian approach, and establish a new agenda for social and political action. To do this, the old Left–Right framework for political thinking must be exposed as outmoded. Far too many people still use Left–Right terminologies to assess political ideas. If ideas are not readily identifiable as 'Left' or 'Right', they are regarded as a compromised mixture of elements from both Left and Right. Communitarian ideas, for example, which stress both duties to the civic order and wider involvement of workers in the running of enterprises, could be interpreted as attempting to bring together an element of Right-wing thinking in subordinating individual rights to civic duties, and an element of Left-wing thinking in promoting workers' involvement in the running of private enterprise. With such an interpretation, these ideas would be viewed as an eclectic collection rather than a distinct political vision. The problem is that such an interpretation is itself questionable, relying as it does on a Left–Right topology which cannot be coherently sustained.

From a communitarian point of view, the Left–Right divide, far from offering a useful map of political ideas, locates them inconsistently and distorts their relationships with each other. There are at least five pairs of opposites which may be invoked by a Left–Right contrast, but none of them provides any kind of coherent distinction between the two labels.

Radical versus Conservative

Radical proposals to change society have for a long time been associated with the Left. By contrast, those who want to conserve established traditions and practices are regarded as representing the Right. However, underlying the conservative reluctance to see radical changes are two quite different sets of motivation. One is typified by the thinking of David Hume, who applies Baconian epistemology to opposing proposals derived from abstract reasoning with little empirical support (Hume, 1975). The other is based on the desire to preserve power structures that are beneficial to a ruling group. If changes to society could be seen to reduce the power of the former ruling elite but enhance the well-being of society as a whole, Humean conservatives would extend their faith to the new arrangements and defend them against radical proposals for change. The hierarchical conservatives, on the other hand, would want to change social arrangements back again, and might even resort to radical means in an attempt to turn the clock back.

Correspondingly, for each first generation of successful radicals, there will be those who want to conserve their achievements, and those who want to extend radical changes to new areas. Of the latter group, there could be two further subsets: one which follows the Deweyan analysis of power distribution and aims to remove barriers to unequal power distribution radically, but in accordance with pragmatic assessment of the likely effectiveness of different change strategies; and one which pursues radical change for its own sake as an ideological commitment, the Maoist interpretation of Marxist revolution being an example. The 'radical' and 'conservative' labels do not pick out any significant differences that would add substance to a Left–Right divide. As Anthony Giddens has observed:

> The truth is that no group has a monopoly over radical thought or action in a post-traditional social universe . . . the neoliberals have actively attacked traditional forms of privilege more than latter-day socialists have done; and these forms of privilege have frequently included modes of entrenched power. Conservatives critical of the neoliberals are often so because they see free market models as producing too much of a divided society; they want less inequality rather than more. (Giddens, 1994, pp. 250 and 251–2)

The political debate has shifted from 'either-conserving-or-radi-cally-changing' to what is to be conserved *and* what is to be radically changed. In some cases, as in the relationship between the environment and the global industrial process, radical changes would have to be implemented if an important aspect of what sustains human existence is to be conserved. The same applies to the productive capabilities of human beings. If such abilities are not increasingly to be made redundant, radical changes would have to be applied to the one-way displacement of human resources by new technology. John Gray has suggested that 'Conservatives need to explore, with greens and others, as yet unthought-of dilemmas of life in societies which are no longer buoyed up by the prospect of incessant economic growth or by modest pseudo-religions of endless world-improvement (Gray, 1993, p. 173).

The new debate is about the reasons and tactics that lie behind conservation-cum-change strategies. In this respect, communitarians in the tradition of Hume and Burke, even if some of them still prefer the label 'conservative', will have more in common in their approach to evaluating which strategies are to be adopted for the common good, compared with those who think that politics can continue to relate to citizens as abstract individuals, with little consideration for the impact on community life.

Socialist versus Capitalist

To end the ownership of capital and other means of production by the few, and replace it with ownership by all has constituted the guiding aim of socialist thinking for most of the twentieth century. Nationalization of key industries and fundamental services became a core policy. This was regarded as an onslaught by the Left on the capitalist system favoured by the Right. Has the reprivatization of certain industries simply pushed the disputed frontier in favour of the Right? Or have the terms of the dispute themselves been altered?

The idea that the level of state control of a country's resources mirrors the level of well-being of its citizens has largely been discredited. In its place, there is the growing recognition that state involvement in the control of resources must be evaluated in terms of its real impact on citizens. The passivity engendered by dependency on state provisions is taken into account as a negative factor which needs to be dealt with. Citizens need to be able to look after themselves; the question is, how best can the state assist them when neither the free market nor direct state provisions can provide a long-term solution.

Some socialists accept that a fundamental rethink is required. David Selbourne, for example, has written:

> The old socialism is dead; the new civic social-ism, neither of 'left' nor 'right' but transcending both and resting upon the principle of

duty, is waiting to be born. The overthrow and fall of socialism, with its dogmas, servitudes to class, party, and state, and – in its welfare socialist form – recoil from the principle of duty, especially as it applies to the citizen's obligations to himself, his familiars, and to the civic order in the form of nation, have opened the way to a new social-ism of the civic bond. (Selbourne, 1994, p. 273)

Just as socialists such as Selbourne are looking for a new direction represented by the communitarian drive to develop responsible citizens, the blanket defence of capitalism has given way to more critical consideration of how the state should function in partnership with the business sector. The high level of involvement that East Asian governments have in the development of their economies, and their success in competing for global market shares, have led many adherents of the Anglo-American model of capitalism to look for lessons to be learnt. Even more fundamentally, the structure of capitalist economies is rapidly entering a new phase of development. Peter Drucker has described the new phase of world economy as 'post-capitalist':

Instead of the old-line capitalist, in developed countries pension funds control the supply and allocation of money . . . The beneficiary owners of the pension funds are, of course, the country's employees. If Socialism is defined, as Marx defined it, as ownership of the means of production by the employees, then the United States has become the most 'socialist' country around – while still being the most 'capitalist' one as well. (Drucker, 1993, p. 5)

The Left–Right divide can no longer accommodate the new breed of civic-minded capitalists and market socialists. A completely different dividing line needs to be drawn between those who seek a citizen-led reorientation of government in relation to the market economy and those who still hold that the role of the state can be defined without the genuine involvement of citizens.

Public versus Private

The concepts of 'public' and 'private' have in the past helped to substantiate the Left–Right divide. The Left supported the public domain, and the Right defended the private. Yet the nature of the 'public' supposed by this opposition has come under growing scrutiny. Is the public domain simply the domain under the coercive control of the government? If there is a different understanding of the 'public', involving public-spirited citizens and a public forum for conflict resolution and collective policy development, how would this be located on the old Left–Right spectrum? David Hollenbach has warned against the polarization of the public and the private resulting from narrow interpretations of the public realm, and which in turn marginalizes the importance of civil society:

> We must rethink the sharp division between the private and public spheres of social existence . . . Civil society is the more encompassing reality, composed of numerous communities of small and intermediate size . . . these communities are not political in the sense of being part of government, they are not private either. (Hollenbach, 1994/5, pp. 18–19)

Although the communities composing the kind of civil society that writers such as Hollenbach and Walzer wish to promote are not part of government, they are political in the sense that they offer citizens opportunities to deliberate and determine matters which affect them collectively. Rather than trying to locate this dimension of human existence somewhere along a rigid Left–Right continuum, what is required is a reconceptualization of the 'public' which would put an end to any simplistic correlation between the public–private and Left–Right divides. Along these lines, Leo Panitch has urged caution in the face of simplistic demand to cut back the 'public' sector:

> the strength of the monetarist assault should not have become the occasion for a knee-jerk defence of the Keynesian/welfare state . . . but rather treated as the occasion for proposing – for insisting on – the fundamental restructuring of the state and its relationship to society so that the communities it is supposed to serve and the people who labour for it together have great involvement in the public domain. (Panitch, 1986, p. 92)

Panitch's admonition to his fellow socialists has been echoed by David Osborne who, far from using socialist ideas as his starting point, has been highly influential in advocating government reforms in America. According to Osborne, while Washington is still caught up in a futile debate about 'more' or 'less' government, government institutions at both state and local level are already creating a third way which combines the activism of the Democrats with the Republican aversion to big government (Osborne, 1992). This new kind of government is characterized by the authentic empowerment of citizens to shape policies in resolving public issues. The ideological battle-line is not to be drawn between more or less conventional government, but between those who confine politics to a conventional form of government and those who want to practise communitarian governance.

Social Liberals versus Social Traditionalists

If economic liberals stand behind the banner of the Right, social liberals are normally classified under the Left. In opposition to attempts to liberalize moral and social views about how people should live their lives, the social traditionalists lead the Right's demand to protect, and if necessary revive, old moral traditions. For a time, this polarization did indeed divide up the political agenda between these two distinct camps. However, one of the notable contributions of communitarians to contemporary political debate is to challenge this division. Not all moral traditions are worth preserving, but neither should they all be discarded. In place of the outmoded confrontation between dogmatic support and rejection of moral traditions, communitarians have brought into the open the debate about the kinds of social practices and common values that are really needed to build inclusive communities.

David Marquand has written of the emergence of 'an alternative response based on the notions of community and social capital', which 'stands for a stakeholder economy, in which markets work for the public good instead of against it; for a vibrant public domain . . . [and] for bottom-up, locally-led development instead of a centralist Fabianism of the past'. He calls it the 'vision of a communitarian ethical socialism, combining individual empowerment with social solidarity' (Marquand, 1995). The new challenge is to decide how markets are to be supported so that they can serve the communities on which they rely to function, and how the public domain is to be sustained by traditions of civic virtues, and strengthened by networks of community institutions (see Willetts, 1994).

Dictatorship Based on Self-proclaimed Equality versus Dictatorship Based on Self-proclaimed Superiority

The Left–Right labels have also been much utilized in explaining differences in policy decisions in relation to dictatorial regimes. Critics of American foreign policy have consistently protested against American support for rebel forces against Leftist regimes in countries such as Cuba, Vietnam and Nicaragua, while it was tolerant (if not at times suspiciously supportive) of the Right-wing regimes in Chile and Argentina. On the other hand, there are critics of Liberation Christianity who charge the world's Churches for the opposite approach. For example, Edward Norman criticized the Churches' involvement in supporting the people struggling against what he viewed as being Right-wing as opposed to Left-wing regimes (Norman, 1979, p. 20).

The Left–Right labels suggest that there are more important differences between the two types of regime than there are between their dictatorial nature and democratic politics. But what are these differences? To some extent, it might be argued that the Left is associated with some form of self-proclaimed equality, and the Right is associated with some form of self-proclaimed superiority. This suggests that there is something inherently wrong with the notions of 'equality' or 'superiority'. Yet such concepts are only suspect if they are wrongly applied. Where people have equal claims to something, discrimination against one or the other deserves to be ruled out. Where someone has demonstrated superior abilities to take charge of certain functions, those entrusted with the task of selecting the best candidate would be right to appoint that person. However, if a regime acts in the name of equality, when that equality is in fact denied to its citizens, or that power is exercised in the name of a superiority which is either non-existent or irrelevant, then that regime has an illegitimate claim to power, and should be opposed. Leonard Schapiro, having studied extensively the nature of totalitarian regimes, concluded that:

> There are probably no two terms in the language of politics which are more imprecise and subjective in the meanings which are attached to them than 'left' and 'right', and which are more misleading in their common usage . . . In short, there is every reason to study both the similarities and the differences between the various totalitarian societies which exist or have existed . . .

but there is no illumination to be derived from the misleading 'Left–Right' classification. (Schapiro, 1972, p. 84)

In this, as in the other cases that have been considered, it is not the Left–Right polarity which provides an instructive framework for political discussions. It is far more important to recognize the political differences between communities that are governed by varying degrees of dictatorship, on the one hand, and communities which govern themselves through real democratic involvement of their citizens, on the other.

The Progressive–Regressive Axis

In place of the artificial and outmoded Left–Right divide, a continuum which focuses on epistemological authority and power distribution should be considered. Instead of Left and Right, it would be a vertical axis, with neutrality at its centre, representing the non-interventionist, anarchic position which maintains that there is no reliable guide for collective political action, and that things are thus best left to individuals. Below this point are located on a descending, regressive scale, ideas which suppose that some absolute authority can be invoked to command the obedience of people without their informed involvement. The further one goes down the regressive scale, the more extensive the use of absolute power is advocated. By contrast, above the central point are located on an ascending, progressive scale, ideas which suppose that political action should be taken to improve society, provided it enables all citizens to deliberate as equals in how their collective power is to be exercised. The further one goes up the progressive scale, the more thoroughly the participation of citizens is advocated.

Communitarian ideas outlined in Chapter 1 would thus be located along the progressive scale. There are conservatives, liberals, socialists, feminists and environmentalists who will be at home on this scale. At the same time, some of their counterparts will be more appropriately located in the central zone, and others will be found on the regressive scale. After all, there are *laissez faire* conservatives who want to see more freedom given to individuals in choosing how to spend their money, regardless of wider implications, and there are dogmatic liberals who dictate to society the limits of collective action solely on the basis of what they declare to be the inalienable rights of individuals. In view of the decline in conventional party politics, the adequacy of any conceptual grid to map out the contrast between communitarian and opposing ideas, will become increasingly important. In the next two sections, we shall look at the ideas in the central zone that are characterized by their individualist power distribution, and ideas below that along the regressive scale that are characterized by their reliance on authoritarian power distribution.

Individualism

Unlike the conventional 'centre' which is regarded as a mix of moderate versions of 'Left' and 'Right' ideologies, the central zone of the Progressive–Regressive axis picks out a distinct body of political ideas. These are the ideas which adopt as fundamental the claim that there can be no legitimate way of declaring how a group should live, and therefore individuals should be left to decide how each of them is to live. This does not exclude the possibility that individuals may under certain circumstances agree that they would all adopt a common system to safeguard their respective personal interests, but the legitimacy of such a system would rest solely on the fact that it is the choice of the individuals concerned.

As for why it is claimed that there can be no answer to the question 'How should we live?' as opposed to the question 'How should I live?', we need to look at the sceptical roots of individualism. According to sceptical analysis, there are three possibilities regarding the legitimacy of claiming to know what is to be done for *all*:

(i)   Everyone can rightly claim to know;
(ii) Only some can rightly claim to know; or
(iii) No one can rightly claim to know.

Option 1 is self-defeating, because people have conflicting views. If *A* is right to claim to know that *x* should be done for all, and *B* is also right to claim to know that *x* should not be done for all, then either it is true that '*x* should and should not be done for all' which is a self-contradiction, or at least one out of the pair *A* and *B* cannot rightly claim to know in this case, which contradicts the premise.

Option 2 raises the question of how anyone can rightly claim to know whether it is *A* or *B* who rightly claims to know. If it is claimed that C can rightly know that it is A, because C uses criterion z, then it can be asked how anyone can rightly know that C is right to use criterion z. If the answer refers to criterion z again, then the whole chain of reasoning is exposed as being circular. If it refers to another criterion, then the same question would be raised again, and this process of epistemological interrogation would go on until either (a) it terminates at a point which is blocked off from further questioning – which would be seen to be arbitrary; or (b) it goes on without end, in which case the quest for a foundational point is found to be futile.

From the sceptic's point of view, only Option 3 is left. No one can rightly claim to know what is to be done for all. One can, of course, state what one wants to see done, but such a demand has no greater epistemic force than any other demand made by individuals. It follows that no one should be given the authority to decide what is to be done for all. The power for collective action should be left to individuals, so that only where their self-interests coincide would there be a legitimate use of collective arrangements. The problem with such an anarchic distribution of power is that it assumes that individuals would naturally arrive at conclusions which are indeed for their common good. In reality, some individuals will get away with achieving what they want far more than do other individuals. For pessimistic sceptics, there is no independent perspective from which an alternative can be constructed for the redistribution of power. Like the Epicureans and Taoists of old, or followers of the contemporary drop-out culture, they prefer to retreat from political issues, and get on with their own lives by avoiding interference from others as much as possible.

For optimistic sceptics, however, Option 3 does not imply that nothing can be done to overcome the problems associated with anarchic power distribution. On the contrary, they would argue that only one type of political system can be legitimate, given that only Option 3 is tenable – namely, an individualistic form of market democracy. Individuals must be allowed to pursue what each of them considers to be the best way to live, provided that does not obstruct others from their own pursuit. To ensure that this happens, all would, out of their own self-interest, support a government that is removable by them if it fails to act in their interests. Such a government would have no authority except what is vested in it by individuals, and would have no remit except for the protection of the coincidence of individuals' interests.

However, the question can be raised as to whether the state should only concern itself with the lowest common denominator of private interests, and not enable citizens to think and develop beyond those interests to considerations of what is truly for their common good. What has hindered many Western democracies from developing significantly in a progressive direction, and helped to entrench the individualist position, is the 'Mandeville's Twist', which in many ways encapsulates the essence of market individualists' opposition to reconstructing democracy through community development and citizen participation. It owes its origin to the eighteenth-century writer, Bernard Mandeville (Mandeville, 1989).

Anticipating many attacks on the moral limitations of minimalist government, Mandeville argued that individuals should concentrate on doing what each instinctively desires. He claimed that this would be the most beneficial arrangement and that any alternative attempt to get everyone to work for the sake of some common good would only make things worse for all. Significantly, Mandeville did not suppose that the self-interest of human beings was so much guided by natural virtues as by vices. What is alarming is Mandeville's sense of complacency concerning the type of society he would like to see. The twist he gave to individualist political thinking projects anarchic power distribution not so much as something we have to accept reluctantly because of our epistemic limitations, but as something we should all embrace positively because it alone can give individuals the maximum of what they desire.

In the nineteenth century, Mandeville's ideas were expanded by Herbert Spencer, who misinterpreted the social implications of Charles Darwin's theory of natural selection and paved the way for the sanctification of the free market. Whereas Darwin's ideas showed that co-operation between members of the same species was an important factor in giving that species competitive advantages over other species, Spencer interpreted natural selection as a paradigmatic process for eliminating members within any given species. On this basis, he objected to political intervention to help the weak and vulnerable in society (Spencer, 1884, p. 358). When in the twentieth century, these ideas were linked with the economics of theorists such as Milton Friedman (Friedman, 1962; Bosanquet, 1989) and the political philosophy of Robert Nozick (Nozick, 1974; Paul, 1983), the ideology of market individualism was established. Mandeville's notion that individualist behaviour is biologically inescapable remains influential in defending this ideology as the only one that fits with human nature (Ridley, 1996).

Friedman argued that the trade-and-let-trade vision of Mandeville was best realized through a stable market system protected by an otherwise minimalist government which would keep public spending, and hence inflation, low. Any government action which adds non-commercial considerations into the workings of the marketplace would be deemed to be disruptive. Citizens should not think about how collective action could be taken by their government to deal with what appears to be problems for society; instead, they are to think only of themselves as individuals and express reluctance to support any action that does not have any direct benefit for themselves as individuals. This Mandevillean attitude which permeates the writings of Spencer and Friedman was woven into a pseudo-syllogism by Robert Nozick.

Nozick argued in *Anarchy, State and Utopia* that only a minimalist state could be legitimate. He held that there are principles of rights which imply that all collective enterprises can only be validated by individuals contracting in or out on the basis of their assessment of the likely harm/benefit to themselves. However, as many critics have pointed out, what Nozick invoked as fundamental principles of what should or should not be the case generally turn out to be little more than the shared intuitions of libertarian thinkers (Wolff, 1983). For example, he claimed that 'there is no *social entity* with a good that undergoes some sacrifice for its own good. There are only individual people, with their own individual lives. Using one of these people for the benefit of others, uses him and benefits the others' (Nozick, 1974, pp. 32–3).

At the heart of Nozick's arguments is the denial that human beings are social entities who are capable of sharing in the common good. Just as most parents – except perhaps those with extreme libertarian attitudes – would not regard spending their time and money on bringing up their children as allowing themselves to be 'used' for the 'benefit of others', so people with any sense of moral decency would not regard a proposal that they should contribute to a fund to help the innocent victims of a flood as a proposal to 'use' them for the 'benefit of others'. By reaffirming the sceptic's denial that anyone can rightly claim to know what is to be done for the good of all, Nozick reinforced the view that politics is just about bargaining over the distribution of resources. Some individuals may be worse off than others, but whether those who are better off should help them depends on the latter's assessment of what they might get in return. If a convincing case cannot be made by appealing to their own personal concerns, then there should not be any changes involving the redistribution of what the marketplace has already distributed.

Thus anarchic power distribution in practice means that those who benefit most from that distribution are given every encouragement to veto any agreement which might cause them to lose out as individuals. Across a wide range of problems which only collective action could help to resolve, individuals are given the choice to opt out, which in effect prevents any collective action from taking place. In line with this approach, men are allowed to dismiss injustices and biases against women as fringe feminist issues; short term investors are allowed to block-off development that depends on long-term investment; those who can afford to pay private suppliers for their housing, healthcare, education and insurance against unemployment are allowed to withdraw their public contributions through reduced taxation, so that public support for those who cannot afford private schemes is cut back; those who have never suffered from racial discrimination are allowed to ignore the need to change social arrangements which have for so long discriminated against racial minorities; those who live in rich countries are allowed to veto changes which are necessary to fight starvation and malnutrition among millions who live in the poor countries; and, last but not least, present generations are allowed to leave an irredeemably polluted and depleted environment to future generations.

Not all thinkers who are located in the central zone take anarchic power distribution to the extreme that Spencer and Nozick exemplify. However, without a community-based political epistemology, their thinking is trapped by their self-imposed moral neutrality. John Rawls, for example, tried to devise a way out of this without violating the individualist assumption that no one can rightly claim to know what is to be done for the good of all. He could see that what individuals would say in practice could in many cases be shaped by their power positions, and hence not get society very far above the level of the minimal state. Instead he constructed an argument to show how individuals would choose if they were not influenced by the positions they occupy in society (Rawls, 1973, pt 1).

In essence, Rawls' argument puts forward two principles of justice which could be invoked to guide public policies, on the basis that these principles are the ones that individuals in an idealized position would choose. In the idealized, or 'original position', as Rawls calls it, individuals do not know what abilities, resources or access to power they would have in real life. All they know is that whatever principles they agree to would be binding on how they would in fact live. According to Rawls, any rational individual would choose those principles which would neither sacrifice individuals for some unspecified greater good nor allow the worst-off systematically to be neglected.

Apart from the debates over the applications of his principles to practical issues of wealth redistribution (Machan, 1989; Rasmussen, 1989; and Sterba, 1994), Rawls' strategy has met with some fundamental opposition, on the grounds that it relies ultimately on an asocial conception of individuals as the determinants of guiding social principles. Robert Fullinwider has defended Rawls against the charge that he views people too narrowly as unencumbered selves (Fullinwider, 1995). He argued that the highly abstract individuals invoked by Rawls in the original position is only a procedural device, and not meant as an analysis of the nature of political beings. However, from a communitarian point of view, it is the resort to this form of procedural device as opposed to any practical process involving citizens in the community, which casts the most serious doubt on the validity of his whole argument.

It is essential for Rawls that every step of the way he could reasonably claim that individuals in the original position would make this or that choice concerning proposals on what principles are to be adopted when they are uncertain about how they might in practice be affected by the applications of those principles. But what is to be regarded as reasonable when different people can, quite understandably, choose to anticipate uncertain outcomes in different ways. Some individuals are clearly, but not unreasonably, greater risk-takers than others. As Benjamin Barber pointed out:

> Rawls must import into his original position covert special psychologies of the kind it was explicitly designed to exclude. Rawls in fact leaps from the original position . . . to the unwarranted conclusion that this uncertainty will produce in them a rational preference for minimizing risks . . . it can be contended that some men may choose rationally to risk starvation and even death for the chance – even against the odds – to be very rich or very powerful. (Barber, 1975, pp. 297–8)

Rawls' strategy has been the most promising (for those who occupy the central zone) to find a legitimate basis to tackle the social problems that individualism, of whatever form, seems ill-equipped to address. However, if Nozick's attempt to defend the structure of anarchic power distribution rests ultimately on his abstraction of the anti-welfare attitudes which typify libertarian thinkers, it is no less true that Rawls' basis for transcending the limits of anarchic power distribution turns out to be his abstraction of· the cautious pro-welfare attitudes that are common among liberals with a strong social conscience. What he claims would be the choice patterns of individuals in the original position are merely the choice patterns that people such as Rawls would adopt in those circumstances. This does not in itself invalidate those patterns, but it still leaves open the question of why such patterns should or should not take precedence over rival patterns.

Authoritarianism

While Rawls failed to find a way for individualism to tackle the disintegration of communities into haves and have-nots, the ideas of Thomas Hobbes had for a long time shown how easily anarchy can give way to authoritarianism. Having invoked a totally individualistic conception of human beings who care only for their preservation and self-satisfaction, Thomas Hobbes argued that such human beings would only be able to live in peace and security if they all entrusted the right to rule over them to an absolute authority (Hobbes, 1968). As for how this could be justified for individuals who, in his view, would have a low level of trust for others in general, let alone someone who would be handed absolute power over them, Hobbes resorted to a hypothetical covenant which in some ways anticipated Rawls' argument. According to Hobbes, people would agree to the institution of such an absolute authority because if they were in a position to think through the relevant factors, they would – or at least, if they were 'reasonable', they would (Hobbes, 1968, p. 227).

Hobbes' judgement that it would be reasonable for people to weigh up the different factors and share his conclusion, is no more convincing than Rawls' belief that any reasonable person would share *his* assumption as to how they would choose in the 'original position'. The inescapable fact is that people will assess differently what appear to be threats and opportunities, and will opt for different strategies if the conflicting points of such strategies are not subjected to discursive resolution.

What Hobbes did show convincingly was that, psychologically, if leaving people to please themselves proves to be too distressing for too many people, then there would be a strong collective temptation for an authoritarian distribution of political power to be accepted.

In practice, variants of the Hobbesian state have secured power at one time or another in many parts of the world, precisely because the anarchic chaos of warring factions or economic disorganization call out for drastic solutions which the rule of *Leviathan* appears to offer. It is a symptom of the individualist–authoritarian dichotomy that so many of those who rightly feel that even Western democracies allow too much absolute power to be exercised by the state, assume wrongly that the only alternative is to dissolve the mechanism for collective action in an increasing number of areas and leave it to individual interactions in the marketplace to deal with them. Against this prospect, authoritarians argue that the problem lies not with there being too much absolute power, but not enough. Hobbes himself suggested that a ruler can gain such absolute power either by convincing everyone that, all things considered, it is best to entrust that power to an absolute ruler, or by threatening everyone with the use of force to make them submit. Under the first option, an argument would be required to dispel the scepticism that underpins the restrictions on the use of absolute power.

In order to discredit the sceptical position, authoritarians seek to claim that there are indubitable truths. This quest originally took the form of metaphysical interpretations of prevailing beliefs about supernatural forces. The priestly class and anti-democratic philosophers such as Plato put forward their understanding of the universe, on the basis of which absolute rulers could dictate what is to be done for all in their domain. Theologians took over this task when they provided the Church authorities with rationalization of their actions. This form of total explanation went largely unchallenged until the seventeenth century, when the rapid development of research communities and the spread of Baconian ideas on experimentation exposed the emptiness of much of what had for centuries passed for profound knowledge. However, the structure of total explanation remains attractive for many people, and the contemporary surge of fundamentalist politics which seeks to impose an absolute agenda in the name of 'traditional' values, bears testimony to the enduring force of authoritarian ideas. One of these 'traditional' values is the value of the power of the nation-state to demonstrate its superiority over other states. Heinrich von Treitschke, for example, provided many of those who came after him with a fairly adaptable script when he wrote, 'war is justified because the great national personalities can suffer no compelling force superior to themselves, and because history must always be in constant flux' (Treitschke, 1916, pp. 597–8). His emphasis on the value of confrontation and the need for constant struggle characterizes the authoritarian mode of politics. Absolute power is to be exercised to attain absolute supremacy over the 'opposition', and success in achieving this supremacy then helps to preserve from criticism the conceptualization of this achievement as worthwhile. Sceptics would regard this as clearly circular but, from an authoritarian point of view, it is a closed circle. If this weakens its logical appeal when seen from the outside, it strengthens its immunity from criticisms from within. Anyone inside seeking to criticize it is by definition a traitor – an enemy to be silenced, cast out or even destroyed.

Of course, in defining the enemy, in place of other nation-states, one can substitute other races, religions, the opposite sex, or a rival economic class. Karl Marx was no less filled with conviction than von Treitschke when he declared that it is inevitable that workers and their families will be crushed 'beneath the wheels of the Juggernaut of capital', and that it is the historical mission of Communists to be the vanguard of the final revolution, in support of which they must 'openly declare that their ends can be attained only by the forcible overthrow of all existing social conditions' (Marx and Engels, 1977, p. 120).

Whereas individualists demand that deliberations about collective action are left to individuals to carry out, authoritarians rule this out because they believe that the answers are already available for those who can appreciate them. Conceptually, anyone wishing to challenge their answers are thereby classified as members of the 'opposition' at whom the struggle must be directed. In practice, power must then be concentrated in the hands of the few who know the answers and fully understand their implications. Whatever outward party labels politicians wear, if they try to impose their personal convictions of what is right or wrong as the root of their campaign to undermine other power bases which may criticize them, then they need to be guarded against as authoritarians, whose subversion of independent systems of evaluating knowledge claims must not be tolerated. As Hans Schemm, the Nazi Minister of Culture, said when he addressed university professors in Munich in 1933, 'From now on, it will not be your job to determine whether something is true, but whether it is in the spirit of the National Socialist revolution' (quoted in Bracher, 1978, p. 336). Similarly, under the Stalinist regime, 'a complex system of centralised administrative and political controls was imposed on the scientific community' (Holloway, 1972, p. 156).

Contrasts between Western and Eastern outlooks also have little bearing on the structure of regressive political thinking. Once the premise is accepted that 'ordinary' people are only to follow and not to question the judgements of those who will decide all that matters on their behalf, repression of co-operative enquiry will follow. When the ultra-nationalists became the dominant political force in Japan in the 1920s, a 'Peace Preservation Law' was passed to limit the rights of free speech and political action, students were thrown into prison for possessing 'dangerous thoughts', and acts of aggression abroad and political murders at home were carried out in the name of the true imperial will (Reischauer, 1964, ch. 11). In China, Mao Tse Tung decided in the 1960s that the development of ideas in universities and party departments could lead to the emergence of an independent intellectual establishment that could pose a challenge to him, so he devised, first, a Socialist Education Movement to send academics and intellectuals to the countryside to 'learn from the masses', and when that proved ineffective in disrupting the structure of learning, he unleashed the Cultural Revolution which promoted widespread persecution of everyone who could be remotely interpreted as criticizing or doubting his ideas on political and economic management (Hsu, 1983, ch. 28).

Authoritarian politics is essentially the same whatever package of 'values' it seeks to impose. The fact that more extreme expressions of it have been held in check in modern Western democracies does not mean that it is not influential among many who feel that they do not have enough power, even when they are in government, to push through their agenda. They are the ones who are most suspicious of, if not fundamentally hostile to, communitarian demands for greater decentralization of political power and more extensive citizen participation.

There is also a growing danger that, in reacting to the surge of fundamentalist ideas around the world, Western societies might fall into the trap of thinking that extremism is to be combated with extremism. Umberto Eco has coined the term 'Ur-Fascism' (or 'Eternal Fascism') to show both the historical and conceptual continuity between contemporary extremist movements and those which spread in the first half of the twentieth century. His list of fourteen features typifying this phenomenon are useful for picking out authoritarian politicians whatever party or religious labels they happen to adopt. These include: the cult of tradition; rejection of all that the Enlightenment stands for; distrust of the intellectual world; hostility to the critical spirit in discussions; intolerance of difference; appeal to anger and frustration; group identity defined through common enemies; hatred of those to be defeated; the Armageddon complex of absolute confrontation; contempt for the weak; the glorification of heroic death; disdain for women and non-standard sexuality; the Leader embodies the Divine/General Will; and a restriction of the vocabulary for expression. Eco's warning must be taken seriously:

> Ur-Fascism is still around us, sometimes in plain clothes. It would be so much easier, for us, if there appeared on the world scene somebody saying, 'I want to reopen Auschwitz, I want the Black Shirts to parade again in the Italian squares'. Life is not that simple. Ur-Fascism can come back under the most innocent of disguises. Our duty is to uncover it and to point our finger at any of its new instances – every day, in every part of the world. (Eco, 1995)

In lifting authoritarianism out of the muddled Left–Right topology, it can be seen much more clearly why it is epistemologically untenable and sociopolitically dangerous. In contrasting it with individualism, even with the latter's shortcomings, it is understandable why so many democratic-minded thinkers are reluctant to move from the individualist position for fear that it would lead to some form of authoritarianism. What the progressive–regressive axis makes it much easier to grasp is the fact that communitarian dissatisfaction with individualism does not imply a move towards the regressive scale of authoritarian politics, but rather a move in the opposite direction.

Political Disorientation and the 'Post-Everything Syndrome'

The approach of the new Millennium coupled with the radical changes to socioeconomic patterns brought about by technological advancement and globalization, have fuelled a sense of total disorientation, which can be termed the 'Post-Everything Syndrome'. Conceptual frameworks that have guided us up to now are everywhere being left behind. Businesses have moved into the post-industrial age; economic structures have gone into the post-capitalist phase; philosophers have to cope with post-foundationalism; culture has become post-modernist; ideologies have to readjust to post-communism; and just about everything the Second World War was supposed to have safeguarded for the world has now been superseded by some unprecedented development (Lyotard, 1988).

The Post-Everything Syndrome paints a picture of comprehensive uncertainty which calls for a political response. If the prospects for education, employment, housing, healthcare, care of the elderly and so on, are all thrown into doubt, people will demand to know what is to be done. For the individualist-minded, the Syndrome is the result of a culminative process in realizing that there can be no collective mechanism for anticipating and managing changes in the world. Wherever possible, but especially within market democracies, there should be a radical shift towards a reduction of authoritarian power, in government, in the education system and in business, so that deregulated individuals can respond more flexibly and imaginatively to the constant stream of changes.

Tom Peters has attained his super-management guru status by heralding this approach in books such as *Thriving on Chaos* and *Liberation Management: Necessary Disorganisation for the Nanosecond Nineties*. Peters advocated the dissolution of hierarchical structures to enable increasingly smaller teams of individuals to adapt more quickly to changes using their own creativity, rather than relying on any headquarters-prescribed response. However, if the new uncertainty projected by the Post-Everything Syndrome is unmanageable even for the most advanced organizations, what chance is there of survival for most ordinary citizens when they are told more and more that they are to deal with the problems on their own? Peters spoke for a new influential generation of management advisers when he suggested that the only way forward was to embrace the implications of 'nanosecond' individualism:

we're going beyond hierarchy, and trying to liberate almost everyone in the organization. Yet that liberation leads to many a sleepless night . . . the problem is that the starting gate in our fashionized marketplace is constantly shifting position. Only opening yourself up wide to perpetual destruction (beyond Beyond Hierarchy?!) offers hope for renewal. How do you do that? Willing exposure to the market's fickle gales is the only answer that seems to make sense. (Peters, 1992, pp. 473, 475)

What Peters offers is a stronger squeeze on the Mandeville Twist. Yet just as many found Mandevillean complacency appallingly unacceptable in the face of the Industrial Revolution, many more will now find the prescription to thrive on chaos somewhat hollow when all too many people are simply in no position to survive the chaos of unemployment, benefits cuts, and social exclusion. The disgust with this ultra *laissez faire* mentality is providing the fuel for the fundamentalist and Fascist movements to burn. In pronouncing all moderate attempts at managing society as being incapable of dealing with the new uncertainty, and in rejecting the Enlightenment as a guide for moral and political action, the Post-Everything Syndrome has cleared the stage for authoritarians to step forward with their absolute certainty, their total belief, and their comprehensive prescription for how we are all to live.

Some individualists still believe that a politics of justice and compassion can be developed without departing from their sceptical central position. They invoke value-pluralism as a means of justifying their support for more collective action to help the weak and to protect potential victims of intolerance, while maintaining that they are not supposing that they are right to support such action as opposed to any other action. The value of such action is regarded as incommensurable with the values of alternative courses of action. Their commitment to pluralism is presented as a passport to press for social action and political reforms, without falling into the trap of self-proclaimed authoritarian righteousness. Isiah Berlin summed up this attitude when he wrote:

Pluralism, with the measure of 'negative' liberty that it entails, seems to me a truer and more humane ideal than the goals of those who seek in the great, disciplined, authoritarian structures the ideal of 'positive' self-mastery by classes, or peoples, or the whole of mankind. It is truer, because it does, at least, recognize the fact that human goals are many, not all of them commensurable, and in perpetual rivalry with one another. (Berlin, 1969, p. 171)

While it is understandable how the values of playing cricket and playing baseball, or the values of climbing a mountain and singing in an opera, may be regarded as incommensurable, it is difficult to see how the values of respecting other people regardless of the colour of their skin and of torturing others precisely *because* of the colour of their skin, or the values of promising to look after every frail elderly person in our community, and of telling all frail elderly people who have not got enough savings to get nursing care that they deserve to die, can be regarded as being incommensurable. The difficulty which liberals such as Berlin cannot avoid is that they are so obsessed with the idea that authoritarianism is the only basis for asserting the rightness of any set of values, that they shy away from making unequivocal pronouncements on moral and political issues. Ernest Gellner has forcefully exposed this weakness:

The truth of the plurality of incommensurate values might perhaps help liberty, by showing that no values must be imposed on anyone. Alas, this won't work, for this position must also allow illiberal values their place in the sun. This is the basic trouble with the initially tempting idea of enlisting incommensurateness on the side of tolerance: the values and visions endorsed by the procedure also include total and intolerant ones, which are neither inconspicuous nor unimportant in history. (Gellner, 1995)

Richard Rorty has defended the position Berlin adopted, on the grounds that there is no independent framework with reference to which liberal values can be described as being preferable to anti-liberal values. According to Rorty:

We cannot assume that liberals ought to be able to rise above the contingencies of history and see the kind of individual freedom which the modern liberal state offers its citizens as just one more value . . . Only the assumption that there is some such standpoint to which we might rise gives sense to the question, 'If one's convictions are only relatively valid, why stand for them unflinchingly?' (Rorty, 1989, pp. 49–50)

Rorty's attempt to defend Berlin ends up revealing that, from their 'pluralist' perspective, it cannot be asked why we should stand by some values but dismiss others as being unworthy. In this view, those of us who are opposed to racism are morally no different from those who torture and kill because of it. We may choose one course of action or another, but there is nothing to differentiate between them morally. So, without laying claim to the legitimacy of one's actions as being for the good of all, the Berlins and Rortys of the world do what they can to help the vulnerable, while accepting that the neo-Nazis and fundamentalist extremists, in waging their campaigns of hatred and terror against their chosen victims, are morally no different – or, more precisely, it would not even make sense to ask about their moral difference. This is the unwavering neutrality which now dominates the politics of individualism.

It is this neutrality that leaves society open to the advances of authoritarian groups. Witness the proliferation of such groups and their demands for oppressive policies against homosexuals, single parents, foreigners seeking political asylum, women workers, the homeless, and people on low income or welfare support. At the same time, opposition to these groups is fragmented, at a time when a united front is needed to safeguard common human values from the attacks of bigots and extremists. To overcome the political disorientation engendered by the changes underlying the Post-Everything Syndrome, and the inadequacies of current thinking on ideological conflicts, there is an urgent need to discover how a progressive alternative is to be formulated to combat both political individualism and authoritarianism. In the following chapters, we shall look at the implications of communitarianism for education, work, and protection, and consider how communitarian politics can be taken forward through action in the state, business, and third sectors.

3
Education for Citizens

Education and Citizenship

Communitarian citizenship requires all members of inclusive communities to develop the understanding and abilities to participate as equals in determining how decisions affecting them are to be made. It is the educative function of communities to develop the understanding of each new generation of citizens to enable them to engage in co-operative enquiries, evaluate knowledge-claims that affect their well-being, and pursue common values. This function is carried out, not just by schools, colleges and universities, but also by research institutions, the mass media, and above all, parents.

Communities that make no systematic attempt to educate the young to become effective citizens run the risk that relativistic individualism would by default come to dominate their outlook. In the absence of any consistent guidance about what is to be done for the good of all, the young could easily grow up with the impression that one choice is as good as an other, and that in making their choices they do not owe any duty to the wider community. Although it is not always easy to establish any definite correlation between one form of cultural outlook and the manifestation of antisocial behaviour, many observers of the United States of America, which exhibits one of the most individualistic cultures in the world, are struck by the growth of callous crimes in that society. For example, Frederick P. Close, the director of education at the Ethics Resource Centre in Washington, DC, believes that in place of the do-as-you-please individualism that has become dominant in American culture, education must be reorientated towards the cultivation of intelligence and character. Close relates 'some sobering statistics from the FBI's latest Uniform Crime Report (1991):

'Between 1965 and 1990, the murder arrest-rate for juveniles steadily increased, up 332 percent for the period . . . Between 1980 and 1990, the arrest rate for white juveniles for forcible rape jumped by 86 percent (compared to a 9 percent increase for African-Americans). In this same period, the arrest rate for aggravated assault for young people was up 59 percent for whites and 79 percent for African-Americans, while cocaine-and heroin-related crimes increased 2,373 percent for African-Americans and 251 percent for whites. Nothing suggests an end to these trends' (Close, 1993/4).

As the USA has considerable cultural influence over the rest of the world through its global marketing, it is not surprising that the American experience is beginning to be replicated in other parts of the world, especially in those countries which follow its individualistic example. What makes the reorientation of education towards the holistic development of young people as citizens difficult to achieve is its susceptibility to being hijacked by authoritarians. The latter would advocate combating moral fragmentation by imposing a set of values and behavioural norms on the young. They would demand harsh disciplinary measures to ensure compliance, regardless of the justifiability of the values and norms in question. Yet, in practice, far from blocking fragmentation, such an approach would only fuel rebellion against what are perceived as being arbitrary standards, and bring any talk of 'values' into further disrepute.

By contrast, the communitarian position puts the emphasis on developing the abilities of citizens' to formulate co-operative solutions to common problems. The general values of love, wisdom, justice and fulfilment do not provide detailed blueprints for what is to be done: they are merely the starting point of enquiries. All citizens need to understand how the values which, in the broadest terms, matter most are to be applied in the way they develop themselves and the ways they relate to others. They need to learn that they share in the responsibility for realizing those values in general, whatever particular skills they may develop in life (Etzioni, 1995b, ch. 3; Crewe, 1997).

The idea that education is supposed to equip different types of people for different positions in life through tailor-made packages was never wholly convincing. What schools and colleges provide is at best a general preparation for coping with life, with job-related skills development being just one element. Unless a society wishes to deny the opportunity of a specified class of people to deal competently with certain types of issue in life, it must view education as the overall development of citizens, and not narrowly as the granting of occupation-specific passports (Tarrant, 1989). As advancement in science and information technology leads to constant and rapid identification of problems and possible solutions, it is not those who possess the most knowledge in a given field, but those who can make sense of the latest knowledge-claims in most aspects of life who are best placed to function as effective members of their communities (Entwistle, 1996).

It does not follow from this that a little of all subjects should be taught, instead of specialization in a few. Mary Warnock rightly warned against teaching everyone the same general range of subjects in the name of egalitarianism. What she held to be far more important is *high quality* education for everyone, where the quality would be 'measured by the degree to which the imagination is exercised. To exercise the imagination is to keep it in practice, by giving it to attend to, in detail, objects which are worthy of attention; and all objects are more worthy of attention in detail than superficially' (Warnock, 1973, p. 121).

So while young people's different interests and technical abilities may lead them to specialize in different subjects, the underlying objective of teaching, whatever the combination of subjects, should contain a core component of stimulating and supporting the growth of the young people's imaginations. By applying their imaginations constructively to the common values of communities, the solidarity of those communities and the development of their members would be strengthened. In contrast to the strengthening of closed communities, which inhibits individuality for the sake of submissive conformity, and alienates other communities, this form of strengthening would allow individual citizens to use their own initiative in a framework that best guarantees the realization of the good for all. More specifically, the cultivation of imaginative appreciation of the four general values provides a measure of the effectiveness of communities in carrying out their educative role. To be effective, education in all its forms must enable successive generations of citizens to pursue those values in every aspect of life.

To begin with, the value of love cannot be communicated except in a caring environment. Although the actual cultural roots may differ in terms of the divergent world views of Islam, Christianity, Buddhism, Humanism, Confucianism, Hinduism and so on – the 'thick' morality that Walzer holds to be culturally fundamental – the fruits are strikingly similar: these being the 'thin' common moral ideas across different communities which for Walzer provide a basis for cross-cultural moral criticisms (Walzer, 1994). All human beings should be brought up and sustained by loving relationships, and sympathy should be extended to those deprived of such relationships. Instead of invoking some neutral procedural process to exclude intolerance, teachers of values should communicate positively the importance of love and compassion, and their direct effects in ruling out as unacceptable the hatred and intolerance of others. If the extent to which one's concern for others is to be translated into practical care for others cannot be determined prior to deliberations over particular issues, it none the less opposes uncompromisingly false values that are built on the arbitrary denial of the equal needs of others for loving relationships – false values which seek to prevent their adherents from recognizing such needs in others just because they have different nationalities, racial backgrounds, religions or sexual orientations.

The value of wisdom, by its very nature, rules out irrationality and indoctrination in transmitting knowledge and understanding to the young. The call for concentration on basic facts in teaching reveals not only a serious lack of appreciation of the nature of knowledge, but also virtual blindness to contemporary organizational behaviour. Knowledge does not consist of a collection of facts: it is derived from the intelligent conclusions of co-operative enquiries, and what counts as knowledge may change as the sophistication of enquiries improves. This evolving dynamic of human knowledge is now a major factor in organizational development. When observers such as P. F. Drucker point to the emergence of the 'Knowledge Society' (Drucker, 1993) they are not saying that society now depends on people who can quote texts from various definitive sources of knowledge. They are explaining that society is becoming more dependent on organizations, which are in turn dependent on their members, who can manage *without* definitive sources of knowledge. The knowledge workers are entrusted with formulating solutions through making their own enquiries, precisely because information and its analysis are developing at such a rapid pace that those who rely on quoting from 'definitive' sources for guidance are the least likely to be able to offer adaptive solutions. In teaching the value of wisdom, no educative community can allow dogmas and prejudices masquerading as traditional knowledge to be preserved. No knowledge-claim, be it about the motives of one's nation's conquest of another, or the accuracy of Newtonian physics, can be granted a special status if it cannot be validated under conditions of co-operative enquiry. The value of justice is one which requires imagined reciprocity to develop. Far from assuming that actions taken in the past, and practices that are prevalent in the present, are all correct, young people should be able to imagine how they would feel if they were at the receiving end of those actions and practices. They cannot fully appreciate the importance of justice in how they behave towards others, if that aspect of the behaviour of adults, past and present, is shielded from critical appraisal. In understanding why adults who subject others to treatment they would not tolerate themselves, deserve to be censured, the young could more easily accept that they too would be deserving of censure if they were to act unjustly. Of course, in practice, what would constitute justice may not be easy to determine.

The more complex the relationship between what one gives one's backing to and the impact on other people, the more difficult it is to discern what should or should not be revised. The many kinds of disagreement between Rawls and his critics illustrate the controversial nature of defining justice beyond the 'thin' level of direct reciprocal respect and mutuality. However, whereas Rawls tries to resolve this by stipulating what individuals abstracted from all moral considerations would adopt as guiding principles, an inclusive community would rely on citizens with a deep appreciation of their common values to consider together and choose the principles with which they could live. Such a process should become a familiar one from a young age. It can be learnt from discussing and agreeing to the rules of a game, to the arrangements for keeping a classroom tidy, or to the procedures for tackling bullying. Justice, instead of materializing from speculative abstractions, would in this model grow out of the maturing experiences of young people, who can identify manifestations of unfairness and appreciate the need for discipline.

Communitarian emphasis on discipline, such as that of Emile Durkheim, should be understood in the context of self-mastery being an essential component of justice (Durkheim, 1961; see also Etzioni, 1995b, pp. 93–5). Authoritarians may demand discipline for discipline's sake, but in inclusive communities, the discipline to challenge dogmas is as important as the discipline to obey commands that are issued through the appropriate channels. Recognizing discipline as an ability to act justly with others carries with it implications for how that discipline is to be encouraged and enforced. To base it on fear would promote resentment and evasion, whereas locating it at the centre of fair dealings with others would show it to be a positive aspect of character development, indispensable in communities sustained by justice.

Finally, the value of fulfilment involves teaching how fulfilment is to be sought. More and more young people are complaining about boredom. This is partly because of the decline in traditional employment opportunities, which leaves more spare time and less money to spend on leisure activities, and partly because it flows from the proliferation of quick-fix pleasures – 'nanosecond' consumer products, status symbols with ever-decreasing life-cycles, short-term stimulants and so on – which leave young people with no grasp of what would give them a real experience of fulfilment. Subjects that are taught mechanically just to convey basic facts offer young people's imagination nothing at all. By contrast, those of us who have been fortunate enough to have learnt from teachers who made their subjects fascinating, know how the joy of appreciating and cultivating appreciation in relation to those subjects can last a lifetime. This is not just limited to subjects taught in schools – but extends to the experience of developing an interest through which one can develop oneself – such as, public service, film-making, voluntary work, bringing up children, mountaineering and so on.

In addition to introducing young people to the experience of fulfilment through meaningful activities, the teaching of the value of fulfilment will also involve preparing young people for the attainment of the means to achieve fulfilment. In some cases, this will concern hard work, such as vigorous practice, which is not pleasurable in itself but is a constitutive part of the fulfilment. In other cases, it will concern developing abilities so that one can secure the income required to engage in the activities from which one finds fulfilment. True fulfilment cannot be prescribed. Young people must therefore be encouraged to explore within a responsible framework what forms of fulfilment they might pursue (for discussions of fulfilment as a key moral value, see Cooper, 1986; and Campbell, 1995). Such a framework would carry with it other general values, so that activities which promote hatred, rely on false assumptions, or treat others unfairly, would not be acceptable. Beyond these, guidance and enthusiasm should be brought to bear on what could give young people a sense of purpose and meaning in their lives. Not to teach this value is to leave young people to the quick-fix experiences that inevitably lead to disappointment and disillusionment. As Mill pointed out: without conscious nourishment, all too many people will sink to the lowest pleasures, which have no duration or substance (Mill, 1972, pp. 8–10).

The Need for Enquiry-led Education

The shift to greater value-orientation in education can be helped by applying the approach of co-operative enquiry more extensively to teaching. Unlike authoritarian values, which are imposed, communitarian values can only become the shared values of each new generation of citizens if they participate in examining and developing those values in the context of their own experiences. It is the development of such an approach which should form the focus of what is often described as 'citizenship education'. Citizenship cannot, and should not, be packaged as a stand-alone subject alongside history, mathematics, chemistry and so on, and taught in addition to the other subjects. Learning to become an effective member of an inclusive community involves the development of attitudes and abilities which must come through the whole educative experience. This experience should not be confined to classroom teaching either, but needs to be extended to all interactions between educators and the young (Lemming, 1994; Fogelman, 1996).

The moral vacuum left by academic relativism has meant that any talk of developing the 'right kind' of citizens through education is treated with suspicion. Rather than risk putting forward a model that could be criticized for supporting a particular authoritarian vision of control, a more superficial form of introduction to citizenship could be considered as a safe substitute. Young people may be encouraged to do a little voluntary work, find out about the availability of public services of interest to them, donate money to charities, and hold mock political debates which mirror outmoded political systems (Haste, 1993).

Unless the activities at this level are developed considerably, the young are not likely to attain any real appreciation of democratic citizenship. They need to know that not only is it important to help those less fortunate than oneself, but also that there are issues concerning power structures which must be addressed if that help is to be really effective in the long run. Similarly, debating skills may be useful, but politics needs citizens who can enquire after the truth with an open mind and not just defend their own current beliefs.

Enquiry-led education would apply the insights of co-operative enquiry to the development of young citizens by ensuring that all educative experiences provide a real opportunity to deepen the understanding of the young. This means that all teachers should be charged with the duty, and given the necessary training, to develop their pupils as enquiring citizens whatever subject they may happen to teach. Developing young people's competence and confidence in searching for the basis for ideas, without misleading them into thinking everything can be challenged arbitrarily, requires skills and patience.

Matthew Lipman's work on developing the 'Community of Enquiry' approach in the teaching of children provides an example of how young people can be taught to expand their understanding of an issue through shared enquiries with others. By following a structured discussion format, children come to understand better why certain ideas and principles should be believed, and also why in some cases it is necessary to recognize that there is no definite answer. Lipman's work, not surprisingly, draws heavily on the ideas of Dewey and Peirce. Instead of positing a set of truths on any subject for children to receive passively, the children themselves are encouraged to participate openly in determining what would or would not be an acceptable claim (Sutcliffe, 1995; Healy, 1996). It is important to note that such processes do not leave their participants thinking that they can legitimately cast doubt on anything they individually may wish to reject. On the contrary, the processes introduce them to the epistemological reality that knowledge is embedded in discursive communities, and knowledge claims should therefore be evaluated and, where appropriate, modified in the context of co-operative enquiries with other community members. As a result, they are able to differentiate more clearly between what they can rely on as a guide to practice and what they cannot. Children and young people need to appreciate that guidance on moral behaviour is based on the cumulative experiences of past generations, and that it is the duty of the present generation to develop it further where there is sufficient evidence and reason to do so. This allows them to take ownership and responsibility for acting in accordance with moral guidance, and not seek to avoid responsibility whenever coercive sanctions are absent (Pybus and McLaughlin, 1995).

Enquiry-led education can also be developed through community service learning. Instead of just studying texts, or even discussing them in groups, young people are to be given opportunities to identify problems which they can make a real contribution towards tackling. Although focus on text-based curriculum debates has often overlooked the value of service learning, many schools have initiated projects which clearly demonstrate the effectiveness of development through action in communities. Such projects have been undertaken by a wide range of schools, and include support for younger children by older students, joint environmental projects with local community groups, offering a service of peer group mediation in schools, action research to understand where voluntary help is most needed in a neighbourhood, mutual support between students and elderly residents they visit, and involvement in community broadcasting (see Institute for Citizenship Studies Report, 1994; and Mulligan, 1995).

Through working in communities of enquiry, young people learn that although questions in life do not always have ready-made answers, possible solutions discovered by co-operating with others in their search; that people with different views should be respected; that people who refuse to comply with the rules of co-operation cannot be allowed to override the wishes of others; and that the most acceptable course of action at the present time could still be subject to revision in the future. Such an approach to education would provide a bridge to inclusive communities dependent on citizens who are inclined, and able, to deal with their common concerns by means of co-operative enquiry.

The idea of allowing young people to learn by asking questions and having group discussions could, however, be criticized on the basis that it weakens learning, reduces respect for authority, and causes confusion among the young when they need firm guidance. After all, an inevitable consequence of applying co-operative enquiry to education is the opening up of more issues to the critical deliberation of those being taught. Opponents of 'progressive' education would argue that such an approach leads to a decline of standards in schools. The more time that is spent on deliberating what might be the case, it is suggested, the less time is spent on telling pupils what the case is. The more they are encouraged to question what they see before them, the less likely they are to have faith in what they are taught. This would produce adults who do not have enough knowledge or ability to play their part in society, but who question what is on offer and undermine social stability. Although Dewey pioneered the approach that has come to be known as 'progressive education', he had also seen the misunderstanding of that approach leading to serious misapplications in the classroom. In *Experience and Education*, he put the record straight by criticizing explicitly those who distorted the progressive approach into an anarchic mode of teaching. He wrote:

> Sometimes teachers seem to be afraid even to make suggestions to the members of a group as to what they should do. I have heard of cases in which children are surrounded with objects and materials and then left entirely to themselves, the teacher being loath to suggest even what might be done with the materials lest freedom be infringed upon. (Dewey, 1963, p. 71)

For Dewey, the teacher's experience must be utilized as appropriate guidance for those who are seeking to learn. Provided it is recognized that guidance does not preclude questioning and discussion, it has a crucial part to play as a catalyst in bringing the ideas of the children into a process of joint deliberation. What teachers need to find in the school community is an effective approach bringing pupils together which can be sustained by political leaders in the wider political community involving all citizens – an approach that can only be found when open discussions are supported by a framework of common values (Tam, 1996b).

There is a danger that those who believe that all values are relative would allow discussions to turn into personal attacks or arbitrary exchanges which add nothing to the participants' understanding of the issues in question. What is required is not the imposition of authoritarian values, but rather the insistence that the common values sustained by co-operative enquiries must serve as the guiding principles in citizenship education. Sceptics should be reminded that the displacement of ancient authorities on natural sciences by the open exchange of information and criticisms between co-operative enquirers led, not to chaos, but much more advanced understanding of natural phenomena.

This has three key implications for the political direction for education in society. First, it reinforces the view that in the early years of young people's lives, funding to support smaller class sizes would be desirable. It is difficult to facilitate an open discussion with 30–40 participants. It also suggests that changes to class sizes alone would not alter the quality of education significantly unless teachers are trained in the development of pupils' understanding through co-operative enquiry.

Curriculum development would need to look beyond the contents to be taught for different subjects, to provide clear guidance on how to conduct enquiries that draw on the problem-solving abilities of every member of the class. This approach would not rule out, for example, the teaching of key historical dates or standard chemical equations. What it would require is that, in teaching such facts, the context in which they gain their significance comes through in the associated discussions. A consequence of this is that the importance attached to such facts cannot be declared to be indispensable for social cohesion. Our understanding of our past, as much as of chemical processes, should be kept under review as new information and interpretations emerge. To deny this and to prevent some children from appreciating what others can see as appropriate changes to our interpretation of various knowledge-claims, would be a factor in undermining social cohesion. Furthermore, the crude measure of how many pupils pass examinations based on recollection of facts must be counterbalanced by more sophisticated measures which look at, for example, how many pupils from different socioeconomic backgrounds succeed in going on to higher education or in getting jobs, how often and how well they engage in co-operative projects within their own schools as well as with participants from other schools and the wider community, or how effective they are in enhancing the performance of everyone in their group by a shared commitment to improving standards.

Second, although the growing threat of unemployment has led to an even greater emphasis on the vocational dimension of education, the way citizenship skills are taught to the young must be given a high priority. To function as effective citizens, they will need to understand how the public domain works. Their entitlement to public services, and how they can best access the support they require, are not issues to be left until their school years are already behind them. Neither are issues concerning their responsibilities to others in their neighbourhood, and to the wider community. The reciprocal relationship between what they can call on their fellow citizens to provide and what they accept as their duties to others in return must be made clear. Schools should therefore work with public agencies to enable young people to discover how they fit into the public domain. The considerable learning experience on offer has been demonstrated by the active involvement of young people in key roles in projects such as residential care with the Normington Heights Group (Lightfoot, 1990, pp. 19–21), community development with the Haverhill Regeneration Group (Tam, 1996c), and strategic placement in local authorities which translate the young participants' findings into new public action (Hockey, 1997). In all these cases, young people have been able to learn from their experiences why they, and the positive changes they make, are valued by their fellow citizens.

While commercial organizations should be encouraged to have an input into the development of vocational skills training, they must not be allowed to dominate the formulation of course contents. Indeed, with so many rapid technological changes taking place, they should come to see that the skills of understanding issues in the absence of ready-made solutions, and of co-operating without the rules of rigid hierarchies, are as important as skills for particular technical operations.

Skills to gain paid work, or to provide unpaid service to others in the home or in one's community, should be developed in this wider context, and not treated as an end in itself which squeezes out the other skills of democratic citizenship. It follows from this that it would be a mistake to suppose that schools and classes should be differentiated into categories which mirror the different levels of employment skills requirement. Businesses may have an interest in a system which segregates young people into such categories so that they can target their recruitment from certain schools or classes. However, fitness for employment in different organizations is not the only socially significant factor in education. Citizens of inclusive communities must also learn to work with each other in considering issues that no single aptitude can monopolize as its own exclusive domain. Differentiation according to a narrow range of academic abilities would produce citizens who are ill-at-ease with co-operating with others who possess different skills and abilities. Although streaming for each subject may have the advantage of developing pupils with diverse potentials, total segregation would mean that a culture of co-operative citizenship could be seriously undermined.

The third implication for the giving of political direction for education lies in the recognition that the purpose of education cannot be divorced from the kind of society citizens collectively want to bring about. If the young were taught to think above all about how they could fit into the commercial world, and how they could make profitable transactions with the skills and resources they possess, they would overlook the importance of the public domain. They would see the world in terms of producers and consumers, and, failing to appreciate the interdependence of citizens and public services, grow up with little motivation to be involved in activities for the public good. If, on the other hand, they were taught to believe in the supremacy of certain hierarchical positions, and not to question them whatever the circumstances, those inheriting these positions would assume that they had an unquestionable right to keep others down; and those who are at the bottom of the hierarchy would become blindly submissive. Alternatively, the iniquity of the system might be exposed and violently overthrown. An inclusive community would not tolerate any hierarchical supremacy based on wealth, race, religion, sex, or any form of group allegiance. Nor would it allow the marketplace to displace public action. To insist on the former is not a matter of being unreasonably 'politically correct'; and to maintain the latter is not being anti-business. Against those who decry every reference to common values as dubious moralizing, schools should be given an explicit role of communicating the values which civic life demands of all citizens. Since we do have a clear consensus on many ethical issues, we should act on these rather than suspend all attempts at moral education just because we cannot reach agreement in some areas (Dewey, 1966, ch. 7; Etzioni, 1995b).

Moving education in this direction could be attacked as undermining traditions. If the traditions concerned are those which hinder the development of inclusive communities – for example, the tradition of white male domination, the tradition of passive subjects obeying whoever holds the power of government, or the tradition of the merchant class which puts the right to trade above all else – then it is just as well that those traditions are undermined. However, if it is argued that such a form of education would undermine all traditions and leave communities with no sense of a meaningful past or a cohesive future, then the argument is untenable. When we looked at the evolution of communitarian ideas in Chapter 1, we saw how those ideas have interacted with social and political outlooks through the ages. There is clearly a tradition in communitarian thinking, a tradition which respects problem-solving through co-operative enquiries, and the pursuit of common values validated by such enquiries. It may not be the dominant tradition in every aspect of life in the West, but it is a tradition which has had a long presence in history, and its expansion in the future would serve to support the cohesion of inclusive communities.

Parents and Schools

Enquiry-led education needs to be supported by parents as well as teachers. Without the approach being reinforced and sustained at home, children could find it difficult to relate consistently to the spirit of co-operative enquiry. This is why the role of parents is so important in inclusive communities. However, communitarian concern with the citizen's approach to parenthood can be confused with the demand made by authoritarians, who would like to bring back selected packages of 'traditional family values'. Yet, characteristically, authoritarians seek to impose values which are only selected through their personal prejudices without any form of co-operative validation. They want to retain or revive a form of society wherein they could be comfortable regardless of the oppressive consequences for those who have to bow to their demands.

From a communitarian point of view, any so-called 'traditional' value which adds to the fragmentation of communities into the powerful and the powerless, could not be accepted. This does not mean that the way parents behave is of no concern to their fellow citizens. Even the most extreme libertarians would concede that parents who are violently abusive towards their children should be prevented from controlling the lives of those children. Other acts and omissions may also be unacceptable if they deprive the young of the opportunity to grow up as healthy, confident and responsible citizens.

Parents should not resort to abuse to settle arguments, put their own pleasures invariably above the needs of their dependents, neglect their children's reliance on them to provide a caring environment in which to develop relationships, advocate hatred and intolerance, or allow them to drift into drug dependency, theft, obsessive gambling, or any other habit which can be destructive of a responsible life. Instead of assuming that parents must be right in whatever they demand of their children, or that they must always give way to their children, the authority of parents is to be derived from how their actions could be validated under conditions of co-operative enquiry. As Anthony Giddens has explained, while this is a requirement which may not be tested directly in practice, since the children may be too young to engage in a critical discussion, it still establishes an independent criterion indicating how parents should relate to their children:

> A democratic parent–child relationship is one of counter-factually bargained authority. The parent in effect says to the child: if you were able to discuss our relationship with me as an adult would do, in a free and open way, you would accept my reasons for treating you as I do . . . To the degree to which it develops, a democracy of the emotions would have significant implications for the futherance of formal, public democracy. (Giddens, 1994, p. 119)

Instead of allowing individual parents to do as they please, regardless of the consequences their behaviour may have on their fellow citizens, inclusive communities must ensure that clear duties are linked to the role of being a parent. Just as citizens seeking public office are expected to take on greater responsibilities in return for the influence they exercise over others, citizens seeking to become parents should acknowledge that how they bring up their children would have an impact on the lives of others, and they must therefore accept their need to behave as responsible parents. The need to develop the educative role of parents, however, cannot be met unless three related issues are dealt with satisfactorily. These concern the debate about family structure, the confusion over the concept of parental freedom, and clarification regarding what can in fact be done to strengthen parental responsibility.

Reactions against authoritarian attempts to attack non-traditional forms of family life have made it difficult to focus on the real problem. At one level, the two sides resort to observations which are neither controversial nor incompatible. One would say that, other things being equal, two-parent families can look after their children more effectively than one-parent families, if for no other reason than the former having more time and energy to spend on the children. The other would say that children brought up by loving and responsible one parent families are better off than those raised in uncaring and abusive two-parent families. It is only at a deeper level that the conflict becomes clear when one side insists that departures from the two-parent family model must be censured even though in some cases separation of the spouses – particularly when one of them is neglectful or abusive towards the needs of the family – would be desirable for the children concerned, and the other side refuses to accept that there should be any criticisms directed at those parents who choose to desert their children so that they can have a more exciting relationship or a more interesting career. Against both the authoritarian and individualist positions, communitarianism targets its criticism, not at old or new forms of family structures as such, but at parental behaviour which undermines the needs of children.

Divorce, not unlike marriage, cannot be right or wrong regardless of the circumstances. The values of looking after one's children are values which matter, not just to the family itself, but to the whole community, and unless the reasons invoked point to values which override the former, then the parents concerned should put the needs of their children first. What citizens should praise or blame is not particular family patterns, but the extent to which their fellow citizens carry out their responsibilities as parents. If people in Western democracies are still prepared to challenge those who turn a blind eye to neighbours who beat their children or put their lives at risk, inclusive communities would require an extension of that readiness to challenge those who insist that the ways in which others may neglect the interests of their children is none of their business.

Having children does not give parents the right to treat them in any way they please. Indeed, whatever their own personal motives may be in deciding to have children, they have an inescapable duty to ensure that the children they bring into the world have an environment at home which is conducive to loving relationships and open enquiries. (For an analysis of the reasons which may be, rightly or wrongly, invoked for having children, see Gibson, 1995.) If they could not provide such an environment because they are either unwilling or incapable, then they cannot be shielded from criticisms just because they are the parents.

This brings us to the second problem. If inclusive communities require the manner in which parents bring up their children to be considered as a matter of public interest, how is it to be reconciled with the concept of parental freedom? From an individualist point of view, it would indeed be difficult to identify a basis on which to criticize the actions of parents. However, for communitarians, what is right or wrong depends not just on what an individual thinks, but rather on what passes the test of co-operative enquiries. On a wide range of issues, therefore, where forms of neglect and abuse can readily be identified as being harmful to the development of children, citizens would be justified in seeking collective action to train potential parents in ways of avoiding such harm; give children independent educative support where their parents do not provide it adequately; and remove children to new homes if their parents have clearly failed to discharge their parental duties.

Before going into the practical implications of such an approach, we should consider a deeper political question about the restrictions it would impose on parental freedom. After all, some parents may feel that the commitment to care and respect for all citizens, and to resolving differences through open discussions, represents a position they could not tolerate. For example, there could be parents who consider it wrong that their children should be brought up believing that their family's moral tradition – which regards people with different religions or racial backgrounds as being significantly inferior – could legitimately be challenged. Should such parents be given the freedom to teach their children to oppose the general values of inclusive communities? And if this entails the freedom to reject contrary teaching, should they be granted the right to withdraw their children from classes or schools which teach equal respect for all religions and races? (See, for example, the *Mozert* v. *Hawkins* case, as discussed in Macedo, 1995.)

For those who cannot see any basis for defending common values, the importance of respecting the diverse traditions of different people must push towards a concession to these people. However, traditions are not valuable in their own right, and one of the most important implications of recognizing the general values of inclusive communities is precisely to rule out as unacceptable any viewpoint that opposes those values directly. This would pose a dilemma for anyone following the individualist line of reasoning. Individualists are bound by their procedural neutrality to tolerate even those who preach intolerance. From a communitarian perspective, however, any attempt to foster or sustain a culture of alienation of other religious or racial groups is not to be tolerated. Parents would therefore not be allowed to withdraw their children from classes or schools on the grounds that they do not want their children to be educated into adopting the values of inclusive communities. The adoption of these values by the young would be a core purpose of education. Parents should be allowed to teach their children about their own cultures so long as that does not involve directing them to oppose these values.

Theoretical confusions over parental freedom could lead to the perpetual undermining of citizenship education. Instead of models of neutrality, which have to be adjusted to cope with social intolerance woven into cultural diversity, what is needed is a political commitment to develop the understanding by all citizens of why and how they should evaluate issues through co-operative enquiries. Amy Gutmann has pointed out that:

> At issue here is not mere exposure to different ways of life for the sake of giving children more choices among good lives but, rather, teaching future citizens to evaluate different political perspectives that are often associated with different ways of life . . . Teaching children to think about social justice entails teaching them that it may be reasonable to disagree with their parents and teachers – and every other authority – on politically relevant matters. (Gutmann, 1995, pp. 577, 578)

In essence, parental freedom is conditional on the exercising of that freedom responsibly. Parents can no more be allowed to insist on giving their children an education that would make them believe that they are superior to others to whom they should pay little regard, than they can be allowed to teach their children to burn the property of those they hate. This argument also applies to parents who feel that they should do whatever they judge to be the best for their children regardless of the consequences for other children. Some parents, for example, may insist that children of lesser academic ability than their own should be segregated, even if it means that the latter would have their self-esteem damaged at an early age, and thus be pushed into a lower status of citizenship. The choice of such parents, and their individual judgements, cannot override the concerns of parents in general, and the admission policy of schools must ultimately help to meet the needs of the community as a whole and not just some parents who do not care about the needs of others.

In practice, much will depend on the development of responsible parental attitudes and abilities. This raises the final problem of the parental role in education, which concerns the extent to which citizens can do anything collectively in a domain which many people still regard as essentially private. In order to ensure that the intervention undertaken is not exploited in support of particular authoritarian demands, the processes must be open and subject to democratic reviews by those concerned with its operation.

The options would include both action through government institutions and action organized by the citizens themselves. As far as government institutions are concerned, they can play a significant role in making all young people aware of the complex responsibilities that go with bringing children into the world. Even if they had not lived consistently by the values of inclusive communities, having children would mean that there would be new political expectations brought to bear on them as parents to live by those values. They would not be allowed to take for granted that they could keep their children regardless of their own behaviour, or that they could walk out on their children to suit an alternative lifestyle they wish to pursue. People who have made no adequate preparations when they (intentionally or accidentally) have children should be required to make those preparations or their children will be adopted by people who have made appropriate preparations. Divorce for couples with children should involve a mediation period to consider the interests of the children with their active involvement. This would require a detailed re-examination of the legal definitions and procedures covering parental responsibilities. Such an exercise would provide an opportunity to clarify what interventions children are entitled to from the wider community in support of their educative development as citizens.

Government bodies can also help parents to fulfil their educative role by ensuring that there are enough nursery education places and child care facilities where the interest and respect for co-operative learning would be stimulated. They can also encourage employers to provide flexible working arrangements to accommodate the needs of parents to balance their work and family responsibilities. Citizens themselves can promote parental discussion groups at local schools, both for existing parents and for those of the future at these schools. Children generally relate to the importance of learning about parenting when their experiences with their own parents are brought into the discussion. They can be assisted by peer group service learning projects to tackle the subject of having and bringing up children. As we have seen, the peer group approach has the additional advantage of developing the young people's abilities to learn through discussions among themselves.

Citizens can also invite voluntary organizations devoted to promoting better understanding of bringing up children to talk about, for example, the need to prevent cruelty to children, the importance of family relationships, the value of expressing love, and the developmental needs of infants. Other voluntary groups, Churches, or humanist bodies can be brought in to advise on ceremonies and practices to reinforce the commitment to provide loving care for children. The politics of both authoritarians and individualists ignore the value of interpersonal relationships. But instead of regarding talk of love and care for others as issues external to the hard political domain, communitarians would locate such concern at the heart of politics. Without the appreciation of love, one of the four key common values, the development of citizens would ultimately be deficient.

Parents, schools and other local bodies can further co-operate in the provision of neighbourhood advice and support. Such local networks would not only help to minimize the chance of individual parents or teachers wrongly assessing the needs of a particular child, they would also provide a consistent message and offer of help to the young who may otherwise be at a loss as to what they should or should not do. It is true that such local voluntary action may do little to change the behaviour of abusive vandals, but the purpose of such action is to help to develop the next generation as responsible citizens even if it is too late for some members of the present generation. To achieve this, parents, teachers and community groups should work more closely together in understanding the areas in which different children in their locality need greater support.

Reforming Educative Institutions

If parents need to be more aware of their responsibilities, they in turn are dependent on the many institutions that play a significant role in educating citizens. In place of authoritarian controls and market individualism, a systematic course of reforms would need to be implemented if citizens are to get the educative support they need. These reforms should cover public policies on schools, universities, the media, the information superhighway, and lifelong learning for adults.

Above all, schools and colleges must set themselves the key objective of teaching their pupils how to learn through co-operative enquiry. To do this, teachers will need to be given considerably more support. First and foremost, teachers' pay must be sustained strategically at a level comparable to that of doctors, lawyers and accountants. The status of teachers in society must be raised to reflect the key role they have in the development of inclusive communities. The teaching profession must be able to offer remuneration which would attract and retain those who are outstanding teachers. To argue that teachers do not need to go through as difficult a training process as required by the legal and medical professions brings us to our next point. The training of teachers must incorporate the development of their understanding of how co-operative enquiries work, and how they are to be introduced to young people in interesting and instructive ways. The training will also need to cover the application of child psychology to the teaching of common values, not through any particular subject, but rather through teaching in general. Just as the commitment to save lives is fundamental to the medical profession, teachers need to be trained to devote their careers to the development of young people into citizens who understand how to pursue common values through co-operation. Finally, following their training, those who enter the profession should be given opportunities to be involved in deliberations over the way that decisions are to be made in their schools. Teachers who are themselves marginalized in the process of decision-making would understandably find it difficult to inculcate a culture of participation among their pupils.

For those who fear that this approach would lead to a rigid homogeneity across all schools, it should be pointed out that the successful implementation of the approach would in fact make it possible for greater diversity to develop. This apparent paradox can be explained with reference to the difference between guiding values and comprehensive values. Guiding values, such as those identified as being central to inclusive communities, do not prescribe how individuals are to behave in every situation. They point to the factors which need to be taken into account, and the manner in which they should be weighed to determine how one is to behave; but they do not exclude what other factors may be taken into account, provided these do not conflict with the guiding values themselves. Comprehensive values, by contrast, purport to cover every situation, and instead of giving individuals the autonomy to deliberate with other community members to consider what is to be done, they specify what must be done.

Schools dominated by a single set of comprehensive values would suffocate cultural and intellectual diversity. However, by anchoring schools with a common set of guiding values, society can more confidently allow different schools to pursue a significantly different ethos. Compared with schools which try to maintain neutrality and give no direction to any set of values at all, the communitarian approach would stimulate different schools to go in a variety of directions in building on the guiding values thicker sets of beliefs and values which reflect the interests and traditions of those schools and the local communities. Catholic and Hindu, Muslim and Buddhist schools would all be able to develop their respective pupils without either having to dilute their teachings to mix with all other moral traditions, or undermining social cohesion through depriving them of a common core of guiding values for all citizens (Ormell, 1996; McLaughlin, 1996). In place of the false dichotomy of either teaching children commitment to a single set of comprehensive values or teaching them no commitment at all, schools would have the freedom to develop their excellence in relation to different moral traditions, on the basis that they all teach commitment to the guiding values. Through its global Associated Schools Project, UNESCO has already achieved considerable success in promoting the development of schools as inclusive communities in countries as diverse as Costa Rica, France, Korea, Senegal, Hungary, Colombia and the Philippines (Meyer-Bisch, 1995). Any suggestion that schools cannot enrich their pupils' sense of moral purpose on the basis of common guiding values would fly in the face of the evidence.

However, this approach could be criticized by market individualists for assuming that schools should aim at the development of citizens with a clear understanding of citizens' common values. They would maintain that the purpose of schools should be determined by the marketplace. This philosophy is translated into pressures on schools and colleges to sell themselves to attract commercial sponsorships, to attract children of rich parents, and where numbers alone count, maximum intake of pupils to secure government grants (or even public-funded vouchers). The argument we have considered in relation to parental freedom applies here too. If parents who want their prejudices to override the common values of the wider community should not be given the freedom to choose how their children are to be educated, neither should those with a higher proportion of society's economic resources be allowed to steer the direction of citizens' education. Small-scale sponsorships may be harmless enough in themselves, but a culture of commercialized education can be extremely divisive. The problem with individualist ideologies, as we have seen, is that they in fact leave prevailing power relations, however unjust, firmly in place. This may, of course, be the main reason why they are advocated by some of those who claim to promote them for the sake of defending individuals' freedom. In reality, the public funding of education for all must be secured at the level deemed necessary by schools in joint deliberations with local communities. To commercialize the funding base would be to divert schools from their civic duties to income-generation projects which may have little to do with the citizenship development of all pupils regardless of their socioeconomic backgrounds.

The commercialization of universities can also have undesirable effects. Businesses which stand to benefit from their research findings should quite properly be encouraged to fund such research. However, it would be wrong to go on to suggest that public funding of universities should be cut back so that they can be made more responsive to business needs. The work of universities covers a vast intellectual and cultural terrain, and only parts of it concern the world of commerce. To force universities to rely more and more on business funding would be to reduce the development of human understanding to nothing more than items that can be sold for a profit.

Most damaging of all, the co-operative spirit of enquiry, which consolidated the scientific discoveries in the seventeenth century into a permanent revolution in our outlook on knowledge, would gradually be destroyed by increasing commercialization of what should be an open and independent research establishment. The very basis and model of co-operative enquiry would be eroded until the validation of knowledge-claims drifts to a pre-Baconian state, wherein the only alternatives are sceptical ignorance or dogmatic pronouncement by those in powerful positions. For fear of losing funding to competitive bidders, researchers would be discouraged from sharing information; to gain marketing advantages, research findings would be withheld from widespread discussions and criticisms; ideas which might extend human understanding but have little potential for commercial exploitation would be marginalized; collaboration for the common good would give way to fragmented attempts to secure patents and other financial benefits to further one's research at the expense of others; and research which might produce findings unfavourable to commercial interests – particularly those dependent on the consumption of their potentially harmful products – would be blocked altogether.

Inclusive communities can only be built on a research infrastructure devoted to co-operative enquiries. Such enquiries produce research findings which can then be fed into schools and other educative institutions. Where improvement really is needed is in the communication of such findings to the wider community. When those engaged in research erect barriers between themselves and others whose understanding they are supposed to assist in expanding, new channels must be established to involve both sides in considering how they can work together to achieve better understanding in different fields.

One avenue through which researchers and others can communicate more effectively is by greater utilization of the mass media. This is an area where the pressure for more commercialization has also been generated by proponents of market individualism.

Instead of recognizing the role of the media to communicate information that enhance citizens' understanding of a wide range of issues that affect their lives, the model of the commercial market is invoked in support of deregulations. In this model, the contents of the media are best determined by commercial forces. Like the research establishment, but perhaps much further down that road, publishers and programme makers are motivated to concentrate on commercially attractive products, and ignore the need for educative information. Even the internationally respected BBC, an example of television with a commitment to educative broadcasting and funded by a community-wide licence fee, has been subject to the serious threat of being reduced to another market commodity.

More direction must be considered for the future development of the mass media. If, unlike schools, they do not have a primary concern with the development of citizens, their output none the less has a major impact on that development. This is an impact which no inclusive community should ignore. Of course, any suggestion that the contents of the media are to be subject to independent scrutiny raises the issue of censorship. In practice, it is widely accepted that incitement to hatred and violence, and the promotion of activities which could harm those engaged in them without their knowing, should not be allowed. Arguments which seek to defend representations of violence in the abstract have to concede that it would be wrong to show a programme which glorifies a figure who tortures and kills women and children to the cheers of his followers. The issue is whether the specific showing of acts which transgress the common values of society are likely to lead to more transgression.

Attempts to sidestep this issue by suggesting that individuals should be allowed to choose for themselves inevitably fail. If what is contained in the media could not have any negative influence on our beliefs and desires, then what people choose to read or see would not in itself lead them to harm themselves or others. If, however, the media could project imagery or stories which through their impact on people's beliefs and desires lead them to behave in ways harmful to themselves or others, then the fact that some people may ignorantly or irresponsibly choose to consume such media output would be precisely why the output should be subject to wider scrutiny. Although psychologists may argue over the impact of particular programmes, the existence of a vast global advertising industry is sufficient testimony as to how significantly the things seen and read in the media can shape people's beliefs and desires – which ultimately affect the way they behave.

It may be argued that if experts such as psychologists cannot always agree among themselves, then any attempt to draw the line between what should be censored or not would fall into some form of arbitrary authoritarianism. This argument invokes the kind of epistemological relativism we looked at in connection with individualist ideas in Chapter 2. Such relativism would demand the acquittal of all who are accused of criminal offences, since it is always possible to find experts who disagree about a particular charge. What should happen is that the mystique of evaluating media content should be taken away. Censorship panels should be set up along the lines of jury selection, and hear evidence from experts before deciding on whether particular cases brought to their attention should be censored or not.

In parallel to scrutinizing the negative effects of the media, the enormous potential they provide for instructive information to children, public service information for local communities, and information to enhance global understanding, should be utilized more. Underpinned by a recognition of our common values, the media should be encouraged, by the institution of major civic awards, for example, to assist the public in gaining a better understanding of how people can lead caring, fair and fulfilling lives. The innovative European Communities Project, for example, has succeeded in bringing schools from all the different European Union (EU) countries together to respond to the challenge of using audiovisual or video techniques to produce a portrait of the participating schools' home area, 'showing its character, the community at work and, particularly, the way that it relates to the rest of Europe' (Haigh, 1995). Imaginative use of the media will generally contribute more than formal speeches to the breaking down of prejudices, by dispelling ignorance, suspicion, fear and hatred. The development of information and telecommunications technology makes the review of media output even more urgent. Without clear direction on what the media are to bring to citizens, the opportunity for more of it to be brought to even more citizens raises many questions. We cannot simply stand back, because contrary to those who have a utopian vision of anarchy, the absence of collective controls would leave those with the commercial power, and those concerned with propagating extremist messages, the freedom to target their output regardless of the consequences for others. As technology is opening a global network of communications, the collective deliberations cannot be confined to national boundaries. In opposition to the threat of the world being further divided up between those who have the power to access more information and those who do not, the advancement of information technology should be used as a tool to assist with the equalization of power relations across all communities in the world. In the emerging knowledge society, the range of information as well as the speed at which it can be accessed, processed and passed on will be crucial in applying the approach of co-operative enquiry on an unprecedented scale.

The network should extend to every household, school, library and business in every community. This cannot be left to the free market. Governments must step in to ensure that cable connections cover all areas. Beyond establishing and securing the future maintenance of the infrastructure, attention must focus on the kind of information to be communicated through the network. Citizens should be given opportunities to shape strategies for securing affordable, universal access to the new source of educative information. Support should be given, in particular, to the production of imaginative educational packages, and to promoting awareness of their availability. Special effort will have to be put towards explaining to those least familiar with information technology what information can be obtained for their benefit, and how they can access it. This can be achieved with the help of community-based computer training resource centres (Smith, 1997, pp. 14–15). Interactive technology should also be used to balance the conventional two-way debates between rival experts or politicians, by developing opportunities for citizens in general to participate in group discussions, and to question the experts on technical issues.

If the global information highway is not to isolate people into individual cells, and displace face-to-face interactions by impersonal transactions with mechanical information systems, it must be used as a bridge for cultivating human relationships. Geography, which has in the past kept so many communities apart, can now be transcended instantly by pressing a few keys. The claim that a global community of inclusive communities cannot be developed because of the distance separating people can no longer be sustained. Instead, citizenship education should make the most of the superhighway to cultivate joint projects by citizens in different parts of the world. Such projects should include collaboration on exposing the ideologies and activities of extremist groups who themselves are exploiting the unregulated network to form new alliances.

Finally, there is a need for all citizens to have learning opportunities throughout their adult lives. In part, this is caused by changes in employment demands. Schools and universities can no longer be expected to provide the basic learning that will see individuals through to retirement. Job content and skills requirements change rapidly, and people have to learn new ways of doing things all the time. In part, this is because of the increase in leisure time which can be enriched through more understanding of what can be enjoyed. The contents of courses and their accessibility will become increasingly important as citizens need them to manage their lives. From a communitarian point of view, this extends to understanding the political activities that go on around them. It is therefore vital that courses which are necessary for the ongoing development of citizenship skills and critical understanding are developed and made available in an affordable form to all citizens.

Once again we need to guard against the fallacy that courses that are 'worthwhile' would attract enough buyers to secure their development. Unless there is a collective push for lifelong education, many businesses which need better trained staff would still rely myopically on others to train them, and people who need more education would remain oblivious to their needs. Taking into account what is available through schools, universities, the mass media and the information superhighway, every government, in partnership with employer and union representatives, should map out unmet education needs, channel resources into the development of new provision, and regularly make their availability known to every citizen. At the local level, local authorities can take the lead in promoting the culture and practices of lifelong learning in their areas (Mudd, 1997). In order to ensure that there are sufficient resources from the economy to fund the different educative reforms, not to mention the financial abilities of citizens to access educational support throughout their lives, we need to look at how an economy which respects the values of inclusive communities is to function. We turn to this issue in the next chapter.

4
Work for Citizens

Work and Citizenship

Citizens need work in inclusive communities for three main reasons. First, there is the requirement to convert resources into goods and services sought by the citizens themselves. Second, work which contributes to the generation of income provides citizens with greater degrees of autonomy so that they can participate in collective deliberations without being dependent on others. Third, work is an important means of achieving the value of fulfilment; without any form of meaningful work, citizens can lose their self-esteem and sense of purpose in life.

The three reasons correspond broadly to what may be called the 'economic', 'social', and 'moral' dimensions of community life. The economic dimension is concerned with how the community as a whole enhances its well-being by working on the available resources. Ever since the Industrial Revolution, communities that have adapted their divisions of labour most effectively to the development of new technologies have succeeded in enhancing their well-being in terms of life expectancy, literacy, diversity of goods, reliability of services, and numerous other indicators. However, as the pace of technological development accelerates, the equilibrium achieved following each phase of adaptation has become increasingly difficult to sustain.

This poses the problem of the inefficient distribution of work. When people have the opportunity of working together, making their respective contributions which lead to a better quality of life in which they can all share, it is relatively easy to bring out the best in everyone. However, if after each adaptation, an increasing number of people are left with no valuable work to do, while others are required to work even harder than before, then the distribution of work must come under question.

Any community that does not address this problem effectively would certainly fall behind communities that reintegrate their members continuously into a productive role. This is not just an issue of relative decline, but the more active conversion of resources by the more productive economies could leave others with less of what they could previously secure with ease. Access to food and other basic goods could become more restricted, either because the sources of their supply have been taken over by stronger economic powers, or because they charge more in response to what the richer communities can afford, and in so doing make it less affordable for others. This has happened to many countries in the developing world, where the inefficient distribution of work has meant that citizens run repeatedly into shortages of food and other basic necessities. It is also happening within developed countries, where communities with high unemployment sink into 'Third World' conditions within 'First World' borders.

Furthermore, the overall productiveness of any community does not depend solely on the productivity of those paid directly for their work. The paid workers rely on the support of other members in their community to engage in their activities. This support ranges from the unpaid work of those who look after the families and household arrangements of those who get paid for their work (informally, some partners recognize the income received by either as joint income, but employers make their cheques out only to those directly on their payroll), to the acceptance of prevailing employment arrangements by those who are unemployed even though they are most disadvantaged by those arrangements. A community which neglects the importance of such support, and marginalizes those who give it, would inevitably create divisive tensions which diminish the productiveness of the entire community.

The failure to consider the role of those without paid work leads not only to an imbalance between economics and social concerns, but also to bad economics. One of the key issues in the renewed debates concerning T. H. Marshall's concept of citizenship is how the role of those without paid unemployment should be incorporated into economic as well as welfare policies (Bulmer and Rees, 1996). Communities need to consider how anyone without paid work can most effectively be involved in working with those in paid employment in generating the output to enhance the quality of life for the whole community. This is not a question of welfare or, for that matter, workfare, but a question of co-operative employment that would enable all members of the community to have the incentive and opportunity to play a role in improving their collective economic strength.

Regarding the social dimension, paid work enables those who have a legitimate share in the income it brings to think and act relatively autonomously in their social interactions with others in their community. Without a reasonable degree of social autonomy, people who are dependent on the 'good will' of others – be these charitable donors, distant but generous relatives, or taxpayers – would suffer from a double handicap. Instead of possessing an income that allows them to look beyond their own needs and to engage in deliberations about the needs of others, they have to worry about securing an income of their own so that they are not reliant on the discretionary 'generosity' of others. Moreover, even if they find themselves in a position where their views are sought, they have to be careful not to offend their 'benefactors'.

It may be argued that the state's benefit system is set up as a form of entitlement which is non-discretionary, unlike charitable donations. In practice, the views of those who are sensitive about paying taxes, and of the politicians who target their votes, can play a very influential part in cutting back on the benefits to which the needy are entitled. Deferential appreciation of whatever is given may at least avoid rocking the boat, but outspoken criticism of the inadequacies of state provision could provoke those in power to hit back. In the name of countering the 'dependency culture', those who are in fact dependent on the state for such basic support as food and shelter, would have that support further reduced. The constant threat is that if they do not learn to be compliant, the support would be cut even more.

It could be claimed that this threat, which undermines the autonomy of those without paid work to have their say as citizens, also applies to those who suffer from job insecurity, or from being the spouses of irresponsible earners. This is in fact what divides citizens who are nominally equal before the law into unequal segments along the spectrum of political power. Those who do not have the means of substantial income generation may not be as totally excluded as the slaves who were denied Athenian citizenship, but their ability to participate as autonomous citizens is undermined in direct proportion to their lack of command of a secure and sufficient source of income. In addition to those who are unemployed, people with underpaid work, insecure jobs, and those without the help of an income-earning partner to help bring up a family, or relatives or other carers to sustain them when they cannot work to pay for the costs of meeting their own needs, are all under pressure to cope with their predicament. Without a system which distributes productive abilities as well as the fruits of labour so as to avoid creating a class of vulnerable social dependents, inclusive communities cannot be built.

When we turn to the moral dimension, we should consider the relationship between the nature of work and community life. Inclusive communities value work which gives people a sense of responsibility and fulfilment. One of the key aims of such communities is to make it possible for their members to take pride in what they do, and respect each other for their worthy contribution as artists, parents, builders, strategists, doctors and so on. It would therefore be quite unacceptable to insist that work that is demoralizing and alienating should be carried out relentlessly for the sake of making society wealthier. In the absence of any recognition of the value of fulfilment, it might make sense for society to demand that people work harder at whatever they are asked to do, even if it is not clear how the increase in wealth would in fact benefit anyone. But once it is accepted that communities should enable their members to achieve meaning in their lives through their work, a purely materialistic conception of work is no longer tenable.

People's work, as an application of their skills and energy to their interactions with their environment, can in itself be a source of satisfaction. Unfortunately, it can also be a meaningless process which leaves us feeling numb about our role in producing whatever finally emerges. This alienating potential of work needs attention. Not only does it pose a threat to one of the most important values any inclusive community would wish to pursue, it could block the development of a inclusive community in the first place. Through draining workers of their energy in a negative, meaningless manner, alienating work could leave people with a moral void which inclines them more towards nihilism than active citizenship. Organizations that want to encourage their workers to engage with the wider community support the integration of their work within the organization with a developmental programme covering work in the community. By contrast, organizations that are only interested in getting the most out of their workers without any reciprocal concern about work fulfilment, are likely to make such excessive demands that workers with energy left to participate in community activities would be deemed to have spare capacity, which must not be left unexploited in the future.

The challenge of ensuring that everyone will have enough rewarding work – in the economic, social and moral sense of the term – to do, is compounded by what in Chapter 2 we called the Post-Everything Syndrome. Economic observers and management experts compete in describing the radical nature of the changes to our global productive arrangements (Drucker, 1993; Handy, 1994). Technology has broken down barriers which have hitherto given varying degrees of protection to prevalent modes of working. It has achieved this by making the simplification of operations transparent at the organizational, inter-organizational and global level. Within organizations, workers are made redundant by labour-saving technology; to compete against such organizations which have cut their labour costs, other organizations turn to technology-driven solutions to reduce their workforce; and on a global level, technology further facilitates cost-cutting by making it relatively easy to shift production operations to countries where workers are ready to accept lower wages.

Those who are at the forefront of developing and applying such technological innovations will increasingly expand their influence and power. These 'knowledge workers' do not need land or capital, because they carry their commercial assets in their heads, and they are shaping a world in which resources and operations are literally moved around at the press of a button. In so far as the world has never witnessed such a rapid global spread of technology-driven reorganization, people are caught up in a Post-Everything Syndrome which has shaken the very foundation of their understanding of how work is allocated. Learning routines, acquiring skills, providing communication links between organizational layers and so on, are routes into paid work that can now be wiped out instantaneously by an innovative computer programme. This does call for adjustment within an unprecedented timescale (see Giddens, 1994, ch. 3).

Without the necessary adjustment, which in the case of the Industrial Revolution the world had over a century to make, all those who do not rapidly attain the ranks of knowledge workers will find the future offering them a stark choice – to become low-wage service workers, or to get no paid work at all. However, the need to confront this development is not something that is unique to the late twentieth century. Far from its being a 'post-everything' experience,

changes in social arrangements as well as technological advance-
ments have in the past wiped out in succession different forms of
work opportunities that had developed over many years. Nomads
gave way to farm workers, and work on farms diminished as
manufacturing took over – and now design of production is over-
taking direct involvement in production itself. If history offers any
lesson, it appears to be that any attempt to neglect or marginalize
those who lose out in such changes is not sustainable. It leads
inevitably to an inefficient distribution of work and weakens
economic competitiveness which, if left unresolved, might stoke up
revolutionary pressures. Communities that allow themselves to be
divided into increasingly antagonistic parts become self-destructive,
unless of course the different parts are brought together again
through some genuinely unifying process.

The Need for a Participatory Economy

The 1989 revolutions in Eastern Europe marked the end of the
Communist experiment in overcoming class antagonism. The experiment was supposed to prove that everyone would be better off
when the control over the means of production was taken from the
capitalists and given to representatives of the workers. From the
perspective of market individualism, the experiment failed because
any attempt to control the economy centrally, instead of allowing
those with a direct interest in business successes to interact freely
with each other, would lead to distortions in the market, which
would, in turn, weaken its efficiency and damage its productive
potential. It would follow from this that the best safeguard for a
successful economy would consist of enabling people who own
businesses to compete freely and honestly in the marketplace.

Such an interpretation of the fall of Communism does not in fact
go far enough. While the Communist experiment did transfer
economic controls away from owners of capital, the political elite
that took over the power was no more representative of the workers
than the emperors of the past were representative of *their* subjects.
When members of that elite tried to determine the variables that
affected the functioning of their economy, they did so from a remote
position which prevented them from fully interacting with others,
whose experiences were vital in identifying and assessing the many
factors that needed to be taken into account. Epistemologically, the

Communist elite, like all authoritarian elites before them, acted as if they possessed infallible knowledge which could not possibly be corrected by the input of other people. Inevitably, the effectiveness of their judgements fell behind other political communities whose key economic decisions were not made by only a remote core of people. This does not mean that passing such decisions to people who are in charge of businesses would be the best alternative. It only means that it would be better than the authoritarian model. In fact, the lesson to be learnt is that the exclusion of those whose experiences and ideas have a role to play in economic decisions is detrimental to the reliability of those decisions, and thus to the strength of the economy. So if only those who are established business owners and managers are entrusted with making economic decisions, the outcome would be less desirable than if other stakeholders were also involved.

Market individualists may attempt to draw an arbitrary line at the level of the heads of businesses, and characterize these as the 'individuals' whose freedom to interact in the marketplace would bring about the best of all possible economies. But since there are other people involved in the economy, to exclude them is to commit exactly the same kind of error as did the Communist elite – namely, to pretend that they can come up with the best decisions, regardless of what others may contribute if their experiences are allowed to be brought to bear on those decisions.

The obsession with deregulations to give increasing power to heads of businesses has blinded market individualists to even the most obvious counter-example provided by the success of East Asian economies. Instead of recognizing that these economies have shown that the government has a vital role to play in bringing together different groups to work for common goals, they conclude that what has made the East Asian businesses particularly successful is their strong sense of family values, which make them less disposed to be reliant on any state system. This simplistic focus on the East Asian communities' belief in family values overlooks two important points. First, families could be valued because they provide a caring and nurturing environment in which the young can grow up into responsible adults, and adults can grow older among loved ones. Businesses which recognize the value of supporting their workers in carrying out their family responsibilities in effect help to sustain a society with strong family building blocks. However, families could also be valued because they preserve traditional units which favour their own and distrust outsiders. Family businesses anchored by such values would encounter both internal tensions when traditional family hierarchies stand in the way of more able family members just because they are not male or first born, and external tensions when commercial trust is undermined by family rivalries and favouritism. Family values of the second type would hinder rather than support the development of businesses.

Second, East Asian cultures, especially where Confucian influences have been strong, tend to view their countries as an extended family, with those in a ruling position assuming the role of the head of the family. Far from the state stepping back from the economy for fear of being too paternalistic, East Asian governments expect, and are expected by their people, to play a key role in steering their economy in the right direction. If prevailing economic policies start to leave more and more people without any paid work to support themselves and their families, their governments would be leading the way towards finding a solution to what would be treated as a very serious problem. After all, the head of a family must not neglect the plight of members of the family. What is open to debate is how that duty is best discharged. Here we return to the question of how economic decisions are to be made. East Asian countries have learnt that their rulers are not always able to find the right solutions on their own. They need to work with the key groups who affect the economic performance of their countries to set out the way forward. Authoritarian tendencies that have worked against them in the past – for example, consider the economic stagnation brought to China by the arrogance of the Ching Emperors, who would take little notice of the concerns of the merchant class and others who pressed for economic modernization (Hsu, 1983) – have not disappeared completely. If they retreat from the process of democratization (which China is still refusing to embark upon except in a limited sense in the economic sphere), then the progress that has been achieved so far could be undone by an authoritarian edict of the future.

What the failures of authoritarian economies really teach us is that the arrogance or complacency of any single group must not be allowed to dominate economic decisions which affect everyone else. This applies not just to the old Soviet leadership or inner circles of imperial rulers, but also to heads of businesses. What is needed is a participatory economy wherein citizens and the many communities to which they belong can feed their input into a collective decision-making process. Without the effective participation of all the stakeholders, those who have the exclusive right to shape all the key decisions will unavoidably neglect others in society. Through ignorance of what others could have brought to their deliberations, through apathy towards others they are institutionally encouraged to ignore, and through greed which drives some of the elite to heap benefits on themselves regardless of the negative consequences on others, work will become organized to suit the few, while others have to suffer economically, socially and morally.

There is every sign that those who stand to benefit most from the present global economic structure are already concentrating on protecting their own interests irrespective of what is happening to other people. What they want is a political system that guarantees their freedom to trade their resources with as little interference as possible from others who may question their trading arrangements. This approach has led to the marginalization of full employment as a policy objective. More and more people who need paid employment are discovering that their ability to earn a living for themselves and their families, is neither utilized nor developed by those in a position to make use of it. The business elite, without any sound epistemological basis, wish to maintain that this is the price to pay for the best form of economic system. But who is to say it is the best, and indeed best for whom? Such claims cannot be validated when the co-operative enquiries necessary to test their validation are structurally ruled out by the exclusion of many whose experiences are relevant to the evaluation of these claims.

Meanwhile, the exclusion of large number of citizens from making a productive contribution to society adds fuel to two interrelated problems. First, the failure to enable them to contribute to society's resources means that society's pool of collective resources is less than it would otherwise be. Second, this depletion of collective resources comes just when more citizens are needing to draw from these resources for support. If it is suggested that the pressures on collective resources should be relieved through cutting back on the support for jobless families, are the latter not entitled to challenge the arrangements that deprived them of their jobs in the first place?

The so-called 'pension time bomb' provides a useful illustration. As people in the West are living longer, they put more pressure on the collective resources required for old age pension payments. With more early retirements occurring concurrently with loss of jobs that would have been filled by younger workers, the dwindling band of paid workers would have to carry a heavier and heavier burden to support the expanding class of pensioners. At this juncture, the typical market individualist prescription of switching the focus to private pensions demonstrates clearly the callous divisiveness of this form of economic thinking. Unless the state gives a communitarian commitment to underwrite everyone's pension contributions to a satisfactory level, those without paid work would end up with virtually nothing to support them in their old age. If the collective pension system is allowed to deteriorate to a level where it is of little worth without additional private contributions, it would be rejected both by those sufficently well-off to view it as irrelevant, and those who are disillusioned with its financial feebleness.

Instead of reforming the system which gives rise to growing socioeconomic exclusion, market individualists want to strengthen it by taking away the remaining controls which may still enable those who lose by it to have a real say. Public scrutiny of wage levels, safety standards and working conditions is to be minimized so that those desperate for paid work, and those fearful of losing it, are both made even more dependent on those in charge of large-scale resource transactions. Those who fall out of the system are then stigmatized as being unwilling to work, and therefore undeserving of public support. In reality, there are many ways to help those who lose one kind of paid work to make a dignified transition to other kinds of paid work. Japanese firms are known for their commitment to finding value-adding work for their workers if the demand in one area drops. If fewer workers are needed on the production side because customer demand has fallen, for example, workers are given the opportunity to switch to providing service support to customers, which would help to maintain customer loyalty until overall demand picks up again. Apart from providing workers with options within organizations to make alternative contributions, enterprise training can also be given to help them set up their own businesses. Michael Kitson has found that new businesses started by people who had become unemployed generally performed better than those started by people who were not out of work (Kitson, 1995).

What is in question is not whether unemployed people can be helped, but whether society as a whole is going to face up to its responsibility to help its members (see Ormerod, 1994, pp. 203–7). The significance of this responsibility may be challenged by those who, following the line that runs from Mandeville through Spencer to Friedman and Nozick, would argue that nobody owes the unemployed a living. In their Nozickian world, we have the right to appropriate whatever no one else has already appropriated under the agreed market conditions. Beyond that, we have no duty to help those who have not succeeded in appropriating anything. But what are these market conditions to which there is supposed to be universal agreement? Did they spring into being with *a priori* validity, or did they evolve through history, commanding varying degrees of legitimacy?

In contrast to the Nozickian world, where seemingly God created the free market on day one and decided there was nothing more to do, the human race has never universally consented to giving up a form of life in which everyone could gather fruits or hunt to feed themselves and their families, for an alternative in which food and other basic necessities cannot be obtained without the purchasing power associated with paid work. The productive arrangements of societies change over time, and if citizens do not collectively take on the responsibility of minimizing the harm brought about by these changes, then those who lose out are entitled to challenge the institutions which facilitate the changes.

In practice, all too many of those in charge of businesses have chosen precisely to pretend that we live in a Nozickian world. They constantly proclaim their rights to own and control resources, but they can see no responsibility for the plight of those who suffer from their corporate decisions. To secure downsizing, mergers, decentralization, or whatever else that might enhance their personal wealth, large-scale redundancies are becoming the norm. Workers are treated as dispensable tools, and are discarded with no support for them, their families, or the communities which have relied on their productive capacity for their vibrancy.

This callous attitude among employers in turn breeds distrust among their workforce. Loyalty to the organization ceases to be identifiable with personal career interests. Just as fixed-term contract staff spend more of their time towards the end of their contract period preparing for their next move, more and more employees in general are feeling that they must make contingency plans for themselves. Instead of concentrating on what they can do for their organizations, they are preoccupied with what their organizations can do for them before they move on. This infectious short-termism weakens the organizations. In response to this, employers cut back on long-term investment in the development of their staff. They do not see the point of training staff if they are to take the benefits of their training elsewhere. Gradually, the skill levels of whole sectors decline, because everyone tries to take advantage of other organizations' training provision, and no one invests in their own.

However, businesses driven by market individualist thinking would seek to overcome whatever problems they encounter by buying the services of individuals they most need at any particular time. The minority who find themselves in this shrinking pool of the well-trained would then command higher and higher pay, and thus widen even further the purchasing power gap between those close to the economic elite and those whom they declare to be redundant.

The reluctance to make a long-term investment in the workers in businesses is mirrored by the reluctance to invest in those businesses. Businesses which do not care for their own long-term success by developing a strong and committed workforce should not be surprised that investors are only interested in making short-term gains out of them. Superficial 'growth' through laying-off workers does not attract investor loyalty. Furthermore, once a culture of short term exploitative investment takes hold, businesses are forced to respond by focusing on short-term performance. Capital investment for the future and the maintenance of spare labour capacity to provide flexibility are cut to maximize profits and dividends for the present. When demand rises, there is not the production capacity to support a demand-led recovery. Instead, inflation and balance-of-payment deficits threaten, interest rate pressures are kept up, and unemployment remains at a high level.

At the international level, whatever fragile interest in global co-operation may exist, it takes only a few nations driven by market individualism to keep fragmentation on the agenda. Controls, which might work for the good of all, are dismissed as being barriers to free trade. Countries that have allowed free trade to wipe out their own food crops are told to dismantle their social support systems even further so they can pay their debt to immeasurably richer countries. Countries which have combined export successes with protection of their home workers are told to relax their controls to allow more external competition to undermine the employment of those workers. The cult of competition blocks every attempt at co-operative solutions. As more human resources lie idle, non-renewable natural resources are depleted for short term profits with no regard for the long-term implications. The vicious circle of market individualism is thus complete.

Democracy at Work

It is tempting to think that the only way to overcome the spread of market individualism is to overthrow the system completely. Yet a revolution would solve nothing if it simply substituted an authoritarian regime for the business elite, which would be no better at solving the distribution-of-work problem without the support of co-operative enquiry.

To break the downward spiral engendered by individualist thinking, what must be done is to build up inclusive community relationships at all levels of economic decision-making. This proposal has to face two related difficulties. First, given its inherent commitment to avoiding top-down prescriptions, how can a communitarian approach be formulated to reform the economy? Second, there is the argument that countries such as Sweden and Germany, which are relatively more communitarian than English-speaking nations, are encountering economic pressures that are forcing them to consider deregulatory actions favoured by market individualists. Before tackling the second of these difficulties, let us consider what changes are needed for economic institutions to develop into inclusive communities. Jonathan Boswell has argued that a communitarian approach to the economy requires a radical rethinking of the levers of reforms. In *Community and the Economy: The Theory of Public Co-operation*, he writes:

> Instead of always thinking first and foremost of economic or welfare policies, then of co-operative instruments, we would have to spend a lot of trouble doing the reverse. We would have to be at least as committed and systematic about the co-operative 'processes' as about their conventionally perceived 'outcomes'. We would have to salute as a key subject in its own right, even as an overarching priority, the quality of sectional interest-public relationships. (Boswell, 1990, p. 187)

Communitarians' preference for restructuring the processes of decision-making, over recommending specific economic decisions, could be criticized for obfuscating the issues. When there are people suffering from the failings of prevailing policies, there are pressing demands for clear, alternative policies, not proposals for developing communities of enquirers. Such criticisms would miss the central

epistemological point of communitarian thinking. Economic policies involve knowledge-claims which, like any other claim, cannot be
validated in the absence of co-operative enquiry. Although the
temptation is to counter current policies with ready-packed alternatives, if one's proposals only reflect the experiences and ideas of
some groups in isolation from others, they are as likely to fail as
other policies that have gone before them. If we are to work towards
a new blueprint of economic management, we must concentrate first
on getting the deliberative processes right.

Far from invoking some vague notion of 'community' as the
model for economic institutions, Boswell, for example, backs his
analysis of economic decision-making with a set of reform priorities.
The gap between current practices and the goals of these reforms
would reveal how much an individual country needs to do before it
is in a position to formulate economic blueprints that deserve to
command the confidence of all citizens. Boswell's proposals can be
grouped into four categories (Boswell, 1990, pp. 190–201). The first
concerns the structural involvement of sectional interests. In order
to prevent the interests of particular groups in society from being
excluded, they must all be given support in forming themselves into
representative organizations that can speak for their members at
both national and international levels. This would pose a particular
challenge for two types of sectional interest. One is the socially
deprived, who can barely get their voice heard in their everyday life,
let alone send a conjoined message to established interests nationally. The other is the public sector which, as Boswell observes, has
been battered by 'restless radicalism', and is constantly under the
'threat of the cult of privatism'. The public service ethos is undermined, and its ability to provide an effective balance to private-
sector demands is put under growing pressure. Stability across
different sectors, combined with structural support for different
interest groups to participate as equals in policy discussions would
be a vital part of reorientating the economy.

To ensure that inter-section discussions are conducted in a
genuinely informed manner, Boswell puts forward a second category
of reforms concerned with the statutory enforcement of openness.
There is to be a massive extension of statutory disclosure requirements. The financial, social and environmental impact of the
activities of large companies, especially when they involve mergers
and takeovers, and of trade unions and pressure groups, would
allow citizens to be aware of the full implications of what different

groups are proposing. Coupled with this would be generally improved social monitoring of sectional organizations. Monitoring to
uncover abuses and discrepancies would be given institutional
support, and the public in turn would be encouraged to follow
and assess closely the work of the monitors.

However, the establishment of sectional groups and the transpar-
ency of their activities would only be paving the way for the
development of co-operative working. This brings us to the third
category, which concerns planned opportunities for inter-group
relationship development. Trust, which is increasingly, if a little
belatedly, gaining the recognition of economists as a crucial factor in
business affairs, needs considerable cultivating. Yet trust takes time
and effort to build up, and with opportunities for face-to-face
interactions in the ever-expanding business networks very much
limited, new arrangements have to be made to maximize the mixing
of different sectional groups. Channels to facilitate contact across
classes, races, regions and economic groups would need to be
improved. Boswell would like to see the concepts and ethos of
working together for the common good being built into job training
and courses at business schools. It would also involve the development of a nexus of strategically located and properly constituted
forums, both at the national level and within organizations. Such
forums would enable those concerned to meet, share ideas, and learn
to resolve their differences constructively.

The final category concerns sustained effort in promoting a
culture of co-operation through civic ceremonies and education.
Boswell believes that society needs supportive symbols and ceremonies to celebrate public responsibility and reciprocity. The value
placed on co-operation is to be further reflected in the educational
norms, and exemplars of partnerships with the common good as
their objective are to replace conventional models which view public
factors as diversions and obstacles to avoid.

The overall effect of these reforms would be the transformation of
economies dominated by zero-sum strategists into productive enterprises driven by the co-operative deliberations of all sections of
society. Boswell is right to acknowledge that in the past it has
usually taken some form of major national emergency to promote
their adoption. When the impact of the emergency fades, and when
competitors who shun co-operation undermine any attempt at a
broader agenda of co-operation, the question has to be raised
whether if such an approach can be sustained in the long run.

The experiences of Sweden, Germany and Austria have illustrated how economies which are *relatively* more communitarian can be both productive economically and effective in addressing the social needs of their citizens. The insecurity and unemployment of one group of citizens was not accepted, let alone demanded, as a fair price to pay for the success of the overall economy. One could argue that the success of such economies could in time galvanize other economies, which find themselves to be sinking into greater and greater social polarization, into adopting the co-operative approach. However, the very difficulties that have emerged, most visibly in Sweden and Germany, may call into doubt whether their model is one to copy after all.

While there are many factors which affect the performance of economies, we should try to ascertain if the processes for co-operative deliberations have really helped or hindered those countries where they are more influential, and then determine what lessons may be learnt by all economies. If we begin with Sweden, the processes clearly have a direct bearing on the strength of the economy. For most of the post-war period, Sweden's system of economic governance, which brings together national businesses, unions and government bodies, kept unemployment below 2 per cent while also sustaining low inflation, high productivity growth, low crime rates, and high levels of health care (Derber, 1994).

When Swedish businesses were badly hit by foreign competition in the mid-1980s, and unemployment rose sharply, the balance between state and private provision was seriously questioned. Critics of the welfare system argued that there needed to be more incentive for citizens to support business success, rather than to rely on an overburdened state. However, the call for reappraisal did not challenge the model of co-operative governance itself. If taxation levels and business incentives needed to be adjusted, they were still to be adjusted by means of inter-sectional discussions. More important, closer analysis of the Swedish economy would reveal that the culture of involvement did not extend beyond the key national players. Swedish citizens took for granted for too long that their national representatives would act for them, and they became out of touch with many key issues thrown up by the changing world economy; at the local level, many began to see paying their taxes as the limit of their civic duty.

The Swedish model has to be modified to make it more responsive to external factors. National economies can no longer be self-contained, and for the networks of co-operative governance advocated by communitarians such as Boswell to work, they must look beyond their borders to ensure that relationships can be built up with other groups that can affect their economic performance. Internally, the model must be extended to every organization and every neighbourhood. Citizens must not be divorced from the decisions that have an impact on their lives. Leaving it to national representatives when the economy is running smoothly may not cause any immediate problem, but by the time the economy hits difficulties – and no form of economy can through some *a priori* principle escape all difficulties – it would be too late to start talking about building relationships. An atmosphere of trust, responsibility and co-operation must be cultivated at every level so that all citizens can appreciate their share in meeting the challenges affecting their common economy.

The need to extend rather than retreat from the model of co-operative governance can also be seen in the case of Germany. It is all too easy to point to the problems that have afflicted the German economy since reunification, and suggest they are caused by the structure for consensus policy-making. In fact, it is more likely that without the well-established consensus structure, a major economic and political upheaval such as the unification process would have caused far more problems, not least the radical polarization of factions which would either force the country into a state of limbo or expose it to the agenda of extreme libertarians or authoritarians. Instead, even in 1992 when the unified Germany was caught up in a recession, it was still the second biggest exporter in the world, with all round high standards of living matched only by countries such as Sweden (see Goodhart, 1994, pp. 33–66).

An analysis of Germany's problems simply in terms of the level of social support it provides to its citizens with paid or unpaid work, misses the more important point of *how* the level of support should be set. To claim that it should always have been set at a lower level to make the economy stronger would be as unfounded as to claim that it should be maintained at a high level in the future, regardless of the economic consequences. The success of West Germany in the post-war period proves that bringing social and economic partners together in a spirit of co-operation is a recipe for social and economic well-being.

However, the unification proposal was a crucial test for the model. Was it too open, or not open enough? In retrospect, it seems that West Germans embraced unification without knowing the full implications for the economy. If they had known, and still decided to support unification, their readiness to make the necessary sacrifices would probably provide a stronger basis to cope with the resulting pressures on the German economy. As it was, the model was not open enough in practice. Yet a further test is facing German citizens. Would they rely on the model, with greater openness perhaps, to rethink the level of social support? Or would they be persuaded by market individualists to jettison the whole model for one that seeks to concentrate power in business leaders? The signs are that the model is being retained. Proposals for privatization and deregulation are discussed through partnership forums, and implemented with genuine consultation of affected parties.

Far from showing that the model is untenable, the German experience supports the view that it is only by developing the model further that any economy can hope to function well as globalization accelerates; therefore Germany is keen to develop this approach with its trading partners in Europe. But whereas Germany sees a federal economic forum as a necessary extension of the model of co-operative governance, the UK, with its aversion to devolving power, naturally suspects that the concept of a federal Europe will lead to a highly centralized super-state. Internally, Germany has to build on its co-operative structures to ensure that workers, and not just their regional and national representatives, are informed and involved in meeting the competitive challenges which may require a new balance to be struck between what they are to put in and what they will draw out of their economy.

The case for further democratization of economic governance does not rest with extrapolating the Swedish and German models. In Austria, the national Association for Endogenous Regional Development has been promoting the practical lessons it has learnt during ten years of regional development. These include extending the partnership arrangements to *all* local and regional players; commitment to consensus on the aims and objectives of regional strategies; and ensuring that local people, supported by local structures for communications, are the ones who produce the strategies.

The importance of developing co-operative networks has also emerged independently from studies of organizations in other parts of the world. In *Foundations of Corporate Success*, John Kay examined companies which have been successful over a long period of time, and contrasted those companies that attained short-term excellence through the presence of outstanding individuals, with those that sustained long-term high performance through their distinctive corporate 'architecture'. An organization with distinctive architecture, according to Kay, 'will often emphasize its dependence on its people. But that dependence is to be interpreted in a particular way. The organization is dependent on them taken as a whole, because the product of the organization is the product of the collectivity. But it is not dependent on any particular one'. Kay goes on to explain that the strength of corporate architecture is derived from the readiness of a firm's members to co-operate, and 'the essential question is how to establish consummate, rather than perfunctory, co-operation . . . Perfunctory co-operation marks the limit of what can be prescribed in a spot or classical contract. Consummate co-operation demands a deeper relationship' (Kay, 1993, pp. 70, 71–2).

Where the deeper relationship has been achieved, in firms in Japan, the UK, the USA or Italy, the result has been a track record of improving quality and maintaining flexibility in the face of changing customer expectations and global pressures. Kay's analysis is supported by many other studies on the theme of the 'Network Paradigm' (see, for example, Cooke and Morgan, 1991). The general conclusion is that organizations that invest in the development of co-operative relationships among their own workforce, with their suppliers, and with their customers, are more able to adapt their productive resources to meeting customer demands. Customer loyalty is built up through responsiveness to their concerns and requirements; suppliers' reliability and flexibility are secured through long-term partnership working; and workers are involved in discussing how best to develop themselves and their working practices to meet the targets that are set for all to see.

If consummate, as opposed to mere perfunctory, co-operation is difficult to achieve for organizations rooted in the opposite orientation, its benefits are valuable enough for concerted efforts to be made towards its attainment. The Mondragon group of co-operative companies in Spain, for example, has established a mutually supportive network which, since its inception in the 1940s, has not had a single compulsory redundancy. Mondragon workers can invest varying amounts of money in their companies, but in terms of their share in decision-making, each and every worker, in the spirit of democratic citizenship, has one vote. Through the companies they control, they channel the productive resources of the Mondragon community into competitive products, provide their members with the opportunity to work, and plough back 10 per cent to 15 per cent of their profits to local facilities.

At a less formal level, firms in the Emilia-Romagna region in Italy have also developed networking relationships that enable them to support each other in sustaining a regional economy with few large firms and little inward investment. The co-operative approach has meant that production cycles can be accelerated significantly across a wide range of industries. Rather than individual firms trying to overcome weaknesses that are beyond their own capability to overcome, firms in the region utilize each other's strengths to minimize the impact of their individual weaknesses. Of course, co-operative firms are not without their problems, but they look to solutions that are formulated and owned by those who have to implement them. Workers have a visible stake in the productive processes they support, and they recognize support for others who might otherwise lose the opportunity to work, not as an externally imposed burden, but part of the commitment they make in conjunction with others for their common good.

The limitations of local and regional co-operative networks are to be found in their susceptibility to parochial isolation. Without wider interactions, innovations and insights may take too long to filter through from outside. Without support from national and international structures, they could be dogged by weaknesses which alone they could not overcome. This obstacle could be removed if the process of extending co-operative economic governance beyond the national level were to incorporate specific support for the development of co-operative networks across local and regional boundaries. Complementing the proposals of Boswell, Paul Hirst has argued that economic development must be decentralized to give encouragement and support to more co-operative enterprises. Hirst's suggestions include tax incentives to help build up mutual capital providers, technology transfer between partners in and across regions, and assistance with the development of employee involvement in the ownership and governance of firms (Hirst, 1994, ch. 5).

Criticisms of communitarian economic ideas tend to attack them as either a return to corporatist thinking, or limited attempts to promote community enterprise. Although neither approach on its own is sufficient to tackle the problems which threaten to deprive more and more citizens of the opportunity to work for a living, a strategy that integrates the two could still produce results that they could not achieve alone. The respective weaknesses of the two strands of communitarian thinking would, in fact, be countered by the other's strengths. Where democratizing policy formulation at the national level is not enough to establish a participatory economy, the process should be extended to sub-national units of productive enterprise. On the other hand, where local co-operation by itself is not enough to tackle problems beyond their control, it should be backed by broader structures, nationally and internationally (see Derber, 1994).

Reforming Economic Relationships

The communitarian framework for economic decision-making at all levels also provides a basis for bringing together a range of proposals that have previously been advocated from a number of disparate perspectives. Instead of relying on incidental alliances to link them together, a coherent programme can be constructed connecting them with a broader agenda that covers the education and protection of citizens in inclusive communities. These proposals can be divided into four categories covering the use of inclusive economic indicators; minimum standards for workers; sustainable productivity enhancement; and the development of participatory investment.

Economic relationships need to be developed with reference to common indicators. Yet if the indicators used focus narrowly on transactions between certain types of individual, they could distort the real significance of those transactions and prevent the state of others from being reviewed at all. For example, gross national product (GNP), the indicator that is used so often to compare economic performance, records the income generated by commercial transactions, but ignores the social and environmental costs of those transactions, and leaves out completely the productive activities of unpaid workers. To channel economic resources into making improvements on the basis of such an indicator would mean that even if they led to consequences such as a proliferation of accidents, which in turn generate a high level of insurance payments, or an increase in the depletion of the world's fish stock through more fish being caught and sold, the outcome would be registered as a positive one.

To avoid wrong goals being set for economies, inclusive indicators have to be developed to ensure that all those who contribute to the productiveness of an economy, and all those affected by their activities, are taken into account. Such indicators would reveal the impact of economic arrangements on levels of educational attainment, the numbers of those who need but cannot get paid work, standards of health in terms of calorie consumption, mortality rates in general and in relation to specified diseases, pollution levels of air and water, access to technological infrastructure (which will link telephones, televisions and interactive computer systems), and the use of non-renewable resources. Furthermore, each indicator should also record the differentials between male and female, differentials between the richest and the poorest, and differentials between any other significant divisions such as tribal, religious or racial groups.

The Post-Everything Syndrome of questioning the concepts of growth and progress stems from a distorted view of what count as 'growth' and 'progress'. The Baconian epistemology that underpins the advancement of co-operative enquiry in increasing our understanding of how the conditions of life can be improved has nothing to do with the narrow materialism that market individualism embraces in the name of modernity. 'Progress' only becomes dubious when the indicators put forward exclude the interests of sections of the community affected by the changes being recorded. More monetary transactions within the economy could be a positive sign, provided they do not undermine the various needs that the work is undertaken to meet. Consumption should be treated as one indicator among many. How consumption is distributed, and whether it prevents productive resources from being applied to help those caught up in slums, poverty and malnutrition must be factors that are also included in assessing whether progress and growth are achieved that matter to all citizens.

Inclusive indicators must also be developed at organization level. Business performance should not be evaluated solely on transactional variations in terms of turnover, profits and market share. In order to judge the overall value of particular commercial operations in society, their impact on all those affected by the operations has to be taken into account. If only some gain from their activities when others are worse off as a result, it would be utterly arbitrary and misleading to ringfence the gains as if they were the only relevant factor to consider.

The development of an integrated audit of the financial, social and environmental effects of business activities would help to provide information that would facilitate discussions between different groups affected by the business, and it would also make available the building blocks of higher-level indicators. Securing the right information to evaluate economic decisions is only one precondition for improving the organization of our productive resources. The second area for reform turns to the issue of minimum standards for workers across the world. Unless citizens can secure the income they need under reasonable conditions, they cannot participate in decisions that affect themselves and the economy in general. Organizational thinking that treats workers as dispensable tools to be exploited and discarded at will constitutes one of the most serious barriers to citizenship development.

In the name of efficiency, workers have been asked to work harder, accept that they would receive a proportionately smaller share of increased profits, and be prepared for redundancies when their loss of paid employment becomes necessary as a short-term option to cut costs and boost profits further. This outlook is becoming attractive to firms that have hitherto operated in countries with more of a tradition of partnership working. It is argued that unless countries such as Germany and Sweden learn to cut back on the entitlements and involvement of their workers, they will not be able to compete against countries that prefer to leave their workers at the mercy of their employers.

The 'sweat shop' model advocated by market individualists focuses on business leaders as being the only relevant players. Workers, far from being their fellow citizens with shared values and responsibilities, are tools to be bought as cheaply as possible. Any agreement that guarantees the autonomy and dignity of workers is treated as an imposition interfering with the free interplay between business leaders. In a sweat shop economy, the more workers are made to feel that they are expendable objects valued only for their cheapness, the more flexibility business leaders have in using them to make more profits for themselves. Contracting out, on this model, is not an opportunity to build a relationship with an independent supplier, but simply a way to drive the costs of labour down by externalizing sections of the workforce. If the model is allowed to expand through greater deregulation of employment conditions across the world, the ability of workers to function as effective citizens in general, and to participate in micro- and macroeconomic decisions in particular would be increasingly undermined. Yet, while it may bring some short-term advantages for those who undercut their competitors by cutting back on the entitlements of their workforce, firms adopting this model cannot rely on it as a sustainable competitive advantage. Strategically, other firms will either reject it as an unsuitable approach, or adopt a similar approach themselves. If they reject it, they would gain the best workers from the 'sweat shop' players, and the latter would gradually become the least capable of offering a better deal to the customers. If, on the other hand, they adopt a similar approach, then a downward spiral would be set in motion. Industrial relations would become more confrontational, workers would be seriously demotivated, there would be a steady increase in days lost through sickness and injuries, and there would be a decline in quality through lack of attention and interest. Before long, some rival firms would see the benefit of investing in their workforce, and any firm that still stuck blindly to its 'sweat shop' approach would become highly uncompetitive. It is worth observing that in the UK, where this model has most consistently received ideological backing, elaborate legislative requirements had to be introduced to support the application of this approach to the compulsory tendering out of local government services. And the very real possibility of the buyers of those services choosing a supplier with a high-quality, well-motivated workforce, in preference to one with low-waged, demoralized workers, was legally excluded by the requirement that, in general, cheapest tenders must be accepted. Without this artificial prop, the ideological wish that services continuously made cheaper at the expense of vulnerable workers might have a long-term future, would not stand a chance of being fulfilled.

However, the fact that long-term equilibrium would favour good working conditions, and workers having a real say and a fair share in achieving successes for their firms, short-term disruptions could prolong the periods of adjustment considerably. Countries gaining a short-term advantage through low labour costs would find that their workers would demand steady improvements in their remuneration and working conditions. Only the most short-sighted managers would refuse to respond to this demand in a constructive manner, as it is essential for the long-term growth and success of their companies.

This process of investing the benefits of their competitive advantage back into their workforce could mark the beginning of a virtuous circle if it is well co-ordinated across the world, and would support a general levelling up of the working conditions of all citizens. Unfortunately, it could equally tempt some to press for a wholesale levelling down, and the more distrust and discord introduced into international discussions about setting minimum standards for workers, the more difficult it would be to secure the necessary co-ordination.

Unless such standards are set, workers would constantly be pushed to the margins of economic deliberation, and many of them would have to put up with exclusion from participation as citizens. One of the most important aspects of such standards relates to the financial position of workers. In every society, with its prevailing cost of maintaining a decent living, there are levels below which its citizens would not be able to cope alone. Whatever consensus there is about a basic level, no inclusive community can allow its members to fall below it. It would therefore be necessary to guarantee a basic income to all citizens, in recognition of their work – paid or unpaid, or, in cases where they are unable to work, as compensation (Roche, 1992, pp. 178–90; Hirst, 1994, pp. 179–84; Twine, 1994, pp. 163–9). In this context, work would cover the activities of citizens who care for their dependent relatives, help their neighbours, or volunteer to support others in need in their home country or abroad.

To prevent this basic income from becoming a disincentive to gain paid work, it could be available in the form of tax credit for those who are in paid employment. A basic income would also avoid the difficulties of imposing a minimum wage level, which could become a disincentive for some employers to hire additional workers. Most important, it signifies a civic recognition of the contributions of all citizens as workers, and enables all of them to have sufficient income to participate in the democratic deliberations of their communities. The proposal for a citizens' income, and the development of worker participation, will incur costs. At the same time, in enabling all to have a real involvement in economic decisions, the overall result could be a net gain in income for all concerned. This takes us to the third area for reform, which seeks to promote sustainable productivity enhancement.

On a communitarian model of economic development, an economy performs best when its constituent organizations work together to maximize the benefits of the market's competitive pressures. In turn, each organization performs best when its constituent members work together to apply their complementary strengths to respond to external demands. Productivity would therefore be enhanced on a sustainable basis when they are able to operate in an environment of trust and dedication, in which the best abilities of each are developed for the continuous improvement of the whole.

Despite fluctuations in management fashions, one theme has remained constant since the discipline of business administration established itself. It is the theme of communicative interaction. It is to be found in discussions of the marketing interface, where the seeking out of customers' views and feeding them into improvement programmes is recognized as being vital to long-term business success. It is to be found in quality assurance, which is at its most effective when it has the fullest involvement of the workforce that has to develop and implement it. It is to be found in the analysis of motivation for employees and suppliers, where co-operative relationships are expected to achieve better results than zero-sum bargaining.

The only way businesses can respond to changing circumstances, and make the most of potential strengths, is to ensure that support is given to effective communications between all concerned. Established practices should not be shielded from critical reappraisals, and ought to be considered for revisions, provided the reasons and evidence are deemed to be sufficiently convincing by the relevant process of co-operative enquiry within the firm.

For co-operative enquiries to work effectively, organizations must tackle internal barriers and engage with wider knowledge development processes through systematic research. Internal barriers may take the form of functional rigidity, job insecurity, inflexible working time, limited delegation of responsibility, or inadequate information sharing. The removal of such barriers would have to take place if workers are to have the ability and confidence to participate in improving the productivity of their organizations. Beyond removing negative barriers, research has a central role in adding to the knowledge base of an organization. However, for research to be effective, it must be applied within a broader framework of research and technology, supported by national and international co-operation. Research which aims for short-term results, and draws back from links with the wider research community (the latter being essential for epistemological validation) would fail to deliver tangible benefits and cause sceptics to reject the value of research altogether.

If research is to contribute to sustainable productivity enhancement, it has to meet three basic criteria. First, it should be targeted. It needs to relate itself to emerging patterns of needs and the advancement of technologies, and to focus on finding better ways of meeting demands. Currently, there are five main areas where demand is likely to grow substantially: products which help to protect the environment; medical and health care for an ageing population; active leisure pursuits; opportunities for spiritual development; and an interactive media mix of education, information and entertainment. In all these areas, it will not be cheap labour costs, but a workforce with an enriched understanding of people's needs and what they can do to meet those needs more effectively, that will maximize productivity.

Second, research needs to be developed with the involvement of all concerned. Those who are to turn research findings into practical improvements must be able to participate in shaping and evaluating research programmes. This would help to bridge the often excessive gap between research thinking and operational application. By ensuring that the workforce as a whole, and not just the 'Research and Development' (R&D) department, is involved, research outcomes would be disseminated more effectively and rapidly, internally through workshops and training programmes, and externally through technology transfer networks. The participation of those who would have to live with its consequences also means that it is much less likely that the research process would treat reductions in employment and non-renewable natural resources as mere variables in the equations.

The final criterion to be met by research is complementary co-ordination. No research can afford to ignore what has been done, or what is being carried out, by other research institutions. To have effective co-ordination, however, does not mean that researchers should be made increasingly dependent on businesses for funding. The links between them ought to be mediated by bodies with broader concerns, to ensure that complementary research is sustained. Narrow links between researchers and businesses run the risk not only of blocking exchange of research findings in the name of misguided zero-sum competition, but also of cutting support for research that has no obvious commercial benefits.

While researchers need to appreciate how they can help businesses to improve their performance, it is their independence from businesses that ultimately makes it possible for them to add value to what businesses do. Researchers have a major role in assessing which knowledge claims are to be accepted and which are not. Just as judges cannot rely on individual prosecutors or defendants to pay their salaries and still pass judgements that command acceptance from all sides, to make research institutions more dependent on business funding would deprive them of the independence that is a fundamental asset in evaluating knowledge claims which could be disputed by different parties. Furthermore, research institutions are involved with much more than just commercially significant investigations. Their contributions to the wider intellectual and cultural dimensions of society clearly should not be submerged by some myopic process of reducing them to being primarily contractors of businesses.

Workers' ideas on productivity enhancement, supplemented by research findings, may well point to areas that require additional investment for their implementation. This is the issue to be addressed by the fourth area of reforms, concerning the development of participatory investment. Investment structures which do not facilitate mutual understanding of potential investors and investees, assume that such understanding is either not possible or unnecessary. Instead, they rely on individuals looking solely to their own interests to maximize overall investment. To the extent that a country's investment is dependent on the concern of potential investors' with what would make them the most money regardless of the soundness of their judgement or the wider economic consequences of that judgement, then the investment base of the country would inevitably be weaker than others that take a more inclusive approach.

The experience of East Asian economies at a national level, and the success of community investment schemes at a more local level, suggest that a structural requirement that increases the understanding between investors and investees builds trusting and supportive relationships which strengthen the investment input. In the case of the East Asian economies, their governments work closely with the industrial and financial sectors to ensure that the investment of capital is not modelled on individual gambling, but on strategic partnerships through which investors and investees pull in the same direction, and which all agree is most worthy of long-term pursuit. In the case of local investment schemes, greater knowledge and trust enable all sides to match capital to projects recognized by local communities as most likely to produce the best returns.

Potential investors, be they large corporations, citizens with spare savings, or workers in companies seeking to improve their performance, should be given information that explains fully and clearly what their investment would contribute towards, and the key factors that would influence the returns they could hope to make from their investment over varying periods of time. The involvement of customers, employees and suppliers in making an informed contribution to the running of organizations is recognized as being vital in developing long-term relationships that benefit all concerned. The principle that participation brings trust and understanding applies also to investors. Investment structures therefore need to be strengthened by more communicative interactions. Investors should not view investees merely as entities that, on the basis of a narrow range of indicators, may make some money for them. Investees should not view investors merely as sources of financial input who are otherwise to be kept as far away from their work as possible. Investment institutions, in particular, must play a more active role in promoting wider understanding between the complete range of stakeholders of businesses, and encourage companies to involve their investors in their strategic and operational thinking.

Bankers and investment advisers should themselves learn to develop a wider and deeper understanding of businesses which turn to them for investment support. They should be more open to taking up equity participation, rather than focusing exclusively on security of loans. For their part, businesses must become much more open with information about themselves, and place a high priority on explaining their market sectors and how their strategies fit in.

For the wider community, the education of citizens needs to include the cultivation of a better understanding of the links between savings, investment and their economies' performance. Instead of being portrayed as a source of quick profit, the purchase of shares should be seen as the building of a long-term partnership in mutual prosperity. This change in perception must be backed by structural changes such as tax allowances to support long-term investment; development of local investment companies; a requirement for fund managers to communicate with fund owners regarding the purpose and implications of investing in particular firms; and a means of enabling citizens, most of whom are pension-fund owners, to deliberate and express their collective views on investment strategies.

5
Protection for Citizens

Protection and Citizenship

Education develops the abilities of citizens, and productive work gives them the resources, to live as effective members of inclusive communities. However, the pursuit of common values can be undermined by a wide range of factors. To enable citizens to defend themselves against these threats and dangers, citizenship must incorporate a system of protection for all. Such a system needs to be based on a common identification of the factors from which we are to be protected. In an individualist model, there are only personal interests. People may bargain about the possible gains and concessions inherent in the varying threats and opportunities relating to their interests, but they cannot work towards a common recognition of what the dangers are for all of them. What results is a series of protective arrangements that would favour those in a stronger position to drive a harder bargain. This may range from the deployment of policing resources to protect the wealthiest, to health initiatives which address the anxiety of the well-off, rather than the sufferings of those too poor to pay towards any system of health care.

Dissatisfaction with the anomalies that are inevitably thrown up by the anarchic distribution of protective resources tends to push this issue in the direction of the authoritarian approach. The protective establishment – in the form of the military, the police, medical experts, or whatever guardian agency – is detached from the protected (see Foucault, 1979; Dreyfus and Rabinow, 1982). The protectors will pronounce on what constitutes a danger, and will act on it as they see fit, regardless of the absence of any shared understanding with the protected. In the name of protecting the passive populace from dangers, the protectors surround themselves with secrecy. At the same time, any actual or potential harm that does not fit in with the establishment's conception of 'danger' would be marginalized as being insignificant or irrelevant. Despite the ascendancy of market individualism, protection of citizens is the one area where authoritarianism is still the dominant approach. Perhaps it is because the consequences of market failures are so much more obvious and immediate to see. However, the arbitrary and exclusionary nature of authoritarian protection renders it quite unacceptable in relation to the building of inclusive communities.

In contrast to the authoritarian approach, communitarian protection would ensure that the power to protect rests firmly with those who need the protection. Allowing a detached band of protectors to hold on to that power carries too many risks. First, total dependence on the protectors could be exploited by some who want to take advantage of the vulnerable – who would have no basis upon which to counter the actions of their erstwhile protectors. Second, allowing the gap between protectors and protected to stand also means that the latter has little understanding of the activities of the former. Although the former's intentions may be well-meaning, without the involvement of those most affected by their ideas and actions, the individuals or organizations charged with protective work may not always know when and how they should adapt and improve what they do to match changing circumstances. Third, even if the protectors were totally honourable and wise, an inescapable consequence of not participating in the process of protection would be the decline in people's sense of responsibility for their own safety. Without this sense of responsibility, people would simply let themselves be harmed again and again, irrespective of the best efforts of the protectors (see Skinner, 1992).

Authoritarian protection offers the superficial comfort that we can leave it to others to look after us. In moving away from it, the question of how we are to secure our protection will quite rightly be raised. A leap to the individualist position would leave people with conflicting views of what requires protection, and those conflicts would be resolved by means of force, or by means of economic bargains. In either case, some with an initial advantage, be it the control of arms or possession of wealth, would secure the protection of their personal interests above the interests of others. The resulting protective system thus generates at its inception an inherently destructive tension – between those who get the best protection and everyone else whose interests are relegated to a subordinate level.

The reason why a shift from the authoritarian approach can avoid the pitfalls of individualist fragmentation is because of the epistemological position that underlies communitarian citizenship. Given the possibility of arriving at a set of common values that guide our behaviour, it is feasible to learn from experience to determine what would undermine the realization of those values. Rather than accepting the pronouncement of some spokesperson for the protective establishment, or of any self-styled moral leader, on what society needs to be protected against, the onus would be on any attempt to identify a new threat or danger to establish it as a real violation of our common values.

As we saw in Chapter 1, our understanding of our common values evolved under conditions of co-operative enquiry. The values that emerge under such conditions include the value of loving and caring for others, and being loved and cared for; the value of wisdom in making judgements, and in understanding when judgements should be suspended; the value of justice and fairness in our treatment and respect for each other; and the value of fulfilment through which we realize ourselves in our responsibilities and achievements. The informed acceptance of these values leads implicitly to the acceptance of their practical implications. In other words, we cannot decry their violations in some cases, and dismiss as irrelevant their breakdown in others.

On the basis of our common values, it would not be acceptable for any individual or authority to declare something as being 'harmful to society', unless that harm to our common values could be established. For example, this may be directed at one form of religious worship which followers of other religions despise. If it is not against any aspect of our common values, then it is a matter of divergent opinion, which those with opposing views should accommodate peacefully. This means that while critics of the religious practice in question may voice their concerns openly, they must not resort to any means, such as incitement to hatred and violence or adoption of discriminatory practices in other spheres of life, that would clearly violate common values. On the other hand, if the religious practice in question does contain elements that injure those involved, build prejudices into their judgement of issues concerning society in general, encourage them to perceive other people as undeserving of equal respect and treatment, or suggest that people should abdicate responsibility for their actions, then it is to be regarded as a threat from which citizens should be protected.

Although there will be areas where no agreement has been reached about particular kinds of suggested 'threat', experience under conditions of co-operative enquiry has led to a consensus over a considerable range of common dangers for members of inclusive communities. The focus on law and order by market individualists turns out to be a myopic obsession with just one form of problem for citizens. In addition to being robbed, which may be a distinct worry for those who have enough money to buy (or so they think) a solution to most of their other problems in life, there are numerous factors that could undermine or destroy things which our common values seek to preserve and cultivate. These can be divided into five levels (for a detailed exposition of human needs, see Doyal and Gough, 1991; also Braybrooke, 1987 and Thomson, 1987):

1. *Threats to life*
   At the most basic level, the loss of life takes away all hope of the attainment of any kind of value. Protection is therefore required against homicide, killings arising from wars and terrorist activities, fatal diseases and accidents, starvation, and natural disasters.

2. *Physical damages*
   Beyond being alive, we need to be in a reasonably healthy physical state to pursue our values. Protection is needed against poor health, causes of disabilities, hunger, malnutrition, accidental or deliberate injuries, unsafe working conditions, bad housing conditions, mismanagement of waste disposal and pollution of the environment.

3. *Psychological damages*
   Physical fitness needs to be matched by psychological well-being if we are to have a chance of living a meaningful life. Protection is thus needed against neglect by parents, mental abuse, torture, psychological enslavement, attacks on self-respect and dignity, discrimination, persecution and humiliation.

4. *Economic deprivations*
   Economic resources are not only necessary to sustain physical and psychological states of well-being, they are also needed to gain access to many of the material means (for example, computer equipment and software) needed to pursue valuable

ends in contemporary society. We therefore need to protect ourselves not only from theft, fraud and other threats to our economic possessions, but we also need to protect ourselves from circumstances beyond our individual control which could prevent us from earning enough from the productive work we are able to do, therefore excluding us from the opportunities available to the rest of our community.

5. *Cultural deprivations*
    Ultimately, the pursuit of our common values requires the development of our intellectual abilities and our participation in cultural activities to expand our understanding. We thus need to be protected from factors that could deprive us of developmental opportunities, such as barriers to learning, lack of literacy and numeracy, exclusion from a cultural heritage, spreading of prejudices and falsehoods in the media, and arbitrary restrictions of artistic and religious expression.

The protection of citizens will take the above identified threats as a common basis for action. Instead of leaving them to different agencies, each with its own views and priorities as to how the threats that fall into its administrative domain are to be dealt with, they are to be managed holistically by the entire community – as both protectors and protected. Before we look at how this is to be achieved, we should consider the problem associated with the lack of agreement regarding alleged threats.

While the consensus based on our common values picks out many threats and dangers that are appropriate for collective protection to deal with, there are issues that are still far from being settled by enquiry and debate. For example, the rightness or wrongness concerning abortion and euthanasia; the dividing line between acceptable demands for respect for religious ideas and unacceptable threats against non-conformity; the implications of different sexual orientations for the rest of society; and the balance between the pleasures individuals derive from substances such as alcohol, tobacco, cannabis and heroin, and the harm such substances may cause those individuals and others in the wider community.

In the absence of any general agreement on the basic principles involved, the only thing we can agree to in practice would be to guard against any single faction dictating to others about what is to be done. However, a call for compromise is not to be interpreted as a signal for quasi-market negotiations that inevitably favour those in a stronger bargaining position. It is a call for the application of what we have so far established as unacceptable violations, to minimize such violations in dealing with issues that have not yet been resolved satisfactorily.

For example, in the case of abortion, the demand for abortion to save the life of a pregnant woman, or to save her from the prolonged trauma of rape, must be protected from those who seek to deny her attainment of those universally acknowledged basic values, in the name of some value – the overriding value of saving the foetus – that is disputed. Equally, the values of bringing new life into the world with care and commitment must be protected from individualist demands to abort a life which has been intentionally conceived, but whose continued existence may now cause inconvenience to what the parents, on further reflection, select as their preferred lifestyle. In between these two extremes, specific cases would have to be determined by those most involved, parents and doctors, guided by their understanding of the details in relation to the common framework of values (Glover, 1977).

Taking action which may cut short one's own life raises different issues. In the case of euthanasia, the value of being able to end one's own life when it is beyond endurance cannot be pushed aside by some supposed value of prolonging people's lives regardless of their predicament. However, there is the question of the accuracy of people's value judgement (Veatch, 1976). The individualist may suggest simplistically that it must be left to each individual to choose, when misinformed choices and decisions clouded by psychological confusions may well distort a person's value judgement. If we in general recognize that those contemplating suicide should be given support in thinking through their predicament, we cannot let individuals opt for the ending of their lives without some minimal advisory intervention. The authoritarian would favour declaring it unacceptable and enforcing its prevention, but this blatantly ignores the possibility that life could become so bad that one can rightly choose to end it.

The tension between conflicting assessments of what threatens our common values is also to be found in relation to our concerns about the consumption of harmful substances such as alcohol, tobacco, cannabis and heroin. We cannot as a rule discard individuals' views of what gives them enjoyment, but if that enjoyment affects their interactions with us and has consequences for our collective health and crime-prevention efforts, then we have to question if their assessment of what they can rightly pursue is sufficiently well-informed.

Advice on the harm to themselves and others that will be caused by individuals' attempts to opt for life-reducing choices must be given, to enable everyone considering such choices to have the best possible understanding of what is involved in their decisions. Furthermore, the pressures that drive people towards such choices – the urge to escape, to be less sensitive to reality, even if others are hurt or distressed by the consequences – must be treated as a common threat to be tackled even if, in the meantime, the difficult choices they generate have to be dealt with in relation to particular circumstances. Thus alcohol and tobacco are allowed to be consumed legally but advised against, while cannabis and heroin are treated as being illegal.

The communitarian approach is inevitably less clear-cut in such cases. But it is better to reflect the genuine indeterminacy, where it exists, rather than impose arbitrarily a uniform requirement which, in the name of protection for all, will rule against many who in fact pose no threat to the pursuit of common values. Having acknowledged that not all apparent threats can readily be subject to a standard response, it is important to remind ourselves that the vast majority of what could be regarded as threatening to us falls directly into the framework of common values, and in these cases the communitarian response is firm and clear: citizens must apply their co-operative intelligence in establishing the most effective system for protecting themselves from such threats. Such a system will safeguard us from the dangers that threaten us, enable us to deal with those responsible for placing us in danger, and empower those of us falling victim to undesirable events or actions, to cope with the experience and recover our well-being.

The Need for Community-based Protection

A community-based approach to safeguarding ourselves from the dangers that threaten us, and enabling us to deal with those responsible for placing us in danger, would need to ensure that the perception of these dangers is communicated widely, detected swiftly if the dangers occur, and rectified effectively. We begin with communication because we need a shared understanding of what we must guard against before we can legitimately expect every member of our community to take responsibility for the part they have to play. The conventional depiction of the 'criminal' as someone who acts apart from the rest of society, projects a simplistic dividing line between law-abiding citizens and wrongdoers. In reality, all individuals are liable to endanger the well-being of other people.

Breaking into other people's houses to steal from them, or physically hurting them out of hatred or anger, are just some of the more obvious forms of behaviour that undermine our common values. When the professionals among us fail to take due care in carrying out their duties, and leave people in pain or distress; when people in business use deception to secure gains for themselves at the expense of others; when employers terminate the contracts of people who have not been trained or prepared for working anywhere else, without giving any serious thought to other possible options; when people make a living out of producing things, the sole purpose of which is to cause pain and death; or when those in public service allow personal financial interests to corrupt their decisions – in all such cases, our common values are being attacked.

Through education and public protection campaigns, we must all be reminded of the vulnerability of what we value, and informed of the practical implications our own behaviour may have. Invoking the norms of particular insular and undemocratic groups, or the prevailing practices within certain organizations, should have no impact in terms of excusing behaviour which tramples on our common values – behaviour which is unmistakably reckless, callous, negligent, selfish or arrogant, when some harm could have been avoided.

Central to the communitarian message is the notion of responsibility. How individuals behave affects the well-being of others. No citizen of an inclusive community can be allowed to entertain the delusion that responsibility cannot be properly ascribed in the world in which we live. Apart from genuine ignorance when there is no indication that a person should or could have found out about the unforeseen harm of his or her actions, and involuntary behaviour arising from the physical force of others or the psychological disruptions within a person, there are no grounds for denying that each individual is responsible for his or her behaviour and its effects on others (for a detailed exposition of the concept of responsibility, see Tam, 1990).

Arguments deployed in defence of harmful behaviour, in the courts or in the media, sometimes seek to exploit the psychological notion of pressure to shield wrongdoers from the consequences of their actions. Of course, some people have severe psychological problems which render them incapable of controlling their own behaviour, and they should be treated as victims who deserve the wider community's help to resist behavioural patterns they struggle to reject. However, this is not to be confused with circumstantial pressures which particular individuals, reflecting their own preferences and dispositions, respond to in a manner that is unacceptable to others (Tam, 1995b). The pressure may take the form of a tempting bribe or a disturbing threat, but society cannot simplistically accept one and not the other as removing responsibility. Neither, in fact, absolves responsibility, although how the individuals responsible should be dealt with should vary according to the character, judgement, and intention manifested by the behaviour concerned.

For example, accepting a large sum of money to buy a luxury apartment in return for information which would lead to an innocent person being murdered cannot be treated on a par with accepting financial assistance to give one's child an expensive but crucial operation in return for eradicating compromising file information on someone who has cheated others of money. Similarly, giving away commercial secrets to prevent one's family from being harmed is not the same as agreeing to carry out a bombing for fear that one would otherwise be exposed as a former spy. We are all liable to encounter difficult decisions in life. If we are not to deal too leniently with those who clearly go against what is fairly expected of everyone in similar circumstances, nor too harshly with those who succumb to what most of us would understand in sympathetic terms, then we need as full a picture as possible of anyone responsible for wrongdoing to arrive at an appropriate judgement of what is to be done.

This means that members of inclusive communities cannot stand back from the process of collective protection. They cannot turn a blind eye to wrongdoing and rely on someone else to take action. They cannot keep their knowledge and understanding of wrongdoers to themselves, and expect the most appropriate judgement to be passed on their actions without the benefit of the information they withhold. Unless we actively care about protecting ourselves, we would inevitably allow ourselves to become more vulnerable.

This active care should in practice be translated into community safety action. Enforcement agencies are to work with communities on understanding problems and fears, and on identifying those responsible for the problems and how they are to be tackled. While not all community safety programmes are successful, there is clear evidence that they can make a significant impact by reducing crime and antisocial behaviour, especially when they are backed by extensive community involvement. The transformation of Longview's Stamper Park neighbourhood in America, for example, shows that even in an area where there are already serious law and order problems, engaging local citizens in an organized partnership with statutory and voluntary agencies can reduce offences and increase people's sense of security dramatically (Hamner, 1995; see also Browne, 1996, pp. 17–19).

An essential building block of effective community safety partnerships is parental commitment. Parents must ensure that their children understand the boundaries of acceptable behaviour, the harm that could be caused to others, and why violations of the wellbeing of others would not be tolerated. Parents thus need to enforce discipline within their homes so that discipline will also prevail in the community at large. This does not mean that parents should shout at, let alone physically beat, their children in the name of discipline. Nor does it follow that neighbours should express their intolerance by picking on and reporting to official enforcement agencies behaviour of which they personally disapprove. Both suggestions would point to abuses that could only be sustained by individualist or authoritarian ideas. Unlike individualists, who would condone whatever individual parents chose as their way of dealing with their children, or authoritarians who demand that we all treat our children and neighbours in an oppressive manner in support of some 'higher' goal, communitarians maintain that belief in our common values must be matched by action in support of them. In practice, this does mean speaking out consistently against violence, deceit, bigotry and so on, and working co-operatively with those charged democratically with enforcement to stop individuals acting against common values.

Far from leaving them to do as they please, parents are to be reminded of the additional social responsibilities of bringing up children. This does not just cover reinforcing the moral education to be provided by schools, but includes setting an example in terms of behavioural pattern – from avoidance of violence, and of abuse of alcohol and other harmful substances, to showing respect and concern for the welfare of other people.

It is in this context that harmful behaviour is to be watched, reported, and where appropriate, registered, so that precautions against future violations can be carried out more effectively (Etzioni, 1995b, pp. 163–91). People who abuse community safety action and seek to disrupt the lives of other citizens by falsely accusing them of wrongdoing, would be guilty of inflicting unjustifiable harm on others and should themselves be punished. To suggest that such abuse could be ruled out by excluding various domains from citizen scrutiny raises two questions. First, how would the wrongdoing in such domains – be they a neighbourhood, a family, a school, a company or an army base – be detected and dealt with? Is there not a danger that the 'right to privacy' could be used by the powerful in such domains to harm the powerless without anyone outside knowing or doing anything about it? Second, once the wall of privacy is erected, how is the wider community to know if the kind of abuses which are supposed to be ruled out by forbidding external monitoring do not occur among those who claim to monitor their own domains? Ultimately, it is unavoidable that the process of tracking down wrongdoers could be exploited by some to harm innocent citizens. Whereas such exploitation is more likely to be detected and stopped when there are open communications between overlapping communities, the closing off of particular domains to scrutiny by others would in effect be a licence to abuse.

The detection of wrongdoing and the identification of those responsible raise another issue, where external scrutiny is vital. This is the question of punishment. It is essential for systems of punitive action to be accessible to others not directly involved in the system. This facilitates scrutiny by citizens and increases the likelihood that punishment will be administered in support of community protection. From a communitarian point of view, punishment is essentially about how an inclusive community is to relate to its members who have violated the common values of their community (Murphy, 1995). Punishment therefore has to address three issues. First, how reparation for the wrong done is to be achieved. Second, how the wrongdoing in question can be prevented from being committed again. Third, how the wrongdoer can be reconciled with the wider community.

At one level, reparation concerns making good any damage done: whatever is stolen is returned; whatever broken is repaired; and whatever cost has been incurred is paid back. But beyond such visible remedies, there are pain, fear and loss of trust, which cannot be so easily mended. Simply making wrongdoers pay a fine, or even imprisoning them for a period of time, would not necessarily restore the social and psychological states in place before the wrong was committed. This is why wrongdoers must come to see that they should not have done what they did, and ensure that they feel remorse for their behaviour. The importance of this process must not be distorted by the fact that it can be, and has been, abused by authoritarian regimes in forcing ritualistic confessions out of dissidents. While authoritarians subject people who oppose their regimes to painful treatment so that they will publicly retract and bow down to oppression, communitarian punishment gives those who have betrayed the kindness and trust of others a chance to reflect and, through sincere repentance, rebuild the links that have been broken.

Reparation presupposes that there was a social bond to begin with, and communitarian theorists of punishment such as Antony Duff have pointed out that a just system for dealing with offenders must be underpinned by the values of inclusive communities (Duff, 1996). In other words, we would not be in a position to condemn the wrongdoing of others and call for reparation if they were already marginalized by prevailing power structures, and pushed to the limits of endurance.

A similar observation applies to deterrence. If people felt they had nothing to lose, even the most severe threats would not be sufficient to frighten them away from taking drastic action. Throughout history, tyrants have found, too late, that fear of punitive treatment cannot stop those who are deprived of the most basic opportunities to live a decent life from breaking down rules and barriers that stand in their way. Furthermore, the infliction of pain and cruelty, far from being a reliable deterrent, merely engenders an atmosphere of violence which infects wider social behaviour. Rulers who react to every minor offence with an extremely violent response do not make that offence less likely to occur compared with places where such offences are dealt with less harshly, but they do make violence and cruelty much more acceptable in expressing anger in their societies. Since the power to rule in inclusive communities rests with the citizens, they must ask whether they want to use the most cruel and violent instruments to deter themselves from wrongdoing, or if they believe that reliable detection combined with the public loss of specific opportunities to pursue their values would be sufficient.

In general, where individuals are tempted or pressured by circumstances to consider doing what they know to be wrong, the fear of swift detection, the shame of being publicly found guilty, and the unpleasant loss of what they would otherwise possess would be enough to deter most people from doing wrong. Some of them, of course, may lapse on the odd occasion, and give in to a momentary impulse that is later regretted, or miscalculate the consequences of their actions and wish afterwards that they had refrained. On the whole, though, most people would not be inclined to go against their own principles under such conditions.

In practice, this demands a good track record for all three elements concerned. Detection must be genuinely swift. This requires community vigilance, trust, and the effective development and application of forensic techniques. However, to suggest, as authoritarians are likely to do, that the process would be speeded up if we had fewer safeguards against wrongful conviction, would be to miss the whole point of having swift detection – namely, to expose the link between the guilty person and the wrongful act. If safeguards against wrongful conviction were cut back, the chance of innocent people being linked to wrongful acts would be increased, and public confidence in the detection process would rightly diminish.

Regarding the public registering of guilt, wrongdoing in many areas is still shrouded in secrecy. Within religious institutions, professional groups, or large corporations, wrongdoers are often shielded from critical exposure in the wider community. Provided they conform to certain internal practices, their transgression against common values would be kept secret. Such an approach offers an escape route for many who would not otherwise risk sacrificing their public respectability for the wrongful acts they choose to undertake. Finally, on the issue of depriving wrongdoers of what they would otherwise possess, the deprivation must be proportional to the deterrent effect it would have on the wrongdoers concerned. First-time offenders should not receive as severe a punishment as repeated offenders, for example, otherwise there would be no sense of something worse to come should a person offend a second time. In relation to punishment in the form of fines, a flat-rate approach would mean the deterrent effect would diminish in direct proportion to the offender's wealth. To avoid this distortion, the fine for any given offence should be charged as a standard portion of the offender's taxable wealth, payable in person in a public office.

It may be argued that, for those who do not care for enforced deprivations, however swiftly or publicly applied, the above approach would not be very effective in deterring them from wrongdoing. This could arise for two reasons. First, it could be that they in fact have little or nothing to lose in terms of wealth or any other means to a rewarding life. In that case, the question to raise is not how these people are to be frightened into submitting to social practices which do nothing for them, but rather why our social practices have failed to protect these people from the deprivations they are already suffering. The second possible reason points to people who do have, by ordinary standards, plenty to lose, but the possibility of losing their wealth or liberty do not have any impact on their behavioural patterns. For these people, not only are the hurt and distress they may cause others of little consequence to them, but even when the community expresses its condemnation of wrongdoing against its members by means of punitive action, they have no inclination to take it into account when they act. It is not clear how such people can be deterred from re-offending, and in the absence of any way to rebuild trust, it is uncertain whether any form of reconciliation with the wider community can be achieved.

For those who at least recognize that what they have done is against the common values to which they too subscribe, there is the potential for reconciliation. The reasons why they have wronged others could be looked at with a view to understanding why the wrong would not occurr again. This cannot take the simplistic form of forcing offenders to swear to a new way of life. It has to be about enabling offenders to see that there are values they can pursue in harmony with the rest of society. Part of the seeing must consist of accessing abilities and opportunities that were previously either lacking or insufficiently utilized. Skills and self-belief in carrying out rewarding work, the development of aptitude for social interaction, and inclination towards mutual respect should all play a part in the process of reconciliation. For those who have displayed an aggressive disregard for the well-being and feelings of others, support for developing their parental skills and attitudes (whether or not they are parents already) would be essential. In their survey of research findings in this field, Utting, Bright and Henricson discovered that:

> A cohort study of New Zealand children born in 1972–73 found that pre-school behaviour problems were the single best predictor of anti-social disorders in 11 year olds and delinquency by age 15.
>
> Aggressive behaviour in primary school children has, in turn, been linked by studies in Britain and America to harsh early upbringing provided by hostile, abusive or punitive treatment by parents . . . Studies in Sweden and Britain attest further to the durability of aggression in anti-social children as they grow towards adolescence. (Utting *et al.*, 1993, p. 17)

In preparation for life after punishment, probationary advice and community service are also vital in securing a long-term bridge back to full community membership. Along with prison service officials, practitioners in these fields require extensive training and support, and deserve much higher financial rewards than most societies have hitherto given them. As teachers have the important role of educating each new generation to develop into responsible citizens, they have the equally important role of giving those who have not yet developed in this way, a second chance to be a valued member of the community.

At present, the great majority of citizens who have committed an offence so serious as to warrant imprisonment are given virtually no help at all in avoiding re-offending in the future. On the contrary, they are confined in an environment in which suspicion, fear, hatred and anger are the feelings most intensely developed; where violence, extreme and pre-emptive, is an instrument to secure safety and respect; where the low self-esteem of many offenders – an important factor of their criminality – is daily reinforced by the dehumanizing procedures and attitudes in place; where deviant sexual behaviour and the the abuse of dangerous substances receive widespread 'peer group' endorsement; where fear of immediate retribution (which can never be sustained outside a prison environment) becomes the key motivation for self-control; and where the only skills regularly taught are those concerned with intimidation, deception and the trading of illegal drugs. Only when inclusive communities offer the wrongdoers among them a real chance to reform their attitudes, and assist them in developing their skills, would the latter be able to reintegrate successfully into life with their fellow citizens.

However, for those who exhibit an unshakable aversion to caring for or respecting others, finding a way to reconciliation would be much more problematic. In some cases, we have to accept that a full reconciliation would not be possible, and hope that the wrongdoers in question would not transgress against the community again. Yet, in other cases, the risk and the threat of danger are far too serious for the benefit of the doubt to be given to the wrongdoers. It may be a tolerable risk to give people who have stolen once a second chance to prove their trustworthiness, but people who have injured others violently without any provocation, and who show no sign of appreciating that they should not hurt others in the future, cannot be given a chance to prove their harmlessness to others when it is some innocent bystander who would suffer enormously should the gamble not pay off.

The decision to confine any citizen to indefinite treatment because of their pathological tendency to harm others is one that must be made in accordance with the principles and procedures of co-operative enquiry. It is not to be abused as a means of detaining those who oppose a particular regime. Given the need to examine and monitor the operation of compulsory psychiatric treatment, the public must be able to check through an accessible system that those confined do pose a serious threat to others, and that no one is released solely to reduce demand on public resources when the release would endanger innocent people.

Empowering the Vulnerable

Just as we should look at how wrongdoers should be dealt with in our community, on the understanding that we could be wrongdoers ourselves, we should consider how those who suffer from damages and deprivations should be helped, on the basis that we are all vulnerable beings. We must avoid falling into the trap of viewing certain sections of society as victims, whom we may want to help to varying degrees depending on our charitable dispositions. Such a view distorts reality, which does not in fact give anyone any guarantees that they will escape from all possible harm in life.

One of the most pernicious aspects of market individualism is its suggestion that individuals have within them the power to lift themselves out of all hardships, and that those who do not exercise this power deserve to be victims, only surviving at the mercy of those who use their power to the full. Capricious fortune may endow some of us with better initial conditions than others to live a fulfilling life, but it can just as easily throw us into tragic circumstances. It is the deep-seated feeling that we need to care for others, just as we need others to care for us, that lies at the heart of human solidarity. When this feeling is dismissed as unworthy of competitive market heroes, it threatens to undermine the possibility of communal existence.

Rejecting market individualism's twisted view of insular security, communitarianism aims to empower all citizens, should any fall victim to undesirable events or actions, to cope with the experience. Such undesirable experiences may result from the deliberate acts of wrongdoers, or they may happen because the preventative action needed has not been forthcoming. In either case, we need to be able to deal with the immediate problems, and then find a way to prevent them from occurring again.

Rather than compartmentalizing the tools we need into different boxes, we should have a strategically co-ordinated network accessible to everyone in the community. Democratically elected local authorities are well placed to facilitate the development of such networks. If any of us should become victims of crime, accident, ill-health, environmental degradation, poverty or discrimination, we should be confident that through our community-based network, the rest of us would be prepared and able to help alleviate the situation.

One of the most basic forms of support required is the identification of, and response to, significant risks. Our vulnerabilities make us potentially fearful of many kinds of danger. In order to distinguish what we should be fearful of from what does not in fact pose any real threat, we need reliable systems to assist us. Particular problems will be encountered where the risks in question are created by people who stand to lose financially or politically from those risks being exposed.

For example, producers of food or medicine may judge that if only 0.5 per cent of those consuming their products become seriously ill, then provided no one can readily attribute the problem to those products, they would be able to make a substantial profit from selling them. However, if the public comes to believe that there is a 0.5 per cent risk of illness that they deem to be unacceptable, those products would lose market share rapidly. In such circumstances, unless there are public institutions that are above individual commercial funding or sponsorship, the producers would be able to argue that their experts (or 'independent' experts they have commissioned) can see no proof of any link between the products and the illness suffered by only a small minority who have consumed those products. The counter-arguments put forward by experts backing the victims would be portrayed as attempts to extract compensation from the producers. It is therefore vital for there to be genuinely independent risk-assessment agencies, funded by the entire community, which can apply co-operative enquiry to determine whether a causal link can be established.

Public funding should not imply that government departments have exclusive control over such agencies. On the contrary, the public must be able to have access to the work of such agencies, so that everyone can check that their work remains impartial, especially when the government itself is under investigation. Any attempt by governments to privatize public safety agencies must therefore be viewed with suspicion. Such agencies do not belong to the government, but are assets of the community. Taking them out of the public domain would encourage them to use commercial interests as the justification to deny full democratic scrutiny by the public. Furthermore, as they would depend on government contracts, rather than on the strength of public confidence in their work, they would be tempted to give the benefit of the doubt to government bodies. The temptation could surface, for example, when the safety of a railway system is challenged after public funding is cut back; when the safety of developing another nuclear power station is questioned by the public; or when the government proposes to relax the safety requirements in a working environment despite the views of those who will bear the risks of lower safety standards.

With the help of publicly accountable independent risk-assessment agencies, identified risks and the best-known way of dealing with them should be communicated swiftly and openly to citizens via protective networks developed by local authorities and community groups. There should be no veto to protect commercial and political interests, as those concerned with such interests would have the opportunity to put forward their case. What they cannot be allowed to do is to have an automatic delay mechanism operating under the guise of 'avoiding public panics'. Similarly, it would not be acceptable to use the cloak of 'cultural sensisitvity' to block communications on how risks are to be dealt with. For example, Ronald Bayer identified four strands of opposition to public health strategies to warn against the dangers of acquired immune deficiency syndrome (AIDS) in the 1980s: the homosexual community's resentment against linking health risks to promiscuity; fundamentalist religious groups' condemnation of the promotion of condoms; the widespread belief among African-American community leaders that needle exchange programmes would increase the addiction rates of black youths; and old-fashioned male attitudes objecting to women being urged to demand conditions of safe sex. Rather than holding back on the necessary action for fear of offending the sensitivities of these different sections of the community, Bayer concluded that 'in the end, no strategy for effective AIDS prevention can be limited by the demand that cultural barriers to behavioral change always be respected' (Bayer, 1995).

Unless citizens can have direct access to the findings and advice of risk assessors, they would not be in a position to take necessary precautions, or to press for the removal of those risks. This state of dangerous ignorance is what authoritarian protectors often seek to secure. With the absolute authority to pronounce on what is dangerous and what is not, the ruling elite could divert public attention to issues they have tactically picked out. For example, the minor dangers posed by toys made by foreign competitors; the threats from militarily backward countries that fit the 'devil incarnate' role; the fraudulent claims against public funds made by irresponsible welfare dependents; or the sufferings that could be caused by some rare but high profile disease would all get extensive publicity which includes what those in power would do to protect the public. By contrast, threats such as the serious health risks carried by products made by companies that contribute significantly in political donations as well as taxation; the dangerous stockpiling of nuclear, chemical and biological weapons by those in power and their international allies; the damages to public finances made by those who can afford to hire experts to cheat the tax system; or the sufferings being caused by diseases spreading because of poor housing conditions, malnutrition and homelessness would rarely be the focus of attention, even though they are much greater dangers attacking our common values.

Linked to a totally accessible risk assessment system, citizens must support the development of protective measures that would not only counter the risk in question as much as possible, but also help those who are none the less harmed to recover. As no preventative action can guarantee its own success, we have to consider how to respond to our fellow citizens being harmed. Since no approach that systematically excludes some from help would be universally accepted, the only approach that would stand any chance of adoption by all citizens is one that offers help to anyone unfortunate enough to fall victim to any kind of recognizable harm. The notion of recovery presupposes a general norm which all citizens can expect to attain in relation to security, from threats to their lives, physical or psychological damage, and the harm of economic or cultural deprivation. The specification of this norm flows from interactions between communities. Minimum standards are set nationally on the basis of what must be secured in every community in the country. Similarly, democratic interactions between countries will lead to minimum standards that will be applied globally. Within global and national frameworks, individual communities may choose to improve on the minimum standards. In this case, provided their attempts do not make it more difficult for others to attain the minimum standards, they should be allowed to apply themselves to achieving a higher norm for their members.

Crime and illness are common factors that push their victims below the accepted norm. In serious cases, the victims are fearful about their chances of recovery. They cannot see how, by themselves, they could escape the loss, pain, anxiety and despair into which they have been pushed. This is where help needs to be made available, not through dependency, but through solidarity (or 'life-course interdependence'; see Twine, 1994). Victims may lose many things, but in an inclusive community, they do not lose their status as citizens. In practice, this means that victims of whatever kind of harm should have sufficient social support to cope with their fears and anxieties, and access to community insurance that would compensate them for financial losses suffered in connection with criminal damage, accident, ill-health, loss of employment, or any other form of forced departure from the agreed norm. The provision of social support is just as important. Victims of abuse, for example, must not only be protected from those who have harmed them, they should also know that the protection will be maintained because the wrongdoers will be kept away from them. Too many children taken away from abusive parents have been left to their own devices as they are passed from one institution to another. An effective community protection network would assign responsibility to people who will ensure that support is developed and maintained for every child who needs the wider community's help.

The approach also applies to caring for those who may have serious difficulty in recovering fully. Serious accidents, age-related deterioration, or irreversible mental problems, can leave people with little chance of being able to look after themselves in the future. It is then the community's responsibility to give them the help they need, but this help should not deprive its recipients of their sense of dignity and responsibility. Wherever possible, those who need the help must be encouraged to play an active part themselves. This would minimize reliance on impersonal institutions which provide care in a regimented manner, and facilitate citizens to receive support from those closest to them in the community. In Japan, for example, 1989 marked not the triumph of individualism, but the beginning of a nationwide commitment to protect the welfare and health of the country's ageing population, which was translated into the ten-year 'Golden Plan'. Local authorities were given the resources and responsibility to improve the range and standards of services of home help and nursing homes. They were to study the needs of their localities in detail and their findings were incorporated into a revised 'New Golden Plan' announced in 1994. Elderly people are thus assured of a choice of home to meet their particular needs, ready access to specialist overnight care, and support for their relatives in adminstering care in general (Journal of the Japan Local Government Centre, 1997).

This contrasts sharply with market individualist thinking, which encourages those who believe that they have enough resources to protect themselves from most forms of harm, to insist that the protective norm of communities should be set at the lowest possible level compatible with bare survival (King, 1989). From their perspective, apart from paying into a collective fund to prevent people from starvation and life-threatening crimes and diseases, there would be no need for higher standards of common safety. Attempts to achieve higher standards would only cost more, give other people access to support which they do not deserve, and tempt many to become parasites on the wealth of others.

This 'nightwatchman' view of collective security appears to justify the radical shrinking of the public safety net. However, any attempt at reducing the common safety net would require the minimum standards that define the norm to be lowered. It is true that many of the problems previous generations had to face are no longer a major threat for those living in developed countries. Surviving to forty years of age is no longer a major challenge when most can expect to live to their seventies. But unless the nightwatchman state declares that only the rich are to be protected from threats which may undercut their chances of living to their seventies, while the poor are only protected up to their forties, then the safety net would have to take into account all the factors that might undermine any citizen's chance of living into their seventies. And lifespan is not the only standard. The endurance of pain, for example, is another. Should only the rich be guaranteed anaesthetics, with the poor being told that they must be thankful that at least they are operated on with sharper and cleaner instruments?

If it is accepted that any enhancement to the potential for a longer life with reduced suffering is to be incorporated into the general norm for all citizens, then the protective safety net has to cover all the factors that might threaten that norm. This is why we cannot look myopically only at imminent life-threatening dangers, but must extend our vision to underlying causes as well. According to research carried out by Richard Wilkinson, it is not because the rich have to carry the cost burden for the protection of the poor that makes it harder to sustain the protection, but rather the gap between the rich and the poor that causes the problem. Wilkinson writes:

> once countries have reached the standards of affluence of the developed world, further increases in *absolute* income cease to matter very much. Thus the US, Luxemburg and (what was) West Germany are twice as rich per capita and yet have lower life expectancies than Greece or Spain . . . It turns out that what now matters in rich countries is *relative* income . . .

> Income distribution, or how big the differences between rich and poor are in each country, seems to be the most important determinant of health standards in the developed world. The smaller the gap between rich and poor the higher the society's overall standard of health. (Wilkinson, 1991)

While some may suggest that it is the poor's immoral envy of the rich that is the root cause of the problem, the reality of exclusion is created by those who widen income gaps, and not by the poor. Citizens who have neither wealth-accumulating skills nor wealth-accumulating parents do not choose to surrender the potential for a longer life with reduced suffering, which the rest of society could attain. They do not choose to have ever dwindling access to a range of goods and services, which others take for granted, because their own purchasing power is reduced by the escalating income of others. Above all, they do not choose to live in a society where their children are made to feel inferior through the display of status-defining goods by the children of richer parents. It is simply untenable to suppose that 'relative poverty' is an imagined problem, when the gap between the economically powerful and the powerless marginalizes the latter in society; and it is a gap which exhortation to 'work harder' can rarely close. In fact, in non-communitarian organizations, harder work may lead only to higher productivity, which enables management to make more people redundant.

For a protective norm to be meaningful to all citizens, it cannot be set at any level far below the kind of secured existence which, socially and technologically, can be attained by every member of the society in question. To insist that the norm is to be set at a level which only guarantees basic survival is to declare that those citizens lacking the economic power to reach a higher level of safe living are to be excluded from the collective help society can provide. It is to stigmatize them as unworthy of society's support. If this is the case, the excluded citizens would be justified in questioning whether if they really had any shared responsibility with others in securing any kind of common protective norm. Why should they bother to prevent the spread of infectious diseases beyond themselves; to report criminal activities against the elite; to refrain from actions which might sacrifice short-term stability in favour of possible social improvements in the long term;, or to refuse help from people who may in return ask them for assistance in challenging prevailing institutions – through acts of violent protest, espionage, or even terrorism?

A society which does not commit itself to bringing its members together in an inclusive community is liable to fragment into antagonistic factions. Instead of taking responsibility for securing a common norm for all, they develop conflicting norms that undermine each other. The demand by the powerful that the powerless in society should surrender to their view of life is hollow (Culpitt, 1992). In reality, there are many citizens who are not only below the level of secured existence that others take for granted, but they are kept there by institutional barriers and social attitudes. To dismiss all attempts to rectify these problems as gestures of 'political correctness' betrays a callous neglect of these citizens' sufferings, if not also a defective understanding of the difficulties people have to overcome once they are portrayed as being totally responsible for their own plight. All too many citizens suffer exploitation and discrimination because there are people and institutions which look down on others because of the latter's sex, skin colour, age, disability, religious belief, or class background. Citizens vulnerable to such treatment should have confidence that society as a whole is on their side, and not be made to feel isolated as troublemakers who refuse to accept their lot.

Reforming Protective Networks

To sustain protective networks which can deal with wrongdoers effectively and empower the vulnerable to attain a norm for secured existence acceptable to all, a way has to be found to provide and apply common resources to their operations. This would not be easy when market individualists are encouraging the economically powerful around the world to think that they are already contributing too much towards common resources in their own as well other countries. When this is combined with the increasing number of economically deprived people who feel they no longer have any real sense of responsibility for their own well-being, people's abilities to sustain collective protection is seriously challenged.

However, the fact that some politicians have taken to persuading people to believe that paying less for the common good is a virtuous goal, should not mislead us into thinking that the reasons they deploy are necessarily valid. These tend to revolve around the claim that people should be encouraged to create and keep their own wealth, and that they should not be 'forced' to hand over part of what they make to help others who have not 'bothered' to create enough wealth for themselves. In reality, the more inclusive a community is in allowing its members to participate in determining the contributions to their common safety net, the less tenable it is to talk about 'forced' contributions. However, many centralized state systems do exclude all forms of participation, and they should be reformed to allow citizens a real say in the construction of their own safety net.

Only those who naïvely think that their well-being can be safeguarded in isolation from other people who would suffer more than they, could seriously entertain the idea that they might safely opt out of networks for common protection. The co-operative research, social stability and the mutual trust necessary to support any effective form of protection could not be secured if marginalized sections of society are driven to abandon a co-operative stance by the withdrawal of common protection from them. If, instead of being taxed without any real understanding of the purpose of taxation, all citizens are engaged in a process of reviewing their common protective needs, how those needs could be met from collective resources, and the implications of alternative options, then more citizens may begin to develop a critical understanding of the resources needed to finance common protection. This might lead to cuts in some areas, but it could also lead to investment in others. It might also put a stop to spending on prisons which just lock people up and make prisoners even less adapted to social coexistence, and channel more resources into developmental programmes, which evidence suggests are more effective at reducing recidivism. In the UK, where authoritarian demands for incarceration reached new heights in the 1990s, the public is largely unaware of the fact that keeping someone in prison on average costs over twenty times more than a community-based sentence (Howard League, 1997). Far from being a soft option, a closely monitored community sentence forces offenders to think through how they are to change their behaviour. Imprisonment should be a last resort reserved for those who are genuinely incapable of altering their behaviour to refrain from inflicting harm on others.

What is needed is a devolved structure of information and deliberation, so that citizens and their representatives at different levels can consider matters without all decisions being concentrated in vast national departments. The involvement of citizens also means that politicians would not be allowed to intervene in the information dissemination process, or to exploit issues to give themselves party political gains. Most civilized countries already ensure that this is the approach adopted in judicial deliberations. It is time for citizens to take on the role of jury in a wider range of public issues (Stewart *et al.*, 1994). Citizens should be able to have free access to relevant evidence, support to hear and question expert opinions, and a guaranteed input into decision-making processes that determine how best to minimize the dangers posed by factors such as the promotion of alcohol, tobacco and their illegal counterparts; defects in the criminal justice system; effectiveness of preventative health care and treatment; poor housing conditions; social exclusion of the most vulnerable; and other threats to our common safety.

Protective networks should also be integrated from the citizens' point of view (for a selection of case studies, see Osborn and Shaftoe, 1997). Instead of facing diverse bureaucracies which have little interest in or understanding of each other's work, citizens should have access to one-stop assistance points through which all relevant public agencies can be brought together for a co-ordinated response. Instead of having tax collecting agencies which have neither the knowledge nor the inclination to discuss how the tax revenue from citizens will be spent, decentralized assistance points should be able to help citizens to develop a clearer picture of what they are being asked to fund. This may lead citizens to challenge politicians to alter priorities, to give localities greater autonomy in improving their own protective systems, or to bring traditionally distinct agencies together to work on specific projects. What is important is that citizens, rich or poor, should no longer be alienated from the process of deciding what needs to be done for the common safety of all.

The same development must also take place in relation to global protective networks. Just as the rich in any country should not be deceived into thinking they could protect themselves by excluding the poor from a common protective network, richer countries should not mislead their citizens into believing they could protect themselves adequately against all threats to their common values without the co-operative involvement of the poorer countries. Growing communications and interactions across the world are showing that the common values, and the corresponding threats and dangers we have identified apply to people beyond our own national borders. In no part of the world can it be denied that the sufferings caused by starvation and diseases, the disasters brought by climatic changes, the escalation of violence made possible by the arms trade, the torture of prisoners, and the depletion of non-renewable resources are to be deplored and countered. The political elites that have seized power may try to justify their role in contributing to these problems, but no moral culture on Earth would tolerate these violations of human values.

Citizens everywhere must be informed of the global dimension of protective networks. At the end of the twentieth century, there are still 35 000 children across the world dying every day from preventable diseases, and 800 million people going hungry every night. The global community will never be as safe as it could be if its most vulnerable members are not assisted with the best help collective resources could provide. Much more should be done to promote education in world issues, break down religious and tribal antagonism, and give every citizen support in understanding the interconnections of dangers and preventative measures in the global context. The work of agencies such as UNESCO should be supported, so that a global agenda can be developed and implemented in addressing the intellectual and cultural roots of apathy, suspicion and conflict.

Once citizens can see for themselves the scale of the problems before them, and the dismal prospects of tackling them on a fragmented, individualist basis, they would recognize that, far from too much being done to strengthen common protective networks, more needs to be invested in the future. The crucial question would then rightly focus on how that investment is to be made. The criticism that the powerless could be made irresponsibly powerless by insensitive systems cannot readily be dismissed. In fact, authoritarian protection, even when it is designed with the best intentions, tends to treat recipients of assistance as dependents, and not as citizens with a duty to the rest of the community. Welfare provision, in particular, has often fallen into this trap, and ended up encouraging people who only needed short-term help to recover their normal position, to become long-term dependents on state support.

The root cause of this is the failure to recognize citizens' needs in recovering their normal position, and respond effectively to those needs. An essential element of recovery is the attainment of autonomy as a citizen. That autonomy can only be secured with the responsible engagement of the citizen concerned. Just as people who refuse to take necessary medicine, or follow doctors' advice on fitness and diet, would become dependent on hospital care, welfare recipients who do not take action to secure a reasonable income become attached to the state system.

In order to tackle this root cause, we must not be deflected by the market individualists' obsession with commercial operations. To suggest that state protective systems should be dismantled and protective tasks handed to commercial firms, raises questions not only about the democratic accountability and reliability of the fragmented bodies, but also about their effectiveness in addressing citizens' needs to recover their normal position. By their very nature, help would be provided if the providers could get a reasonable financial return. Those who could not afford to pay insurance to cover unemployment, criminal losses and damages, ill health and so on – and having to live in deprived areas, they would be charged higher premiums to match their higher risks – would get no support at all.

What should be done is to carry out an extensive reform of collective protective networks, with the intention of making them much more community-based. This means that centralized state processes must be devolved to levels where real dialogues and partnerships with citizens-in-need would take the place of impersonal transactions. The purpose of such dialogues is not to tell those receiving help that there is a time limit beyond which they would not be given any more help, but rather that they must participate responsibly in a recovery partnership designed to help them attain the norm collectively agreed by society. On the basis that the help on offer would realistically secure them an independent income, it would then make sense to stipulate penalties for refusing to play one's part in the partnership. It is vital that the advice and support offered, unlike some of the token training schemes that have been packaged in the past, provide a real bridge to autonomous living. The refusal to take full advantage of this bridge would then justify the reduction of welfare support, and indeed tough enforcement against those who waste their lives through anti-social behaviour and wanton abuse of alcohol and drugs. Once there is a real option to live a responsible life, deliberate rejections of the option must carry punitive consequences (Andre *et al.*, 1994; Saffran, 1996).

There is, of course, the danger that an authoritarian protective establishment would use a superficial and inadequate recovery programme as an excuse to cut back its support for the most needy. This would be analogous to a hospital telling its patients that unless they all go home and take the medicine it prescribes – which it knows is not likely to help them recover – it would discharge them all at once and never re-admit them. Although community-based protection cannot guarantee it could come up with effective recovery programmes, it does facilitate far greater citizen participation which would scrutinize and press for improvements to those programmes in the light of what would lead to adequate paid work in the area. It would also allow the enforcement, or suspension, of penalties to be related much more closely to the conditions under which recovery may be achieved. For example, when employment prospects in an area are particularly bleak, the penalties should be relaxed for a longer period to allow structural regeneration and developmental aid to take effect.

Community-based protection also means that citizens in need are not left to their own devices, but that their problems and responsibilities are shared with others in their community. Community-based regeneration programmes, implemented by multi-agency partnerships involving the participation of those in need, have had many notable successes. For example, the regeneration of the Holly Street area in Hackney, London, has led to dramatic reductions in violent incidents, fear of crime, bullying of children, and demands on the health service. One survey suggested a one third drop in most of these categories in a 12-month period (Kean, 1996, pp. 20–3).

As citizens can develop a more responsible attitude towards paying taxes for the common good through involvement in shaping the way that the common good is protected, they can also develop a more responsible commitment to getting themselves a decent quality of life, when they are involved with others in their community in the process, and not treated as mere 'claimants' by anonymous officials reporting to a distant headquarters.

Another aspect of protective networks which must be reformed is the built-in disincentive to put more effort into overcoming difficult predicaments. However, rather than cutting down on benefits, which simply penalises people regardless of their chances of gaining an adequate income, a tax credit system should be introduced alongside a basic income scheme, so that the latter can be progressively supplemented when more paid work is carried out (see Roche, 1992; Hirst, 1994, chs 6–7). The details for such a scheme would be easier to work out if national governments concentrated on collecting enough tax revenue to pay out the standard citizen income to everyone, and leave local governments to develop with their respective communities the tax–benefit adjustments they wish to make to maximize work incentives for their citizens.

What national governments do increasingly need to turn their attention towards is the development of global networks which can reliably detect and punish large-scale crimes, and provide consistent incentives for multinational organizations to support global protective goals. The poverty and squalor in which millions of people are trapped in the developed as well as developing countries, are now inextricably linked to global economic pressures. Local community initiatives must be backed by global action to halt the trend of substituting more and more human resources with non-renewable natural resources. Quite apart from the long-term threats posed by environmental degradation to our health, the imbalance in the world's utilization of resources is making it increasingly difficult for millions of people to find sufficient paid work to contribute towards their protection.

Tax incentives should be created for companies to reduce their consumption of natural resources, and to support the development of local workforces. Investment should be channelled, not into short-term profits, but into safer production methods that do not harm people environmentally or socially. Citizens should not allow their governments to tell them to keep out of the affairs of the commercial sector. On the contrary, the performance of businesses against indicators relating to their contribution to common protection objectives should be publicized regularly for all citizens to see and judge. Ultimately, the notion of competitive growth must be replaced by sustainable development to protect our common values, not just in relation to the threats of war between nations, but also to the threats of alienation and confrontation between those who are permanently excluded in all countries, and the rest of the world. Where citizens are threatened by the dangerous by-products of an unregulated world market, they must use whatever instruments for change they have at their disposal to deal with those threats. The action that can be taken in the state, business and third sectors to achieve the reforms which have been put forward will be considered in the next three chapters.

6
The State Sector

Political Citizenship

In Chapters 3–5, we have seen how the education, work and protection of citizens need to be developed if inclusive communities are to be established and sustained. The development in question requires a structure for co-operative enquiry and practical support to carry out informed deliberations. Citizens need to be able to come together to shape decisions on what is to be taught, how production is to be organized, and where the minimum standards are to be set for their common protection.

Conventional politics, of the individualist or authoritarian variety, takes the marginalization of citizens for granted. Political decisions are taken by the state, and citizens are at best given a periodic vote when the small elite who would go on to run the state are chosen. This kind of politics is failing. It raises false expectations, and it regularly turns the spotlight away from the main issues, because it cannot afford to deal with the public disillusionment that might otherwise occur. The difficulties of meeting the educational needs of citizens in a rapidly changing world, coping with the unstable and uneven distribution of opportunities to carry out paid work, and helping those who are the victims of circumstances beyond their control, are not evaluated with the participation of those they most affect.

Authoritarians despise consensus politics as being weak, and insist that their vision should be imposed on everyone, regardless of what others might think of the consequences. The individualist response to this has amounted to little more than seeking out the lowest common denominator as representing the highest number of votes, and building a political platform to appeal to those interests irrespective of what those on the platform really think are important for the common good. The rise of cynicism towards contemporary politics reflects the dwindling credibility of both approaches. The way government institutions are run is losing respect and trust. Citizens are now looking for new levers to manage their public domain (Kooiman, 1993; Dalton 1988).

For a time after the 1989 revolutions, it appeared that market individualism might win acceptance as the best solution the world could hope for. Individualists who distrusted the state sector established a convenient alliance with the economically powerful, who were confident that the former's reluctance to use the state to correct uneven power distribution would ensure that those in command of material wealth would be able to continue to prosper regardless of how the side-effects of their operations affected others in society. Authors such as Francis Fukuyama even concluded that the evolution of political systems had come to an end (Fukuyama, 1992). Under the 'New World Order' of the market individualist, citizens should no longer think about how they could help each other collectively. Instead, they should concentrate solely on how they could help themselves as individuals. Those who succeed in helping themselves to material prosperity are given the protection of the economic establishment – that is, protection from being asked to pay more taxes for the common good. Those who fail are told that it is their own responsibility, and they should not expect to receive help from others. In short, equal political citizenship is to give way to a system of vastly different levels of economic achiever (Macpherson, 1985; Marquand, 1988).

In practice, this has led to the abdication of political responsibility for an ever-increasing number of problems which the economic establishment by itself is simply not capable of solving, even if some business leaders are involved. Without political action, society cannot help its members when they are threatened by permanent economic and cultural exclusion, by everyday dangers from which they do not have the means of protecting themselves, or by extremists who believe that they can achieve their own objectives by hurting others. The widening gulf between those who are still championing market individualism and citizens who are expressing deep discontent with this flawed compromise, points to the need for a communitarian alternative. Rejecting the view that politics is confined to the state sector, communitarianism regards political action as being applicable wherever the issue of power structures arises. Therefore, in addition to what goes on in state institutions, citizens should be concerned with the impact of activities in the business sector, and in the third sector of voluntary organizations and community groups. Instead of relying solely on those in charge of government to bring about changes necessary for the building of inclusive communities, citizens should apply their influences directly to state, business and community organizations to secure the conditions of communitarian citizenship.

We shall begin by looking at the action that should be taken in the state sector, and will consider action in the business and the third sectors in Chapters 7 and 8, respectively. Market individualists have promoted the view that the state is an authoritarian instrument and its use should be confined to protecting the operations of a market economy. All other issues should be left to the profit-driven actions of businesses, or the voluntary activities of individuals. The state sector, in this view, should be cut back by having more and more of its responsibilities moved into the 'private' domain of commercial and voluntary action.

While by communitarian standards most state bodies still operate on an excessively authoritarian basis, the way forward is not to surrender the instrument of state action, but reform it so that it can serve the needs of citizens effectively. Rather than standing back as economic agents and individual volunteers, we must defend our political status and protect the state from incremental privatization. In order to preserve the realm of state action as an essential element of citizen politics, we must distinguish reforms that would deprive citizens of political instruments to secure their common values from reforms which would make state bodies more responsive to citizens. All too often, reforms promised to be of the latter type have turned out to be of the former type. An urgent task for citizens is to unmask such reforms.

Since the 1980s, countries across the world have been told that the state sector has grown too big and unresponsive to the needs of the public, and therefore it has to be reduced in size. As the twenty-first century approaches, the message has established a powerful hold on all major global financial institutions, which are pressing all governments to give up more responsibility. The message has influenced governments of different party political backgrounds. In essence, it wants the state sector to tax less, spend less, manage less, own less, and regulate less (Martin, 1993).

Supporting the good of all by contributing to a common fund is one of the most fundamental political obligations, and this obligation is discharged through taxation. Of course, authoritarians could use a system of taxation to compel people to fund state expenditure regardless of what they know or think about such expenditure. It does not follow that taxation is inherently authoritarian. What is required is greater citizen involvement in taxation planning. At levels that are accessible to citizens, it is not unknown for local authorities to consult the public to ascertain their views on the taxation requirement to meet the expenditure priorities they support. If state bodies are to become more open and decentralized, then it is perfectly possible for taxation to rise or fall in response to the informed participation of citizens in the tax-setting process. Such an approach would give citizens a real choice in considering different public service options (Prior *et al.*, 1995).

It is by refusing to contemplate this approach that market individualists resort to invoking the mythical 'choice' which the reduction of taxation would of necessity create. For them, individuals would have more choice on how to spend their money if, instead of handing it over to an authoritarian state, they themselves decide what to spend it on. But if the state is to function as a deliberative forum for citizens, then taxation in fact offers people more choices than they could hope for individually. Numerous projects can only be achieved if people can rely on binding structures that would secure the agreed contribution from everyone to pay for what would be for the good of all. Without such structures, health care, emergency services, accident prevention, and many other services that support modern civilization would not be available. Indeed, in many countries, the weakness of the state in tackling these issues is the single most important cause of tragic deficiencies in these areas.

The propaganda war against state resources must be countered by citizens. The false dichotomy of allowing an authoritarian state to take more of people's money, or letting individuals keep more of it, must be exposed. The key question is how greater public involvement in the allocation of these resources is to be developed. If the process of public involvement, which requires civic education as well as more public-orientated management, is to have any real chance of success, the scope of influencing state expenditure must not in the meantime be strangled by the dogma that state expenditure must be reduced in any event. Public debates about what might require additional expenditure – such as the education of an increasing number of young people, or medical and social support for the growing elderly population, and what could be reduced – such as forms of punishment which lead to the highest rates of recidivism, and stockpiling of weapons which are not so much needed for the defence of citizens' freedom as for the profits of the defence industry – are stifled by the ideological insistence that citizens do not want to pay more taxes, and should not be encouraged or supported in discussing tax issues.

Instead of reducing politics to a test of the sincerity of politicians in cutting taxation, the public and the media should demand more open examinations of the state's activities. Suggestions regarding cutting back these activities or precluding their application in specific areas must be accompanied by analyses of what the consequences would be for society. Given the difficulties of adjusting to radical changes in a global economy with few communitarian structures for co-operative action, one of the most pressing problems of the early twenty-first century will be the distribution of paid work to the world's population. Without an adequate distribution, large numbers of people will suffer, and their sufferings will affect the moral and physical well-being of others who, in the short-term, might have benefited from the rewards of their share of the world's paid work. If the state is simply going to retreat from tackling these problems, what can be expected from the benevolence of individual charities, and the exhortations to those with insufficient means to take responsibility for their own lives?

Market individualists, however, would turn this question around. They would argue that these latter options are the only viable ones, because the option of state action requires state-sector management, which is inherently inferior to private-sector management. People would be better off, in their view, if more and more aspects of life were managed by the private sector. Thus every opportunity for cutting back state-sector management must be pursued. The core argument for this anti-state stance is that state-sector managers, lacking the competitive forces that drive private-sector managers to improve their services to customers, are inevitably less efficient, less cost effective, and less responsive. This is the basic justification used for contracting out the management of the state sector (Loney *et al.*, 1991). While contracting out has had some benefits, it is important to point out what the benefits and damages are, and why the damages would continue to outweigh the benefits if the contracting culture does not give way to the development of a communitarian alternative to state-sector management.

As a catalyst for shaking up authoritarian state management, the philosophy of market testing has made a positive contribution. Those in charge of state bodies are liable to assume that they know what is best for everyone, and that they are entitled to carry out their work with little, if any, involvement by those they affect. Market testing means that the demands of those receiving state services have to be taken into account when drawing up specifications, and the costs and processes for meeting those demands are evaluated in comparison with others who may come up with better approaches. The testing is not done as an academic exercise, but calculated by organizations that must be confident they can deliver the alternative packages of costs and management if they are awarded the contract.

Experience in the UK, which is not significantly different from elsewhere, has shown that market testing requires a great amount of management information, which makes it more difficult for ineffective management practices to be hidden from critical scrutiny. However, beyond threatening the complacency of many in the state-sector establishment with imminent redundancy, the relentless application of market testing as a policy tool is causing damage that increasingly outweighs the benefits it has brought about. The problem lies with the inherent limitations of market testing. If it is to make a lasting improvement in state-sector management, it must link up with extensive citizen participation. All it is capable of achieving in isolation is the pushing of more public-sector responsibilities into the hands of private-sector management. This has three notable consequences. First, it delivers superficial savings, which masks the underlying problems created. Market testing has revealed that significant savings are only to be found in services which are essentially routine operations. Where professional skills and strategic judgements are the core elements of a service, the private sector has found little scope to cut costs. Where it has been able to cut costs substantially – estimates have varied from 5 per cent to 20 per cent – the cuts have been derived from a combination of lower wages and fewer jobs for manual workers (Walsh, 1994). Those with the least economic bargaining power are thus squeezed by the economic establishment to generate savings for all citizens. With fewer opportunities to earn enough to keep themselves above the protective norm, they also find market individualists demanding a reduction in public support for those who fall below that norm. Furthermore, even the savings figures disguise the fact that costs of developing specifications and monitoring contracts are now added to the state sector even if the costs of the contractors are reduced.

Second, without integration with citizens' involvement at the strategic level, market testing focuses managers' and management consultants' minds only on how to package contracts and remodel processes to maximize their own financial gains. State-sector managers would seek to define the needs of the public in terms that are most suited to prolonging their direct control of services, and managers of state contracts would be under financial pressure to make them interpret contract terms as narrowly as possible, so that citizens' needs, which are not clearly specified in their contracts, are either ignored, or dealt with only if the state is prepared to pay more under the contract. The knock-on effect for people who work in state-sector services is that they will avoid looking at citizens' needs, treating them only as a distraction from what has been specified in their contracts. Instead, they will look inward, at how best to manipulate contract terms and monitoring processes to secure their own financial positions. The idea of becoming more responsive to public needs and improving quality assurance will be pushed further and further down their management agenda. If left unchecked, the opportunity to develop citizen-orientated state-service management would be lost, and the old-style authoritarian barrier to citizen participation could come to be replaced by a new-style individualist management which is just as dismissive of the value of involving citizens in state services.

Third, political accountability would diminish. Individualists may argue that, as consumers, citizens would find it easier to pin down contractors and complain about their failure to comply with contract specifications. But this relative improvement would only be secured at the cost of even greater marginalization of citizens. By handing the interface with the public to a private-sector operator, the state, in effect, reduces citizens to consumers who may express their dissatisfaction to the operator, but who cannot directly hold anyone to be politically responsible for what they wish to query or challenge. Private-sector operators have no political obligation to explain their actions or failures to their consumers, so long as they can satisfy the state representatives who award them their contracts. State representatives, on the other hand, are given a neat buffer to divert citizens' question to those in charge of the day-to-day operations of all kinds of state service. If a private-sector operator fails to deliver a service because their management priorities have changed or they have gone out of business, the blame is left with the private sector and not with state representatives who contracted with them in the first place.

Given the damaging effects of following the market individualists' prescription to hand state services to the private sector, the agenda of repeatedly championing this prescription must be scrutinized, not because the state and its employees should be protected from reforms, but because it poses a serious threat to the development of inclusive communities. If market reforms mean in practice that services must be contracted out to the lowest tender, regardless of whether the citizens relying on those services agree to the contract; if the political power to hold those delivering state services accountable diminishes with managerial transfers; if the complex splits between those responsible for specifications and those responsible for operations confuse the public further about who is to be contacted for what, then the continued pressure to transfer more of the state's responsibilities to the private sector can only be explained in terms of its role in undermining attempts to equalize political power.

Services hitherto delivered to enhance the public good become services carried out for private profit. Services that would have taken extra care of those who were poor or vulnerable are managed more 'efficiently' so that those who reduce the amount of profit are marginalized. Most significantly, citizens who used to carry out these services as public servants would become vulnerable pawns themselves, easily made redundant to boost the profits of those running the contracts. Whereas collectively as public servants they could speak out against the reduction of services to the public – especially when the government tries to hide such reductions from public scrutiny, as fragmented employees of different private contractors they stand to lose their livelihoods if they dare to question what they are instructed to do.

It could be argued, however, that regardless of the power shifts to those in charge of private-sector contracting organizations, the public at large could only gain a more cost effective and responsive delivery of state services if the management in question is subject to the competitive pressures that make private-sector bodies more cost-effective and responsive. On this basis, if not only the management, but the whole business including responsibility for specifications, assets and so on, were to be completely privatized, cost-effectiveness and responsiveness would increase even more. The flaw in this argument lies with its core assumption. Competitive pressures do not make private-sector firms more cost-effective or responsive. It is customer-focus strategies that make market-led organizations more successful. Competitive pressure is just one stimulus to adopt customer-focus strategies, and at times it could also be a distraction which forces companies to adopt short-term measures that damage their long-term customer focus. What is important is the management approach to services that focus on the needs of those they are intended to benefit. Dogmatic insistence that this can only be brought about by commercial competitive pressures, or by treating the 'customers' of state services as profit-generating consumers as opposed to citizens, could only harm the development of state services (Tam, 1994b, ch. 1).

Even the wave of British privatizations in the 1980s, an exemplar supposed to illustrate why governments all over the world should follow its example, reveals on closer examination that it is the adoption of customer-focus practices even when they were still in the state sector, which made many of them more cost effective and responsive. Where the political will existed, selected state instruments were subjected to massive reorganization and investment, incentives were provided for improved management, and 'transformation' being established *before* rather than after privatization (Parker and Martin, 1993, pp. 44–7).

To maintain that only extensive privatizations of management and ownership, combined with widespread deregulation, will provide the incentive to develop responsive state action, is dangerous for two reasons. First, it is dismissing the fact that people could be motivated to serve the public good more effectively by better understanding of their duties as state servants. Propounded by an influential minority who themselves are driven only by personal gains, this dogma seeks to deny the possibility of communitarian state action when, in fact, many people in the state sector have demonstrated their commitment and ability to work more closely with citizens in general because that is needed to enhance services for the public good. Second, allowing the dogma to spread would risk the loss of even more state instruments for tackling public issues. It takes a long time to develop the culture and trust to establish successful state institutions, and if these were to be eradicated, it would be a greater challenge to rebuild them. In the meantime, more and more institutions that citizens once held in shared ownership for their collective benefit, are becoming private concerns in which only a minority share ownership. Providing safe water, adequate energy supplies, reliable public transport and so on, are all ceasing to be utilities to be managed by the state on our behalf, and are being treated as means of making profits for a few individuals. Those who cannot pay the rate demanded would have their supplies cut off regardless of the opinions of citizens who think that such supplies are essential to a minimum standard of living (for a detailed analysis of privatization policies and their global implications, see Martin, 1993).

Those with economic power may think that the radical undermining of the state would give them the freedom to dictate to the rest of society. But whatever short-term gains they achieve, the long-term instability fuelled by the polarization of society is not something they can ignore complacently. In Russia, where the 'reject authoritarianism for the only alternative of market individualism' argument has been immensely influential, the consequences are clear to see. Business elites (including those with major criminal connections) are taking over powers once held by Communist Party elites; opportunities for embezzling public funds are proliferating; citizens who used to work for state institutions are not given any support to become more responsive to the needs of their fellow citizens; and instead of having 51 per cent of privatized company's shares, as promised, proportions for workers were watered down to 10 per cent; large-scale redundancies have followed to boost profits but not to improve the quality of state services, which are in fact seen to be declining for many vulnerable citizens (Conradi, 1994).

The global ascendancy of market individualism, and its reliance on privatization to build alliances with the economically powerful to undermine the state, must face up to its effects on the economically weak. What is left of the state could be used by the well-off as an authoritarian instrument to repress discontent, until it leads to a revolutionary explosion; or the process could be reversed, with the state reformed through large-scale citizen participation, and used as a communitarian tool for building inclusive communities.

Communitarian Governance

Communitarian criticisms of market-orientated reforms of the state must not be taken as support for the state system as it is. Most

Western countries, for all their superficially democratic structures, still retain too much centralized control and legislate continuously on so large a scale that the activities of their state institutions minimize public understanding with their complexities, and exclude grassroot participation with their remoteness. Action is urgently required to develop an alternative form of political governance whereby citizens can participate in the deliberations of their state as equal and responsible members of a shared community. It has to cover three interrelated aspects of state organization. It must distribute power to as many community decision-making points as possible, involve all citizens who might be affected by those decisions in shaping the decision-making process, and enable the localized deliberative communities to come together at regional, national, supranational, and global level to deal with the issues they cannot tackle effectively alone (see Tassin, 1992; Kinsky, 1995).

The redistribution of the power to shape political decisions should begin by demolishing the myth of state sovereignty. Most Western countries still subscribe to the authoritarian view that once the issue of who is to be in charge of the core political institutions of a given country is periodically settled by the electoral process, citizens should have no more involvement in their own governance until the next round of elections. Since most people believe that their votes would change very little in any case, this reduces them to being mere spectators of political events. Politicians encourage them to blame other parties for lack of ideas to tackle the problems facing society, but not to do anything meaningful about those problems.

This patronizing approach was, of course, inherited by Western states when they took over the claims of former monarchs to have absolute sovereignty to rule over their domains. In reality, those monarchs had used force to control an area, and then tried to legitimatize their rule by invoking divine right or whatever else was believable at the time. Those who took over these monarchs' power to rule might think that they had also taken over some form of sovereignty to command the obedience of those who live under that rule. However, as these monarchs did not have the legitimacy to demand the support of many in their own land whom they exploited as cheap labourers and dispensable soldiers, not to mention the indigenous people in America, Australia, Asia and Africa whom they subjugated, they did not have any sovereign right to rule to be taken over by anyone. The right to rule has to be earned from the people in whom sovereignty ultimately rests. Epistemologically, morally and politically, there is no other way to legitimatize any form of government except through the informed support of those being governed. This informed support could not be obtained except by making the workings of the state much more accessible to citizens, who are then encouraged to give their considered views on what should be done. Instead of misleading the public into believing that sovereignty cannot be divided, all government bodies must develop decentralized structures that would allow deliberations on policies as well as operational matters to take place at the level of local communities. It is only where people have a sense of belonging, such as their local town, or their own neighbourhood in a big city, that deliberative communities can be established. Arbitrary administrative zones with boundaries to suit head office planners rather than local community feelings would not be acceptable. Furthermore, the setting up of decentralized units run by centrally-appointed people with no input from local people would serve only to further alienate citizens from the political process.

Authoritarians would argue against decentralization on the grounds that it runs the risk that unacceptable variations would spread, particularly when extremists in some localities would use the power they gain to run their areas in ways which the rest of the citizens would not tolerate. Does this mean that all variations are unacceptable? Or is it the case that there are certain basic standards which should be applied to everywhere that the higher-level state body has jurisdiction? Except for authoritarians who would insist on their political infallibility, no one could accept the argument that all communities must have the same practices and procedures regardless of what their different needs and circumstances demand. Even if standardization helps to produce economies of scale, and the regularity of service delivery, the opportunity to try out different practices in different areas would still be an important source of innovation.

It is not variations as such, but the possibility of certain types of violation to which variations might give rise, which is problematic. If these violations could be defined with reference to threats against common values, and translated into practices that are workable across different communities, then their prevention would help to set minimum standards for everyone. The minimum time for the fire service to reach the site of an emergency; the basic level support for anyone without access to food or shelter; the age up to which children must attend compulsory education; or the core criteria for non-discriminatory treatment of citizens at work, can all be set to rule out violations that are universally unacceptable. With such minimum standards, the collective resources and authority for meeting them must also be secured by arrangements with the higher-level state body.

Beyond meeting these minimum standards, however, there are numerous issues which citizens should have the power to decide in their own communities. Unless their decisions violate the minimum standards, there would be no basis upon which to object to them just because they would be different from what other communities might do. Diversity of political practices is not only a healthy sign within a framework of common values, it is also a stimulus for cautious experimentation and social improvement. Decentralization thus acknowledges the ethos of competitive development but, unlike market individualists who tie competitive motivation to financial gains, it recognizes civic pride as a key incentive. With the autonomy to consider and apply their own resources to improving their communities, citizens would see that they have a real role to play in determining their own quality of life (Crouch and Marquand, 1995).

As to how these units of communitarian governance are to be defined, the starting point should be the local level of government with which citizens are most familiar, and decentralization from established local government to area communities and communities of interests could be developed through consultation with local citizens. Expert analysis of geographical features and population sizes could contribute to discussions on boundary adjustments, but must not be used as a blueprint for some total reorganization as it would only overthrow grassroots systems for a new structure that has no links with either existing state mechanisms or the citizens' sense of community.

Apart from avoiding the imposition of authoritarian visions of decentralized government units, the units must have real powers invested in them, and they in turn must become fully accessible to citizen participation in their deliberations. The legitimacy and effectiveness of entrusting the locally elected representatives with ultimate decisions would be enhanced by their interactions with citizens, who could discuss so much more with them than when they are confined to ticking a name on a list of people they know virtually nothing about. Attempts to bypass local accountabilities by handing state functions to locally-based, but centrally-appointed, agents must stop. Locally elected authorities should take over the running, or at least the monitoring, of such functions, so that local citizens are not misled into thinking they have an input into their own governance when significant elements of it are beyond their democratic involvement. Distributing power to local units of government does not by itself guarantee that citizens would take part in the use of that power, however. They must develop practices and procedures to ensure that citizen participation in fact takes place (Ranson and Stewart, 1994).

Although decentralization helps to remove the barrier of remoteness, citizens may still feel indifferent to becoming involved in political processes which traditionally have been indifferent to their views. Without a culture of co-operative enquiry, individuals may just carry on with their personal reactions to political events without considering what collective response might be appropriate. To borrow the term coined by Walter Lippman, it would not be easy to pin down the 'phantom public' (Lippman, 1927). This is why the task of developing citizen participation must be regarded as a priority rather than as just another initiative to make the state sector more accessible to those it serves.

The reform of the state sector should begin with the training and development of skills among public servants. They need to recognize that merely delivering services is not enough, because those services may not meet the requirements that only a responsible and informed citizenry can help to define. They need to be given the skills and encouragement to involve citizens as partners in their activities, and not to treat them as distractions from their 'real' work. They must also be given the trust and authority to respond to as many enquiries as possible without having to refer back to some higher-level decision-maker. After all, public servants are citizens too, and unless they feel confident themselves in reaching out to other citizens in the shaping of state services, the attempt to bring the public closer to their state instruments would get stuck at the outset (for a guide on how state sector bodies can approach the task of citizenship development, see Tam, 1994a).

Too many state institutions still operate with an authoritarian internal culture, which must be replaced by communitarian practices. Apart from training and development programmes, policies and procedures for the involvement of citizens must be established. It is crucial that citizens are involved, with the aim of facilitating their collective deliberations and not just voicing their unreflected personal prejudices. This calls for sophisticated techniques to engage citizens in co-operative enquiry concerning what their state institutions are to do for their common good. Citizens should be given regular opportunities to influence the design and delivery of state services. Through comments on proposed quality standards, complaints, input into suggestions schemes, feedback from service monitoring, and participation in user groups, citizens will need a variety of channels to put forward their views. The techniques of customer management, so long as they are not misapplied in marginalizing the needs of those with the least purchasing power, can be brought in to help develop a much more systematic approach to bridging the gap between state activities and those they affect (see Tam, 1993a; Prior *et al.*, 1995; and Gaster, 1996)

To ensure that citizens develop their views on an informed basis, there must be long-term strategies for communicating with the public. For fear of producing state propaganda, some state bodies might be reluctant to invest too much in the development of such strategies. It is instructive to consider the parallel with moral education. Just as teachers who refrain from teaching correct moral values for fear of indoctrinating children, in effect let those with immoral views dominate the children's consciousness, so state institutions which refrain from giving the public the information needed to judge public issues, eventually leave the public with falsehoods and distortions to shape their views. Furthermore, if the information in question is not made available in an interesting manner, it would be no better than being withheld, since all information has to compete fiercely for people's attention.

The fact that some people would object to public funds being spent on the provision of public information raises two possibilities. Either they are ignorant of the importance of such information – in which case their ignorance confirms the need to provide such information, or they are aware of the importance of the information being provided, but feel that only those who know how to access the information should be able to receive it – in which case the state has a duty to prevent sections of society from being disadvantaged by the lack of valuable information. As for the importance of the information, it derives from the value of knowing what is being provided for the public using public resources; what obligations citizens have in support of state activities; help and advice they could call on to protect themselves from harm; the problems their communities face; how they could get their views across to those in charge; and what their elected representatives are doing, so that they can judge them on their actual performance rather than on the party political labels they happen to wear.

The regular interchange of information between citizens and state bodies is not only valuable in itself, it is also essential in paving the way for more in-depth involvement of citizens in shaping state activities. Too often, attempts to develop citizen participation have been deflected by apathy generated by a lack of communication. Citizens are hesitant about working with state bodies which they perceive as being unwilling to discuss matters with them. By contrast, living in an area where elected representatives and state officials are generally known to share information and ideas with the public, citizens would be more inclined to take part in deliberative processes that would influence government decisions.

The challenge is to develop processes in which the conditions for co-operative enquiry are met for evaluating rival claims as to what should be done in relation to all those who would be affected by the ultimate decision. Such processes cannot just aggregate individual preferences, but must enable citizens to consider issues as members of a shared community (see Barber, 1992). John Stewart has pointed out that this is an area which calls for considerable innovation (Stewart, 1995). Information on initiatives that have been tested out by various state bodies should be widely disseminated to promote their use by others.

Initiatives such as citizens' juries, consensus conferencing, deliberative opinion polls and standing panels, allow varying numbers of citizens to learn about an issue before delivering their verdict on what should be done. Instead of debating which is the best approach, in practice they provide a range of options that would suit different occasions. A larger number can be involved where the learning process is less complex; and a smaller number may be more appropriate when the evaluation of evidence and cross-examination of expert witnesses would take a much longer period of time. The mix of initiatives would also mean that considerable rotation and random selection of memberships can take place, and contrary to the view of market individualists that most citizens just do not have the time or inclination to participate in their own governance, most citizens in practice welcome the opportunity to participate and learn from their experience (see, for example, Stewart *et al.*, 1994; Stewart and Tam, 1997).

To reinforce the culture of participation, issues which give rise to confrontation should be handled with the help of mediation bringing opposing sides together, and discussion groups which can draw out the views of those who would otherwise feel too alienated or intimidated to speak. Schools should be supported in developing deliberative forums with young people. In parallel with the development of a far more participative approach to decision-making, more decision-making concerning the use of state resources should be devolved to groups in the community. While it is not always necessary for the state to organize the deployment of its resources directly, it is crucial that those setting up groups to discharge state functions should be ready to operate as inclusive communities in their decision-making (see Hirst, 1994; Cohen and Rogers, 1995). Therefore, quite apart from looking for suitable opportunities for the devolution of resources and management, state bodies should assist with the development of information infrastructure in the community, and especially with interactive technology; with providing training and facilities in user participation; with setting up neighbourhood forums and community groups; and with the production of community information to raise awareness and interests (Gran, 1983; Gyford, 1991; Miller, 1993; and Hirst, 1993).

The development of decentralized, community-based units of governance could, of course, give rise to differences between localities. Where these differences threaten to break up the uniformity of minimum standards, unless a process can be found to resolve these differences, fragmentation would spread. Without the counterweight of other communities to check the demands of the breakaway groups, some of them could come to oppress minorities within their boundaries, on the grounds of the minorities' racial ancestry, religious beliefs, economic positions or some other factor.

To avoid the authoritarian imposition of one set of views on others, and the individualist inclination to accept fragmentation, the communitarian approach offers a framework within which diverse communities can bind themselves to a uniform set of minimum standards based on their common values. The framework requires each unit of governance, at the local level, to establish its legitimacy to speak for its constituent citizens by enabling them to participate in their own governance. Without this legitimacy, it cannot participate in higher-level discussions. For those which have established this legitimacy – in most areas this would depend on the willingness and abilities of existing locally elected authorities to cultivate communitarian governance in their areas – they should elect their own representatives to participate in a regional assembly to discuss the common concerns and standards of their region. Depending on the size of a country, there would be a varying number of tiers of local/regional government below the level of national government. At the national level, regional representatives would determine what resources are to be made available to meet the agreed national minimum standards. The framework would be completed with national representatives coming together at the supranational level – Europe, North America, Africa, and other continental blocks – and the supranational political institutions in turn electing their representatives to serve on a global state body, a role that could be carried out by the United Nations (UN), provided it becomes more democratic in its selection and deliberation processes (for proposals on reforming the UN, see Urquhart and Childers, 1990).

In addition to representatives elected by those involved in the units of governance at lower levels, it would be useful for second chambers at all levels to be elected directly by all citizens within the relevant area, for three reasons: it would maintain the continuity of directly-elected public offices at regional, national and supranational levels; it would provide a democratic platform to monitor and influence the activities of the indirectly elected chamber; and it would give citizens not involved as elected representatives in higher-level state bodies a regular opportunity to consider issues beyond their own localities. It would take time for such reforms of state institutions, from the local to the global level, to be achieved. They are none the less necessary to break down enclaves of political alienation and oppression.

However, those who do not want to see their power to control diluted by the involvement of citizens may resort to other considerations. They could claim that their views are rooted in different histories and cultures, and so cannot be discussed alongside the views held by others. In reality, in the history of every tribe, nation and continent, there are chapters which record the prejudices and dogmas to which particular groups succumbed for a time, and there are chapters which chronicle the extension of love, wisdom, justice and fulfilment that echo in all civilizations. Persistent refusal to work on common grounds merely confirms the authoritarians' apprehension that their approach would not be sustained by co-operative enquiry. Alternatively, they could claim that the efforts required for citizen participation at every level of communitarian governance are too great when a much more efficient mode of governance can be delivered by entrusting a single, centralized power to make all political decisions. Yet what is the nature of this alleged 'efficiency'? Does it really amount to anything more than being able to declare what the interests of the public are, even when an informed public would disagree with that interpretation. Ultimately, it is not efficiency but speed in making mistakes that such centralization delivers.

However, it does not follow that the only alternative to authoritarian centralization is individualist anarchy. With Europe, for example, the common interests of European citizens should not, for fear of an authoritarian super-state, be left in the hands of national governments that are structurally indifferent to the interests of people in other countries (see Tassin, 1992; Newman, 1996). To propose a referendum without any parallel development in citizen participation when considering national and European state activities, would be to reduce a major political decision to a contest to discover who can win the largest number of votes using the media to promote or combat the worst form of jingoism. Far from giving citizens a real say in how they are governed, such contrived gestures would only breed further distrust of and contempt for the state sector. An effective European Union (EU), and indeed any supranational or global state organizations, can only be built when state bodies at the national level go down the communitarian route of power-sharing for the sake of pursuing common values.

The Power and Responsibilities of the State

Substantial changes to society's power structures cannot be achieved without an active state. The state is the only mechanism for binding collective action, and to think that community groups could without state support remove all oppressive relationships is utterly utopian. Far from turning our backs on the state, citizens must press the state to focus on taking responsibility for those tasks they know would not be done effectively without state institutions.

The development of communitarian governance and the related support for citizens should be the basis for defining the state's responsibilities. What is needed is not so much a Bill of Rights setting out what the state could or could not do to individual citizens, but rather a Bill of Responsibilities which sets out what responsibilities citizens hold towards each other, and the responsibilities of the state they elect. The power of the state would then be limited, not by some metaphysical right of individuals, but by the responsibilities citizens have assigned to the state. Any attempt by state bodies to go beyond or against their defined responsibilities would have no political legitimacy. The drafting and ratification of a Bill of Responsibilities for each unit of governance, from local to global level, would provide an impetus to involve citizens in determining what they want to achieve through the state sector. With the support of state organizations, citizens can access objective analyses of their collective problems, count on a democratic forum for considering what might be done, and ensure that collective resources are made available to assist the implementation of action plans.

The process would involve setting out the mutual responsibilities of state and citizens. To ensure that the assignment of reciprocal obligations is clear to everyone, it must begin with the process of bringing new generations of citizens into being (Young and Halsey, 1995). It is odd that while one needs to demonstrate one's understanding and abilities up to a set of agreed standards before one can drive a car, one needs to do nothing of the kind to bring up a child. Furthermore, most citizens know the conditions under which their licence to drive could be taken away, but few parents are aware of the criteria by which they could be judged on their abilities to keep the custody of their children. All citizens contemplating parenthood should, with the help of their local state organizations, learn what would be required of them in return for the collective support that would be given to them in medical and educational help for their children. If a citizen's income is insufficient to support the upbringing of an additional child, whether with a present partner, or a new partner following separation, it should be a factor taken into account in considering whether that citizen is ready to have another child. Factors such as knowledge and dispositions towards bringing up children must also be stressed, since ignorance and abusive behaviour could harm children seriously (see Loney *et al.*, 1991, pt II).

As children grow up, they learn from their parents and their schools what they should do to prepare themselves for adulthood. It is at this stage that children should recognize that the support they can call on from society at large is part of a reciprocal package dependent also on their own contributions. The citizen income payable to them when they complete their full-time education needs to be made conditional on some form of citizen service which provides help to the vulnerable in society (McCormick, 1994). It would be compulsory for all adults capable of working, with exemptions granted solely on the basis of recognized paid work or unpaid care work, such as looking after children or elderly relatives. At retirement age, provided a citizen has carried out the citizen service required whenever he or she is not performing recognized paid or unpaid work, the basic citizen income would continue to be paid. This would simplify the issues of old age pensions, deductible savings, and other related benefits.

In addition to setting the level of citizen income, and organizing the activities involved in a citizen service, the state would need to determine the minimum responsibilities in relation to those who choose to drop out of even the most basic social expectations. For example, there are people who would not apply themselves to any form of productive work, would refuse to take part in citizen service and thus would not receive a citizen income, would drift from street to street intoxicated, and persistently ask others for money. As we saw in Chapter 5, an inclusive community would not accept that people should be penalized for their behaviour if they are not offered any real support to lead a responsible life (see Duff, 1996). The state should ensure that if individuals are denied parental love, effective education, or the opportunity to fulfil themselves in a productive capacity, help is given to reverse any sign of anti-social decline. However, once assistance is readily available, the disregard of general social expectations can no longer be tolerated. After all, no one has the right to disrupt the lives of others.

As the economic, technological and environmental aspects of life become more complicated, only the collective responsibilities of citizens can prevent increasing numbers of people from falling into anti-social reactions or numb despair. If too many state institutions have become too big because they would not decentralize, too many of them have also become too small in their vision of what they should do for their citizens (Galston, 1991). It is the state that must codify and enforce regulations to secure the educative, work and protective conditions of citizenship. Confusing legislation deserves to be criticized as unnecessary red tape, but legislation to protect children from harm, disabled citizens from neglect, people from gender discrimination, businesses from lies by competitors, to name but a few categories, is all essential. Moreover, with the speed of changes now taking place, the state cannot afford to sit back and wait until the disastrous consequences of its non-intervention become apparent before it considers taking action. Instead of being the reluctant last resort, the state should encourage and assist citizens to think about their long-term needs, not just at the local level, but also at regional, national and global levels. Infrastructure for transport and communications, co-ordination of research and development, skills training, measures for countering worldwide environmental degradation, would all collapse if left to individualist businesses competing for their own survival.

Failure of the state to take its responsibilities seriously would result in more variations on what may be called 'the tuberculosis tragedy'. State action to improve public health provision almost eradicated tuberculosis in developed countries, and was having considerable success in the developing world, when demands from market individualists to cut back state spending in return for the continued support of global financial institutions, weakened the drive to stamp out the disease. Drug-resistant strains have now emerged as old strains were allowed to survive and mutate. The irony is that the West, home of the market individualists who think that state support for public health could be cut back dogmatically alongside other kinds of state support, is beginning to witness the return of tuberculosis as well. To prevent such tragedies from proliferating around the world, citizens must never again allow their politicians to fool them into embracing the 'responsibility-shedding state' as a political attraction.

To minimize the risk of citizens being duped by demagogues, the state must take responsibility for the development of institutional cultures and structures to maximize citizen participation in the state sector. It may be argued that unless everyone is given equal social and economic powers, people could never participate as equals politically. Such an argument is dangerous because it either leads to more attempts of the utterly discredited experiment to equalize everyone's wealth and social status – an experiment known to destroy incentives and innovation, and turn those in charge of it into a new socioeconomic elite – or it provides a convenient justification for those against equal political participation to dismiss it as an unrealizable goal (Beetham, 1993).

In inclusive communities, how similar or different citizens' social and economic positions are is not something to be fixed by traditions or by those in positions of power in business organizations. It is something that must be subject to open discussions by those who are affected by the differentials in question. The possibility of there being open discussions has to be underpinned by the equality of political power. The principle is already recognized in one vote by each citizen in an election, or one vote by each juror in a trial. What the state has to change in practice are the numerous barriers that keep many citizens from participating in their own governance. One of these barriers is the arrogance exhibited by some professional politicians when they assert that regular elections means that the electorate must trust them, because they can vote them out at the next election.

To avoid citizen participation becoming a vehicle only for those who understand the state system, the state itself must promote participatory opportunities for everyone, especially those who are the most likely to be excluded by prevailing practices. Advice centres and outreach workers are essential elements of any genuine attempt to help those unfamiliar with state processes to feel confident that they can have a real input. New practices that empower those affected by state actions to shape those actions should be adopted widely. These may range from shifting state decisions on child welfare to practices such as family group conferences, as developed in New Zealand to enable as wide a family network as possible to make plans for children (Taverner, 1996), to enabling refugees in the Ikafe settlement in Uganda to elect their own representatives in determining how food sent to them by the international community is to be distributed (Van der Gaag, 1996).

At the global level, it is even more urgent that citizens are made aware of the implications of what their governments are doing in their name, and given opportunities to discuss and influence government proposals. Acute problems of starvation, torture and armed conflict are festering around the world because citizens remain uninformed about them. Across national boundaries, state institutions must co-operate much more to develop lasting processes enabling truly inclusive communities to function. The Commission on Global Governance has pointed out that:

> As events in Haiti and Angola have demonstrated, international support for democratic transformation should not always end with election returns. It needs to be sustained in some cases through a physical presence and almost always by support for long-term development. . .

Many newly created democratic systems have also to devise ways to reconcile conflicting demands and interests before they imperil national stability. Such difficulties are, of course, not exclusive to new democracies, and many countries with long democratic traditions have been troubled by the strains inherent in plural societies. (Commission on Global Governance, 1995, pp. 59–60)

The only way to preserve pluralism without descending into individualist fragmentation is for the state sector to improve continuously the democratic mechanisms for community deliberations at all levels.

The Challenges for Citizens in Government

Apart from pressing state institutions to adopt a more communitarian approach to their responsibilities, citizens may influence government activities even more directly by becoming elected representatives or appointed officials. They would then be in a position to work towards reforms of political power structures. Under the influence of market individualism, the political process itself has become dominated by short-term programmes designed to satisfy the unreflected self-interests of the largest number of voters. In Western countries, this has provoked an authoritarian reaction pushing for fundamentalist agendas to be set regardless of widespread opposition (Eco, 1995). While this reaction has not had too much success electorally, it is combining with extremist groups that are anti-government and with anti-minority groups to put pressures on state bodies to grant them concessions. Against these trends, citizens in government must reject the demands of the extremists, and strengthen the focus on long-term changes which would secure widespread citizen participation in guiding state action.

As the opportunities for citizens to win political offices as independents are limited, much will depend on how political parties themselves are restructured in line with the model of inclusive community. Party politics demands that politicians are not to be judged primarily on their abilities, but rather on the labels they wear. The right to wear a particular label, in turn, depends in most cases on an individual's suitability to be identified with a ready-made package of 'selling points' which distinguish one party from another. From a communitarian point of view, the worst elements of party politics can be removed by the extensive democratization of political parties, allowing all those belonging to any particular party to have an equal say in determining how its policies are to be shaped, and by reforming the rules for political communications with the electorate. A fixed number of public communication opportunities, such as press advertisements and poster sites, would be allocated in relevant localities and in the media. Beyond the allocated numbers, no candidate would be allowed any unfair advantage by being able to buy more opportunities to criticize others when the latter could not afford to respond on the same scale. This would mean that while politicians might still project themselves in terms of the party politics they accept, they would also need to concentrate on persuading other citizens that they really are better than other candidates for the post in question.

The shift from party to citizen politics would also mean that organizations which seek to buy greater influence over state actions, would find it more difficult to succeed. Their contributions would not be of much help once the rules for electoral communications were reformed to eliminate their current bias towards those with greater economic resources. The returns from donating to a party which constitutionally cannot impose specific policies on its members without an open, democratic process of deliberation would also become much less certain. Provided that donations, in whatever form, made to individual candidates or incumbents are disclosed to the electorate, citizens would be able to judge whether they want to trust those politicians who, for example, are happy to accept huge donations from companies which are bitterly opposed to the public call for tighter regulations of their activities (see Etzioni, 1995, chs 8 and 9).

Apart from party politics, the prevailing systems of state organizations have also diverted many politicians from the goal of working with their communities. The same applies to appointed officials who may come to view knowing how to manage the system as more important than helping their fellow citizens to deal with their problems. Both politicians and officials would benefit from ongoing training to develop their understanding of what public service should aim to achieve in inclusive communities. They should attend regular courses to remind them that they are not there to work out all the solutions in isolation from the wider community that would have to live with those 'solutions'. Instead, they are to acquire techniques and experiment with innovations in promoting citizen participation. The state sector would become a more responsive tool for the construction of inclusive communities, when more citizens active in state organizations set an example for others in treating the public as a vital partner in their activities, and initiate extensive reforms of structures and processes which may alienate citizens and cause them to lose sight of how the state should be made to work for the public, and not the other way round. Unless citizens who have attained positions in government make it their top priority to reform prevailing power structures, they may not get another chance. If individualist politics is not comprehensively reversed, it would either reduce government totally to a shallow marketplace for the economic elites, wearing different party labels, perhaps, to buy votes; or it would give way to the destructive demands of Fascist and fundamentalist groups.

7

The Business Sector

Corporate Citizenship

As the business sector must retain a reasonable degree of autonomy from the state sector to operate effectively, the political action of citizens must go beyond influencing state activities, and secure a tangible input into the activities of business organizations as well. The educative, productive and protective aspects of communitarian citizenship need to be supported by businesses, not just in terms of their compliance with legislation, but also in terms of how they interact with the people whose lives could be radically changed as a result of their decisions. Active citizens have led the way in exposing the harm that corporate irresponsibility can bring to the communities in which businesses operate. There are products which harm people but for various reasons are not banned by law. It could be difficult to pinpoint the criteria upon which legislation could be drawn up, but the harm could easily outweigh any benefits the product concerned might offer. There are shifts in market focus which leave those with the least income no affordable option to purchase – variations in insurance premiums which hit those in the poorest areas being just one of many examples. There are businesses which subject their employees to excessive stress and other health risks when they are expanding, and to constant fear of redundancy when they are facing strong competition. Businesses also, directly and indirectly through the products they produce, deplete the non-renewable resources of the world and add to the pollution of the environment (Donaldson and Werhane, 1983; De George, 1993).

The argument that is rightly directed at remote and unresponsive state organizations applies with equal force to businesses which do not sufficiently recognize, let alone care about, citizens' concerns with their activities. Just as having the occasional vote is not enough for citizens to have real influence over the state sector, having the option of purchasing or not is inadequate to influence the business sector. An individual citizen's refusal to buy a company's products or its shares is unlikely to have much impact. However, when citizens organize themselves democratically to decide their joint responses to business activities, they can in many cases make businesses rethink their decisions.

Critics of the notion of corporate responsibility have argued that any attempt to introduce factors other than pure business considerations into management decisions would be detrimental to the success of businesses (Carr, 1968). Businesses are supposed to operate within the existing legal framework, and provided they stay within that framework, they should be allowed to do whatever they judge to be necessary to achieve their business objectives. If they have to resort to tactics they believe would give them an advantage in a highly competitive world then, unless the law says otherwise, no one should interfere or complain about the use of those tactics. The analogy with a poker game is sometimes invoked, to suggest that to insist that business people should behave completely honestly would be like insisting that the players in a poker game should avoid misleading others as to what cards they have. The failure of the analogy brings out precisely the need for corporate responsibility. While the law may prescribe certain general rules for behaviour in games, it cannot be expected to legislate on the rules for every kind of game. It is for those involved in any particular type of game to agree their rules. To suggest that unless one can get the law to change the rules of a given game, one has to accept the rules as they stand, is to demand that the state sector legislates on matters over which it should not have jurisdiction. It is because the state should not get involved with regulating every aspect of business activity that businesses must be prepared to revise the way they operate in response to the views of those affected by their operations.

Furthermore, if people do not like the rules of poker, they do not have to play the game. But the effects of business activities are not so easy to avoid. The range of costs and quality of what we need to purchase to attain various standards of living depend on how businesses are run. So too does the wider impact on the environment and on community life. If there are business activities which, if disclosed, would cause serious concerns to citizens, then those activities *should* be disclosed and be subjected to scrutiny and debates about whether they should continue. If the rules by which a company plays entail certain categories of people losing out under the legal operations of that company, then those people should know about the rules and their implications, so that they may demand their revisions. Just as playing a game which involves 'bluffing' as a key element does not mean that deception in any form would be accepted, so acknowledging that businesses cannot be expected to inform the public of their competitors' strengths does not mean that businesses can always deceive those they deal with to gain a competitive advantage. Citizens should be vigilant to ensure that businesses do not break rules they claim to accept.

Of course, not all businesses refuse to accept that they have to take their corporate responsibilities seriously. There are signs that increasing numbers of businesses are ready to adopt communitarian practices to enable them to act as responsible corporate citizens. Surveys with practising managers indicate that a growing number of them are willing to speak out on issues relating to financial conduct, treatment of workers, and control of information (see, for example, Brigley, 1994). They feel that their organizations have strong expectations in relation to standards of conduct, public morals, and the quality of what they produce for public consumption. There is widespread recognition of the importance of linking moral values, corporate culture and company policies (for a survey of European managers' interest in business ethics issues, see Murphy, 1994).

What businesses need to do is to identify how the concerns of citizens can be brought to bear in revising their policies and their decision-making arrangements. Some business leaders are supporting research into how corporate responsibility can be enhanced in practice. Some are sending their managers on to a growing number of business ethics courses. Others are participating in joint forums to formulate common courses of action, and to put peer pressure on other companies to follow their lead. The Prince of Wales Business Leaders Forum, for example, has multinational members operating in many parts of the world. One of the most notable achievements by a business forum in recent years has been the two-and-a-half-year inquiry carried out by a team of top UK executives brought together by the RSA (The Royal Society for the Encouragement of Arts, Manufacturers and Commerce). The findings of the inquiry have been published under the title 'Tomorrow's Company' (RSA Inquiry, 1995). The inquiry team, which included companies such as Cable & Wireless, Cadbury, Guiness, IBM UK, the John Lewis Partnership, and Thorn EMI, concluded that:

As the world business climate changes, so the rules of the competitive race are being rewritten. The effect is to make people and relationships more than ever the key to sustainable success. Only through deepened relationships with – and between – employees, customers, suppliers, investors and the community will companies anticipate, innovate and adapt fast enough, while maintaining public confidence . . .

The companies which will sustain competitive success in the future are those which focus less exclusively on shareholders and on financial measures of success – and instead include all their stakeholder relationships, and a broader range of measurements, in the way they think and talk about their purpose and performance. (RSA Inquiry, 1995, p. 1)

The findings are not only significant because they have opened a gateway between conventional management thinking and citizenship theory, but because they have demonstrated that it is not true that major companies in the Anglo-American tradition would not embrace communitarian approaches to management which are more commonly associated by their critics with continental European businesses.

Four gaps are now clearly visible. First, there is the gap between how investors' money is used and how investors might want the money to be used if they were more aware of the options and their wider implications. Second, there is the gap between the limited way suppliers and employees are allowed to contribute to the success of businesses involving them, and the way they could be empowered to make much greater contributions. Robert Heller has pointed out that, despite the growing awareness of this gap, managers are still generally slow to act to narrow or close it in their organizations (Heller, 1995). Third, many in the marketing industry have been struck by the widening gap between the widespread rhetoric of customer care, and the growing distrust of business claims for products and services. To overcome this, businesses must stop trying to get away with as much as they can under the law, and learn instead to secure customer loyalty through respecting the value of honesty consistently in everything they do. Finally, there is the gap between the corporate image businesses would like to project in terms of integrity and responsibility, and the general perception of big businesses as being callous by, for example, polluting the environment or devastating communities with large-scale redundancies.

Communitarian Management

According to communitarian principles, the management of a business should enable all those who are affected by the business to influence its deliberations as members of a shared community. In practice, this involves developing a new kind of relationship with those who contribute to the functioning of a business. All too many businesses still operate on the basis that a core of directors are responsible for the functioning of their business, and that everyone else is just a dispensable resource. This authoritarian model dehumanizes the majority of people who make business operations possible, and views them as sources of investment, supplies or labour, to be bought with dividends, fees, wages or other monetary incentives.

The elite core could argue against proposals for change so long as it appeared that the status quo was the best guarantee for social and economic well-being. However, the growth of global competition is compelling those reluctant to change to face up to alternative methods of organization. Businesses which confine the identification of opportunities and threats and the formulation of innovative responses to an insular core of people have always been in a weaker position than those which are supported by a wider network of people who take pride in the contributions they make to their company. What increased competition has exposed is that this inherent weakness cannot be shielded from the necessity of reforms. The problem with authoritarian management is that it marginalizes the role that a wide range of people outside the conventional core could have. It does not take their views or interests into account in its deliberations, and it devalues their significance. Just as government bodies cannot be reformed adequately by breaking down authoritarian structures into individualist fragments, businesses cannot overcome their authoritarian limitations if they simply break themselves up into smaller and smaller components.

While small units may have relatively more flexibility in terms of their ability to change direction quickly, they have less flexibility in terms of being able to divert resources from other parts of their organization to cope with new priorities. It is not small size that holds the key, but the capacity to anticipate and respond to changes. Indeed, a small company which retains a rigid hierarchy would still suffer from slowness to adopt what those on the 'periphery' see as necessary changes. By contrast, a company which operates as an inclusive community would benefit from the trust, understanding and regular communication between all its members, which would ensure that problems are swiftly identified, and innovative solutions can be tried out. Communitarian businesses would therefore recognize that all their contributors – investors, suppliers, workers and customers – can assist with their business development, and should be encouraged to make their contributions without any hindrance.

Debates on corporate governance have concentrated far too narrowly on the controls that investors should have over the people who sit in the management core. Although abuse of shareholders' trust by directors is an issue to be tackled, it should be located in the wider context of power structures for corporate decision-making. A board of directors should be entrusted by the rest of the organization to facilitate their co-operative enquiries, and carry out action plans in accordance with those enquiries. Their power should thus rest with the community of stakeholders who make the company concerned a viable operation. It may be objected that the need for quick decisions would render it impractical to have too many people involved in decision-making. However, an inclusive community does not require all its members to take part in every decision. It maintains a structure for decision-making supported by its members, and within the structure certain decisions need to be based on the input of all members. Others would be delegated to specific teams which the rest of the community trusted.

To move corporate power structures in the communitarian direction, the abilities and motivation of all potential contributors would have to be developed throughout the organization. To begin with, investors must be integrated more into the business they are helping to succeed with their financial support. As Anthony Harris has argued, investors need more, not less, information in order to become more effective (Harris, 1996). To suggest that information could give existing investors unfair advantages over others would only make sense if there were no limits on the number or timing of who can buy shares. Where there are reasons for restricting some investors from making unjustifiable profits from information they can access, it is far better to have specific rules on the purchase and sale of shares in those circumstances rather than to suppress the information in question. After all, suppressing some information would only attract the attention of those who can find a way to access the information and then gain unfair advantages, while the authority argues in vain about whether the suppressed information had, in fact, been accessed.

If investors are to put money into businesses which they honestly believe would perform well, they must have the full picture of what those businesses are up to. If short-term speculation can cause problems when rumours about mergers or takeovers emerge, the cure is more likely to be found in requirements for shares to be held for minimum periods before they can be resold. The insistence that shares are not to be traded for short-term profit would also have the benefit of motivating potential investors to give careful considera-tion to the long-term value of different businesses (see Hutton, 1995). What they should not be denied is the knowledge of what any given business has as its objectives, how it goes about achieving those objectives, and the effects of its activities. Furthermore, investors must be able to put that knowledge to use. If they believe that their company is setting the wrong goals, mismanaging its resources, or causing problems which must be rectified, they should be allowed to raise their concerns, and discuss possible solutions with others involved in the company. Some may suggest that possible 'interference' by investors is precisely why they should not be given too much key information about the company. Yet, unless investors have a real understanding of what a company is doing, they are likely to overreact to rumours about the company, which in turn suffers from a highly insecure investment base.

The information for investors should not be restricted to financial data either, since many factors that cannot be analyzed in accoun-tants' terms can have a major impact on the future success of a company. Companies that arrogantly refuse to acknowledge the relevance of issues touching on their corporate integrity may find themselves under attack from their own shareholders. Abbott Laboratories, for example, had to adopt an extremely defensive position when a Catholic order with shares in the company de-manded fundamental revisions to the company's practices in mar-keting infant formula alternatives to breast-feeding in Third World countries (see Molander, 1980, case 22). Investors should not – and in any event *cannot* – separate themselves from the activities of the companies they help to finance. They must therefore be given real opportunities to question and influence those activities.

The same principle applies to people who contribute, not their financial resources, but their productive capability to businesses. At one time, they could be conveniently divided into two categories:

suppliers and employees, but now the boundaries of what constitute a business enterprise are not so clearly drawn. At one level, this reflects the need for more flexible productive arrangements to cope with technological and market changes. At a deeper level, this reveals the untenability of rigid demarcations among citizens who are engaged in a common productive enterprise. Management, supervisors, part-timers, home-workers, temporary staff, freelancers, project advisers and contractors all have an important role to play in securing success for the company to which they make their respective contributions. If the removal of authoritarian hierarchies is not to leave them drifting into individualist entities each viewing their interactions with others as a zero-sum game, they must be integrated into an inclusive community with shared values and a co-operative mode of working.

Workers, whatever position they occupy, would need to be assured that, with greater flexibility and responsibility, there will also be greater trust and recognition. People who work from home, on a part-time or short-term contract basis, should be given the necessary support to maintain a reasonable degree of stability for themselves and their families. The need to have time and resources to look after one's dependents is particularly important. A business which demands that its workers sacrifice the well-being of their families to achieve corporate success cannot expect much respect for corporate success. On the other hand, businesses which support their workers in looking after their families, with sympathetic parental leave, childcare facilities, and family insurance protection, can count on more devoted and loyal service from their workforce (Hewitt, 1993; Friedan, 1996).

Flexibility must also mean that barriers between departments and divisions, which prevent a sense of community developing, must be removed. Workers should be given every opportunity to join different work teams, co-operate with teammates to work out their solutions to problems they are charged with tackling, and develop the vital trust which only grows out of people working together on shared projects. In the long run, if flexibility is to benefit workers and their companies alike, there must be continuous communication to ensure that arrangements are adapted to the needs of the organization and its members, without turning into rigid hierarchies. To achieve this, workers must have an effective flow of information about their company's activities, and they must be given the confidence to express their views and concerns. Often, when companies have streamlined their lines of communication, communications with staff have not in fact improved, because vital information, instead of being passed down the line, is held back at senior level. Attempts to improve communications must also be backed by clear signals that feedback would be treated with respect. The quality of the feedback is potentially linked to the quality of training and development that companies provide to their workers. Businesses that are serious about becoming learning organizations so that they can adapt to changing circumstances quickly, must recognize that, ultimately, their learning capacity is derived from the workforce. The notion of giving workers the power to determine the best way to deal with their responsibilities, has gained considerable currency under the banner of 'empowerment' (Pickard, 1993; Hogg, 1994). However, authoritarian businesses still have a tendency to interpret empowerment merely as cutting out middle management and leaving the frontline workers to sink or swim as they deal with their assigned responsibilities. In fact, the essence of empowerment lies with the recognition that managerial power must be redistributed in order to cope with intensifying business competition (Tam, 1994c). Citizens who are only able to function as passive workers lack the drive and abilities to deal with new pressures. By contrast, those who are allowed to develop through taking responsibility for their organizational domains, grow in their jobs and strengthen their company.

As Robert Heller has explained, organizations must stop preventing people from using their own initiative to do their jobs. There is no all-knowing chief executive who can dictate to everyone exactly what is to be done. Senior executives depend on the judgements and innovations of other workers to move their businesses forward. Heller observed:

> At Rank Xerox, for example, [the] managing director . . . [and every] top manager knows specifically what is expected of them, their departments and the whole company, and everybody is involved in deciding what they have to do.
>
> That's why youthfully-led project teams in well-run car companies now have total responsibility for new models – and why even chief executive egos can't override them . . . Leaders who don't hear the messages from below won't be listened to themselves. (Heller, 1994, p. 42 and p. 44)

Empowerment applies not just to workers' interactions with customers. There are many other areas where workers can contribute to the success of their business. Their views on what would create and sustain a supportive working environment must be at the centre of decisions concerning work practices. The health and safety of workers, the equity of pay, and protection from discriminatory attitudes and actions are not social issues which businesses should ignore as much they can under the law. Instead, they must be recognized as issues that are integral to business success. The participation of workers in deciding how these issues are to be dealt with ensures that their epistemological input is taken into account, and that they share in the responsibilities for the policies and practices that are ultimately adopted. For example, when General Motors Corporation (GM) developed its Quality of Work Life programme, it was determined to involve all parties in open discussions about how well work was being organized in GM plants. In the best-documented case of the programme, at GM's approach to the Assembly Plant in Tarrytown, New York, 95 per cent of the 3500 hourly-paid employees volunteered to participate, grievances against the company went down by over 95 per cent; and absenteeism fell sharply and remained below 5 per cent (see Molander, 1980, case 12). Successful worker participation in the management of industrial firms in the former Yugoslavia has also demonstrated that the democratization of work communities can be put into practice (see Pateman, 1970, ch. 5).

Critics such as Maria Hirszowicz, however, have complained about the limitations of participation as a tool for organizational reform. She argues that worker participation is either manipulated by authoritarians, or is dragged back by 'the outlook of the most backward and lukewarm allies' (Hirszowicz, 1977, pp. 214–15). At the heart of her argument is the assumption, generally shared by both authoritarian and individualist thinkers, that participation is a zero-sum bargaining game. Either one side tricks the other into handing over all the real advantages, or they end up with a lowest common denominator compromise. She is particularly sceptical about worker participation in managerial deliberations, because she believes that management would not want to lose control, and representatives of the workers would not want to become too involved lest they lose their capacity to challenge management.

Yet the purpose of real participation is to overcome such barriers. Participatory discussions are not battles to be won by one side at the expense of the other – they constitute a gradual transformative process which enables all concerned to learn how to achieve something greater than the sum of their individual interests. Those in charge of management would gain insight and commitment, and the workers in general would have more control over opportunities to improve their lives.

So long as management views the process as a manipulative tool, or union leaders treat it as a confrontational platform for their own power base, the element of trust will not develop, and the workplace will remain an oppressive community. What experience shows is that trust can be built up, and a sense of shared community can be developed. Work councils, so often treated as a make-or-break issue between stubborn employers and radical worker representatives are, in fact, just a small step towards communitarian management. In France they negotiate only about profit-sharing and share ownership, but in Germany, they cover grievance and accident prevention measures as well. What they do provide is a door through which workers can function as free and responsible citizens in the world of business (Gomez and Schneider, 1992). If as a result of the co-operative enquiries conducted in a particular business, all those who contribute to the success of the business decide that everyone concerned should have more direct involvement in decision-making and a greater share in the distribution of profits (or losses), then the business should move with the decision rather than become side-tracked by any outmoded Right- or Left-wing ideologies.

One line of objection to communitarian management, which seeks to avoid invoking ideological ideas, is based on the argument that communitarian ideas are really only suited to continental Europeans, and cannot be transplanted to Anglo-Saxon economies. David Soskice, for example, has suggested that communitarian practices such as allowing workers more say in the running of their respective organizations, which have, in turn, led to more protective measures for workers in general, should not be adopted in Anglo-Saxon economies, for three reasons (Soskice, 1996). First, Soskice argues, such practices would be open to abuse by workers who had not grown up in continental socioeconomic systems, and would need to be balanced by powerful employer organizations. Second, the supposedly anti-communitarian Anglo-Saxon culture is considered to be more suited to industries which have to face fast-changing technologies and global competitive pressures. By contrast, the organizational culture of northern European firms is not. Finally, according to Soskice, Anglo-Saxon businesses, as they are, allow more women to take part in the economy than do other economies. What Soskice, and others who support the myth that communitarian management cannot be imported to Anglo-Saxon businesses, fail to understand is that the question of importing does not arise. Some continental European firms have communitarian practices, as do some Anglo-Saxon companies, but there are many in all parts of the world that are still authoritarian in structure and policies. Significantly, it is the movement away from the management-knows-all approach that is most commonly associated with dramatic improvement in business performance. Admittedly, the Japanese commitment to worker involvement and consensus building has influenced management thinking in the West. But long before Japanese management techniques became fashionable, co-operative and partnership working were taken up by businesses in Britain and other Anglo-Saxon countries. For example, the John Lewis Partnership in Britain established a Staff Council to facilitate staff participation in management decisions as early as 1919. The business growth and the democratic involvement of all workers of the Partnership have both expanded considerably over the years. The competition from other retailers, which do not respect their workers as members of a shared community, has been intense. None the less, by the end of 1994, turnover had reached £2575 million, with a trading profit of £141 million (John Lewis Partnership Report and Accounts, 1995). As for the notion that communitarian practices reduce the ratio of women in the workforce, in 1994 there were as many women as men among managers in John Lewis (compared with about 40 per cent as the private-sector average), and 60 per cent of its graduate intake was female.

The reason why Anglo-Saxon economies may appear to 'favour' women workers is that they are generally more opposed to legislation to protect women and support workers' parental responsibilities. Firms are given the incentive to recruit more women because they can more easily get away with paying women less than they would men. There is also the Anglo-Saxon culture which regards work that earns an income as in some way being more admirable than work that consists of raising a family. Compared with their counterparts in many continental European firms, both men and women in English-speaking countries are given little recognition or support for their parental responsibilities in terms of maternity or paternity leave. Furthermore, women opting to devote more time to their new-born children are perceived as being less 'dynamic' than mothers who want to return to pursue their careers. There are signs, however, that both men and women are beginning to get more respect for refusing to neglect the needs of their families merely to comply with the expectations of their employers and society in general. Culture change is an important factor to consider when reforms of management practices are proposed. However, the need to view proposals in a wider cultural context does not mean that reforms should always be held back. Culture can be developed over time, and the changes which many companies across the world are undergoing testify to its possibility. It would be a different matter to say that the changes would be counter-productive. Yet to claim that making firms more communitarian in their management approach would make them less competitive simply flies in the face of all the evidence. If, in the Second World War, countries such as Britain and America proved that democratic political systems are better than authoritarian ones at resolving armed conflicts, then since the end of the war, countries such as Germany and Japan have shown the world that management systems that approximate more closely to inclusive communities are better equipped to succeed in business competition. Japanese and German firms that work with their investors, suppliers and employees as partners with shared long-term goals, have succeeded in winning market shares from companies that still dictate to their stakeholders, and exploit them as dispensable resources to gain short-term profits. It should be made clear that there is no simple demarcation line over which German and Japanese firms have crossed, and which gives them a permanent competitive advantage. In fact, there is the danger that as global competitive pressures continue to grow, businesses which do not further consolidate worker participation could drift back into polarized conflicts as workers' pay and conditions come under threat from managers desirous of preserving their positions at the expense of other contributors to their organizations. German and Japanese firms would have to face up to this challenge as much as any Anglo-Saxon business (see Handy, 1994, ch. 8).

Just as we argued in Chapter 6 that even countries with basic democratic structures need to develop to attain greater communitarian governance, all businesses need to extend their communitarian management approach to ensure that all who can contribute to their success are able and willing to give their best to achieve shared corporate goals. Many of the industries in which Anglo-Saxon firms are still regarded as having a global competitive advantage are to be found in areas where authoritarian management has long been exposed as unsustainable. Financial advice, technological innovation and entertainment, are all areas where companies with communities of workers entrusted to apply their own creative solutions and build their own project teams, can outflank organizations which seek to impose a blueprint on what everyone has to do. The lesson is not that different national cultures enable contrasting management approaches to succeed in different global markets, it is rather that once any industry becomes susceptible to global competition, the inherent weaknesses of authoritarian management in comparison with communitarian management, would be exposed.

The underlying theme of what American theorists have called 'empowerment', Japanese management has called 'kaizen' (Wellington, 1996, p. 8), and the British RSA Inquiry termed the 'inclusive approach', is one and the same. In essence, people who work as an inclusive community are more likely to make the most valued contributions to the wider community in which they operate. Whatever the national culture is in which a company has to operate, the task of developing communitarian management must still be tackled with the same openness and commitment. If those who have been in the management core, or those who are asked to represent their fellow workers, approach the task with the mindset of conflicting authoritarians, each simply trying to manipulate discussions to secure their own position against the other side, then the task could not be accomplished.

In practice, we must recognize the experience of numerous businesses that have embarked on this journey of communitarian development, and reject the cynics' dogmatic claim that it could not work. American companies can look to the example of W. L. Gore & Associates, founded by Bill Gore in the 1960s, with $950 million worldwide sales derived from high technology divisions producing complex fabrics, electronic connectors, medical implants, and industrial filters (Lester, 1993). In place of management hierarchies which divide decision-makers from those who are to carry out orders, associates of the company are given the freedom to act on their own initiative, they are consulted about all key decisions, they have flexibility in trying out team leaderships, and are all involved in a co-operative system of setting and reviewing salary levels.

In Britain, companies such as NFC have demonstrated that the growing trend for contracting-out need not lead to the fragmentation of ever-dwindling service units, but instead long-term supplier relationship could be established with the purchasers of the contracted-out services. In the case of NFC, a leader in the haulage industry, the purchaser–provider relationship is built on the company's own internal working relationships, which treat all workers as being members of an inclusive community. In 1982, when the opportunity came to establish the group's independence, the directors opted for an employee buyout rather than a management buyout, even though the latter option would have made them 'rich beyond the dreams of avarice' (*Management Today* Report on NFC, 1993). The company managed to achieve over £90 million pre-tax profits consistently through the recession in the early 1990s. In 1993, its employees, their families, and pensioners controlled over half of the total votes of the company. As shareholders, workers and contributors to corporate deliberations, members of the NFC community unite behind the goals they set for themselves, and support each other in their achievement.

The extensive participation that Gore and NFC have shown to be possible and valuable in Anglo-Saxon economies, can also be found in other countries outside continental Europe. One of the most notable examples is that of the Brazilian company, Semco, which makes pumps, valves and other industrial equipment. Since Ricardo Semler introduced changes to the company in 1980, Semco has not only survived the recession in Brazil but, with productivity increased six and a half times, it has achieved year-on-year increases in profits. Semler's changes turned the company from one which operated through authoritarian hierarchies, into one which gave every member of the company the training, confidence and opportunity to participate in its activities. Team members discuss hiring and firing issues in accordance with practices approved by all members of the company. Production targets, pay and bonuses are also set through discussions by those involved in making them possible. Workers decide whether their output can sustain higher earnings, or, when economic prospects are poor, if they should reduce their earnings to support their company's competitiveness. Strikes are accepted as a democratic practice to focus people's attention on major issues to be resolved. Furthermore, workers interested in establishing their independence through a buyout of their units are given every support to set up their own businesses, which in turn become suppliers with a shared ethos (Semler, 1994).

Critics will no doubt continue to pick on individual examples and say that communitarian management cannot be transplanted from a particular business or country. The truth is that examples can be found in a wide range of businesses, in Anglo-Saxon and Latin-American countries as much as in East Asian or continental European ones. The real reason why there is reluctance to adopt an inclusive approach to management is, as Sir Anthony Cleaver, Chairman of the RSA Inquiry, observed, because it is hard work to reform traditional hierarchies, and many companies just cannot be bothered. There is, of course, the problem of vested interest as well. For many directors, if they could just get through to their own retirement with a financial package they can influence, they would rather leave it to others to worry about their companies' future. As global competition intensifies, however, coming generations of senior management will have to face up to the challenge of introducing communitarian reforms, or see their companies squeezed out of the marketplace before they get to retirement age.

The Power and Responsibilities of Businesses

Debates which artificially pitch the freedom of employers to maximize their profits against the freedom of workers to secure the best conditions for themselves, neglect the crucial possibility that the two objectives are best pursued together rather than in opposition to each other. They also neglect the fact that both these objectives should be further harmonized with the needs of the wider community if they are to stand the best chance of being achieved and sustained in the long run. Conversely, businesses cannot address their external responsibilities as corporate citizens effectively unless they have adopted a communitarian approach internally. It is only when a company is capable of pursuing a set of objectives which unite all its contributing members that it can engage openly in harmonizing those objectives with the concerns of citizens outside the company.

The areas where businesses must apply the communitarian management approach to their external responsibilities can be categorized in terms of the powers they possess. These are:

(i)   The power to inform and educate;
(ii) The power to protect and improve people's quality of life;
(iii) The power to generate productive work; and
(iv) The power to facilitate sustainable community development.

The Power to Inform and Educate

Businesses have considerable power to shape people's beliefs and influence their attitudes. They spend vast sums of money on advertising and public relations to persuade more people to recognize and use their services. This power is of great value when it is used to correct misconceptions, overcome ignorance of what is available at more convenient locations, offer more affordable prices, and explain how different problems could be tackled with the help of the services on offer. It is because this power is so pervasive, and its correct use of such great value to society, that citizens should demand its use to be monitored, and action to be taken if it is abused. The rules regulating the propagation of commercial information are not to be left to state bodies and businesses alone. The public should be aware of the limits, and be alert to how manipulative practices could be deployed within those limits. Advertising which fuels prejudices against sections of society, encourages more people to consume what will cause more health problems for the whole community, sales techniques which put pressure on the vulnerable and the unsuspecting, and public relations which deliberately project the support of interested parties as an impartial endorsement of a given product, may all take place within the limits set by the law, but they should none the less be pursued with businesses responsible for them.

To argue that individuals should be allowed to judge for themselves whether the promotional practices in use are unduly influencing their decisions, is to suppose that people are in full possession of all the relevant information, when in fact what is disputed is the extent to which some businesses use their communicative power to prevent people from deliberating on the basis of the relevant information. Some businesses, however, have adopted a different stance, maintaining that it is not their job to give the full facts, and that if people make the wrong decisions or misuse their products because they are not adequately informed, then the fault lies with the consumer and not with the companies concerned. This approach can only be taken as a 'health warning' against the trustworthiness of what companies adopting it want to tell the public. A business which knowingly encourages citizens to purchase products that they may well later consider to be unsuitable, deserves the mistrust of all citizens (for examples of controversies in sales and advertising, see Iannone, 1989, pt IV).

The Power to Protect and Improve People's
Quality of Life

The business sector deserves credit for the contributions it makes to protecting and improving people's quality of life. However, these contributions are not guaranteed. Products could also cause harm to citizens, for a variety of reasons: they may be inherently dangerous if not used properly; users might be misled into assuming that they are protected when in fact the products are not as effective as the users might think; or the products might have harmful side-effects which could significantly outweigh their benefits. In some cases, products may alter the habits and dispositions of their users so that the latter become less responsible citizens, and society is the net loser. Addictions to gambling and unreflective gratifications could be as harmful as becoming uncontrollably disposed towards hard drugs or aggressive behaviour.

Instead of taking the attitude that so long as the state does not restrict products and services, it should continue to maximize their consumption, every responsible business should ensure that it reviews constantly the potential harms and benefits of all its products. Just as an anticipated decline in demand should prompt a business to make products which would be more in demand, a rigorous assessment of the harms and benefits of any product should provide the business with strong indicators as to which products should be promoted, and which discontinued. The complex epistemological issues involved in determining the scale and probability of harm should not be used as a smokescreen for complacency. Instead, they should be treated as central issues which a business would tackle wholeheartedly. In practice, one of the key questions is how the impartial research required is to be funded. Agencies set up directly by interested companies inevitably have to operate under the shadow of suspicion that their funding would be jeopardized if they produced findings which the companies concerned would deny. The alternative is for there to be a binding levy on all the companies involved in the making and selling of the product in question, to pay for the ongoing research into its potential effects on users. To avoid free riders taking advantage of the arrangements, and to minimize duplications of research into similar problems across different product lines, one solution would be for a product safety tax to be set up to fund independent research into how beneficial/harmful any product really is.

In addition to supporting the funding through a specific product safety tax for independent research, responsible businesses should also ensure that the research agency has an investigative arm which can look into complaints brought to its attention either by workers of a particular company, or by members of the public. Learning from the complaints raised by customers is now recognized by many firms as a key to improving their activities.

However, when the complaint has implications for financial liability, or when it is brought by a worker against others in more senior positions in the company concerned, there is the danger that those who do not want to be exposed for mismanagement would try to cover up or dismiss the complaint as being unfounded.

Problems which could give rise to disasters, malpractices which threaten the lives of innocent people, falsification of evidence in scientific research needed to underpin product development, a miscalculated relaxation of safety measures, or the use of unacceptable ingredients, should all be examined critically and speedily so that appropriate corrective action can be taken. Citizens who help to draw attention to these matters, especially when their employment could be directly under threat as a result of their action, should be given advice and protection. Since businesses which act selectively to tackle some of these problems but not others would not secure public trust, the only viable method would be for them to lend their collective support to an independent investigative process. The extent to which businesses in any sector support the development of such a process, serves as a useful yardstick for measuring their corporate responsibility in this area (see, for example, Berkley, 1996; and Dehn, 1994).

The Power to Generate Productive Work

Businesses succeed in so far as they manage to match their productive capability to the demand they identify for their product. The problem of unemployment arises from the lack of demand for the productive capability of certain citizens, and the provision of opportunities to engage in productive work is therefore a vital contribution businesses make to the growth of inclusive communities. However, the power that businesses possess as employers can be abused, and responsible businesses would make a firm commitment to give all citizens an equal opportunity to join them, and apply their abilities with the fullest corporate support.

Not only should businesses adopt best practices in eliminating discriminatory practices, and developing training support for their workers, they should also collaborate with other businesses to ensure that peer pressure is put on employers who do not comply with advice or procedures on staff recruitment and retention. The organization of workers' representation to facilitate the formulation of their collective input into the deliberations of their company should be encouraged. Relationship with unions should also be developed, on the basis that they offer protection to the workers and play an active role in influencing how companies are run, but do not encourage a divisive line between management and workers.

Ultimately, the best safeguard against workers being treated as dispensable tools is their involvement in their companies' deliberations as equal and responsible members. By giving everyone an equal vote in determining how a business is run, all would come to share an interest in developing the abilities of each for the good of the whole enterprise. It is also the best safeguard against workers becoming alienated from the activities of their organization, and undermining, intentionally or otherwise, the ability of their organization to survive in the global marketplace. Charles Handy, having studied the human resource operations of a wide range of businesses across the world, has observed:

> There is nothing more exciting than losing oneself in a cause bigger than oneself, something which makes self-denial worthwhile and where success is shared, not hugged to oneself in secret . . . For that to happen [all concerned in a business], or a sensible proportion of them, must be citizens in the true sense, not mercenaries; citizens who have a shared responsibility for the future of the organization, who are not mere instruments doing the bidding of the board, and who know that their citizenship will not be revoked when times get hard. (Handy, 1996, p. 35)

We have seen that businesses such as the John Lewis Partnership have demonstrated that they can operate successfully as inclusive communities. Interestingly, in a recent survey carried out in the UK by the advertising agency, FCB, into public perceptions of the business sector, the findings regarding the retail sector concluded, 'Nearly all of the supermarket chains and most of the major retailers were criticised, with the notable exception of John Lewis . . . In the research people said the first supermarket to put consumers above shareholders will win hands down' (Snowdon, 1996, pp. 16–17). It is not that the interests of shareholders as such must be marginalized, but if the long-term aims of workers and their organizations to match their productive capacity to the needs of customers are to be effectively achieved, then shareholders must take on board those interests as being vital, either because they are themselves workers in the organization concerned, or because the possibility of making profits from their shares is tied to the long-term market performance of that organization.

The Power to Facilitate Sustainable Community Development

Beyond the products and services they provide to their customers, businesses can also influence how communities develop. Businesses realize that a positive impact on communities affected by their activities is a credit they could readily claim. Indeed, the opportunities for such credit are rightly taken more and more into account in the planning of business activities. However, the power to help communities develop on a sustainable basis can also be seriously mishandled.

At the local level, citizens who work as employees or suppliers of businesses operating in their area, rely on the income their work produces for them and their families. Business decisions which involve drastic reductions in, if not total elimination of, such vital income, must not be allowed to take place without a thorough investigation of how they could be avoided, or at least minimized. Claims that businesses must put their financial performance before any responsibility to local communities raise two issues: first, does the financial situation really necessitate just one course of action? If everyone took a slight reduction, would it not be better than sacrificing those who are least able to cope with the consequences, especially when, in reality, what is proposed is at times no more than a smokescreen to increase the earnings of those at the top by cutting out those lower down the conventional hierarchy. Second, is the low regard for community responsibility a position any company really wants to be associated with? If it is, then it deserves to be exposed to citizens who should subject it to sustained criticism. If it is not, then it must recognize the need to reconcile that responsibility with the financial pressures it has to face. Giving money to support charities and cultural development is commendable, but it is not a substitute for investing in funds to develop people's skills to meet future employment needs, and to support those who have to accept reduced hours, decreased earnings, or prolonged unemployment. Businesses which see the vibrancy of communities in which they operate as an integral part of their strategies should get the fullest support of those communities.

At the national level, businesses should co-operate with each other in identifying activities that have a negative impact on the wider community, and agree on corrective measures. The messages they send out via the media on the kind of lifestyle which should be adopted; the extent to which they make it difficult for their workers to respond to the needs of their families; the investment they channel into different kinds of product development; and the examples they set with their management practices, are all matters for which they are accountable to citizens in general, and they should be discussed in open meetings, not restricted only to shareholders.

With growing globalization, businesses will also have to look at their community responsibilities in other parts of the world. Instead of thinking that they should concentrate on maximizing their output until legislation catches up with them, they should lead the way in developing alternative approaches which can be sustained in the long run. This applies not only to environmental problems, but also to sociopolitical problems of collaborating with businesses and political regimes abroad which do not have sufficient regard for the common values of democratic citizens.

The marketing of pesticides illustrates both sets of problems. Multinationals achieve their commercial objectives when arrangements are made with local agents to make or sell the product. With little experience in managing the dangers of pesticides, large quantities of a harmful substance are then misused, with serious consequences. Examples have included the dumping of pesticides into lakes because it apparently enabled fish poisoned by the substance to be caught, and empty pesticide drums have been used by local people to collect rainwater for drinking. In one of the most tragic cases, the largely autonomous Indian subsidiary of Union Carbide was responsible for failing to carry out a number of checks, any one of which would have been sufficient to prevent the disaster in its plant in Bhopal, in which 3500 people were killed when methyl isocyanate (used to make the pesticide, Sevin) leaked from the plant (De George, 1993, chs 4 and 5). Businesses cannot stand back from foreseeable consequences of their actions. When they allow others to sell their products without the enforcement of a wide range of safety measures, they are aware of the dangers to which local people might be exposed. If they do not revise their practices, then citizens across national boundaries must campaign to bring about the necessary reforms. In this task, democratic citizens will find powerful allies in businesses which have decided to take a stand on such issues.

The Co-operative Bank, for example, demonstrating that co-operative worker relations tend to provide a good basis for communitarian interactions with the wider community, has put forward a corporate responsibility policy which many others should consider adapting for their own applications (The Co-operative Bank Ethical Policy, 1996). The policy covers support for local community initiatives (for schools, community groups and local charities); funding advice for business customers in enhancing environmental protection; collaboration with others who share a complementary ethical stance; a commitment not to invest in regimes or organizations which deny human rights, manufacture instruments of torture, or are involved in animal experimentation for cosmetic purposes; a refusal to finance the manufacture or sale of weapons to any country with an oppressive regime, or to provide any financial service to tobacco product manufacturers, or any person using exploitative factory farming methods, engaged in the production of animal fur, or involved in blood sports; and a firm declaration that it will ensure its financial services are not exploited for the purposes of money laundering, drug trafficking or tax evasion.

The Challenges for Corporate Citizens

While citizens in general should engage in collective action to make businesses adopt the reforms put forward, much will also depend on the commitment and abilities of those in charge of businesses to reform their organizations' culture and practices. Corporate citizens should recognize their responsibilities as key contributors to the development of inclusive communities, and seek out like-minded allies in bringing about the necessary changes.

One of the first challenges facing corporate citizens is the popularization of the idea that outmoded authoritarian hierarchies should be replaced by individuals operating as 'virtual companies' or 'portfolio workers'. It is yet another manifestation of the authoritarian–individualist dichotomy. In reality, the process of anarchic fragmentation would not give us sustainable economies, only stress, insecurity, and long-term unemployment and poverty for many. Economic as well as social problems cannot be tackled by people thinking only 'How am *I* going to deal with this?'. The question 'How are *we* going to solve this common problem?' must also be addressed. Instead of casting people off to find their own portfolios of work, corporate citizens should strengthen the links between all those involved in their common enterprise, and ensure that everyone is aware of the mutual respect and support which can be counted on in their organizational community. To achieve this, they need to secure progress at three levels.

First, those entrusted with the most senior decision-making positions must lead by personal example. Communitarian leaders should only advocate business practices which they themselves can carry out consistently. Such practices would apply to their approach to epistemological judgements. They would make decisions on the basis of the findings that could be validated by co-operative enquiries. They would not allow prejudices or ignorance of the facts to be protected by hierarchical power, therefore distorting their company's understanding of the issues raised. They would also recognize that there are temptations to which business executives are particularly exposed, and would demonstrate clearly that their commitment to the common values of their organization and the communities in which they operate, means that the question of giving in to such temptations does not arise. Such temptations may take the form of financial offers to betray what has been agreed with others; using organizational power to exploit or harass others; or keeping quiet about unacceptable activities that have been discovered. Above all, senior staff should develop their effectiveness as strategists and managers to retain their colleagues' respect for their leadership. Effectiveness in management is something which can be learnt and enhanced (Drucker, 1988).

Second, to ensure that the right culture does develop, corporate citizens should encourage all their colleagues to engage in co-operative enquiry to resolve conflicting claims, and to develop an evolving conception of the common purposes of the organization. The beliefs and values of an organization should not be imposed on it by its leaders, however enlightened they might be. They must be formulated through a genuine exchange of ideas and concerns and involve everyone in the organization. Everyone must feel that what matters to them as members of the company, and as members of other overlapping communities, can be harmonized within a coherent framework. The alternative, as Robert Solomon has warned, is the alienation of 'personal values' from 'corporate values', as if the two could not, and should not, be bridged. Applying Aristotelean ideas on community to business management, Solomon writes:

> To think of ethics simply in terms of one's 'personal values' – and to juxtapose these against something ominously referred to as 'corporate values' – is to miss the obvious, that our most personal values are also social and that we join, stay, and succeed with one organisation rather than another because our values fit . . . *Corporate role identity* is genuine identity, and to deny this is to alienate oneself from the corporation (and probably from any possibility of success or happiness within it) from the start. (Solomon, 1993, p. 161)

Conversely, business leaders must open up the development of corporate values to input from everyone else who contributes to the business. When the latter have a real sense of identity with the values in support of which they work, then the cultural challenge has been met.

Finally, the example set by communitarian executives and the culture developed through sustained participation must be translated into effective management practices throughout the company. The guiding values should be realized in every interaction between the company, its customers and the wider community. These values would have to be linked to the formulation of targets, and built into agreed practices and procedures. Having agreed the way forward, and made available the information and resources required to get the work done, management should then trust those charged with specific tasks to perform them. This does not mean that everyone is to be left to their own devices. There is a close parallel here between the empowering approach to management and the progressive approach to education. In both cases, to misinterpret the approach as allowing individuals to do as they please without any co-ordination is a fallacious trap into which many have fallen. The truth is that both approaches require a constant flow of creative proposals and action plans supported by a stream of reinforcement and, if necessary, corrective feedback.

On the basis of her extensive research, Rosabeth Moss Kanter has concluded that workers can only be empowered to achieve better results for their companies if they are given both more power to take decisions *and* continued support for activities when they seek help. The anarchic approach of abdicating managerial responsibility, leaving workers uncertain as to what they should, or could, do was found to be as counter-productive as the authoritarian approach of dictating every management decision (Kanter, 1992, ch. 9). What corporate citizens should aim for is gradual improvement through processes, which inevitably need to be adjusted in the light of feedback received. It cannot be expected that they alone can in some way transform business practices which may reduce the power of some to exploit the system for their own benefit. They must encourage others in the business sector, the democratically-run unions, and the public in general, to work together for reform. In the face of the most powerful organizations in the world, only strong alliances would be able to mount sustained campaigns and achieve any real impact.

It took six years, for example, for employee representatives from the European subsidiaries of the American firm, Gillette, to press the parent company to agree to a united 'Euro works council' (see Gomez and Schneider, 1992). Pressures on another multinational company, Shell, were equally prolonged, but less successful. Throughout the 1990s, the Ogoni people in Nigeria protested peacefully against Shell's actions, which 'left their soil and water polluted and gave them nothing except a legacy of rusting pipelines, thousands of unsightly wells and refineries, and no material benefits from the oil profits at all' (Steele, 1995). When the Nigerian regime executed the prominent spokesman of the Ogoni people, Ken Saro-Wiwa, arousing worldwide condemnation, Shell proceeded to sign a $4 billion deal with that very same regime. With the combined sales of the world's largest 350 multinationals totalling around a third of the gross national product (GNP) of all the industrialized countries put together (*New Internationalist*, 1993), there will be many occasions when the odds against progressive reforms seem to be overwhelming. However, many corporate citizens have shown that reforms are possible, and an increasing number of them are taking the lead in introducing necessary changes.

8

The Third Sector

Active Citizenship

Apart from organizations in the state and business sectors there are many voluntary and community groups which operate in a third distinct sector. What they have in common is that they are set up voluntarily by their members to pursue non-commercial objectives. The level of activity in this third sector provides an indicator of community vitality. If people are fundamentally constrained to do only what state institutions command them to do, or they are motivated solely by personal gains in a market system, then civic order itself would inevitably suffer as fewer and fewer citizens volunteer their time and resources to pursue their common values (Walzer, 1992; Selbourne, 1994).

As we have seen in the previous two chapters, cutting down the size of the state dogmatically, or encouraging businesses merely to become more philanthropically minded, would not help to create the conditions wherein inclusive communities can thrive. State institutions and business organizations must reform their interactions with all those they affect, and develop new power structures and support mechanisms, so that all citizens can participate as equal and responsible members in decision-making processes which shape their lives. It is only through close partnership with reform activities in the other two sectors that the third sector can develop its own strengths and contribute to communitarian politics. It is also important to remember that third-sector groups can themselves be dogmatic or insular. In the absence of communitarian power structures, such groups could block the pursuit of common values and undermine the possibility of co-operative community life as much as any authoritarian government or irresponsible corporation. The focus of citizen activities in the third sector should therefore, be on developing a form of civil society that exhibits the three characteristics detailed below.

First, it should enable citizens to experience taking responsibility for pursuing values that go beyond themselves. Volunteering is not to be treated simplistically as an expression of volunteers' generosity, but as a political recognition of the values of other people's lives, which call for a response. From the caring support a neighbour may need, to the emergency assistance people abroad desperately require, citizens should be aware of opportunities to contribute to making the needed improvements. Instead of being confined to state instruments or commercial arrangements, the third sector should make it possible for citizens to have the option of offering their services to help secure what would otherwise be denied to those in need. This means that citizens are not only to act in those cases where there is a binding collective agreement on what are to be granted as entitlements, but also in cases where their empathy and compassion for the plight of others can be translated effectively into tangible differences. Such an action would also be a vital learning experience in coming to understand the needs of people beyond an individual's circle of family and friends, and developing the skills to respond to them. While this may not be regarded as politics in the conventional party campaigning sense, it is an important form of political action in the communitarian sense of helping to define and realize the common good.

Second, the third sector should enable citizens to work together, in the form of voluntary and community groups, to achieve what they cannot achieve single handedly. The challenge could relate to problems which require the pooling of resources or the application of co-operative intelligence to overcome. By working together in pursuit of a common set of objectives, citizens experience both the values and practical implications of collective action. It is an experience that can enrich their appreciation of the necessity of give-and-take in human relationships, and their recognition that co-operation can give rise to mutually enhancing development instead of zero-sum compromises. Such shared experience would also help to remove barriers and prejudices, which so often arise from ignorance of what other people are really like (McCormick, 1994, pp. 10–11). Unfounded assumptions about the beliefs and behavioural patterns of others would effectively be overturned when volunteers discover that there is much they can achieve through working together. Furthermore, the growth of community action groups would increase the number of overlapping areas of interest, where bridges to link single issue groups are most likely to be explored. The co-operation of community groups in turn generates a democratizing influence, which helps to check the attempts of authoritarian activists to exploit grassroots support. To adapt Voltaire's comments about religions, we can observe that having a single community group could be oppressive, having two could lead to bitter rivalries, but having a large number would encourage them to be civil and co-operative towards each other.

Third, citizen activities in the third sector collectively should provide a balance in relation to the activities of the state and business sectors. This means that the third sector should be active in its own right, and not be a mere agent to deliver state programmes. Equally, it should avoid becoming dependent on corporate donations for its operation as this could risk it becoming a subsidiary of companies' 'public affairs' division. The strength of the third sector, however, is not to be measured by its capacity to take over from the other two sectors. It is a mark of utopian anarchism, rather than communitarianism, to suppose that citizens should aim for a world in which voluntary groups take over completely from state and business operations. All three sectors are needed, and communitarian reforms are best achieved when they support each other's development without distorting their overall interdependence.

Writing from his experience of Poland's emergence from the clutches of an authoritarian regime, Wlodzimierz Wesolowski has noted that a communitarian injection of third-sector activities is urgently needed to support Poland's transition into a country of inclusive communities. He writes:

> Poland has a serious deficit in intermediate groups that link society and state organs in a democratic way . . . Liberals argue that the state should remain neutral, with respect for individual ideals. Communitarians, on the other hand, say that both voluntary associations and state agencies are obliged to help people in finding the resources for achieving decent lives and social citizenship . . .
>
> In the light of both older and more recent Polish traditions, moving towards some version of communitarian philosophy and socio-political practice may provide a more easily achieved

accommodation of workers and employers to the capitalist economy. A communitarian arrangement may also provide a more certain road to the legitimation of the new democratic order. (Wesolowski, 1995, pp. 126–7)

Wesolowski's observation is an important reminder to those who think that the 1989 revolutions were essentially about moving power from the state sector to the business sector. In fact, without the development of a vibrant, democratic third sector, and parallel reforms of the state and business sectors, a better society would not emerge from the ashes of the collapsed Communist system. The lesson also applies to Western European and other developed countries, where the ascendancy of market individualism has eclipsed the values of the third sector, and where notions of moral responsibility and civic duty need to be promoted actively (see, for example, the Report of the Wetenschappelijk Instituut voor het CDA, 1996).

Communitarian Civil Society

A communitarian civil society is characterized not simply by the absence of state controls, but by the diverse voluntary activities of citizens in improving their communities' quality of life (for general discussions of the concept of 'civil society', see Hall, 1995; and Gellner, 1996). Instead of a single blueprint regarding what is to be done, citizens are engaged continuously in a process of discovering how the values they share can guide their actions, resolve conflicting views they hold on other matters, and provide a basis for co-operating with other groups (Putnam, 1995). The common respect for the values of love, wisdom, justice and fulfilment, enables citizens with different perspectives to participate in mutual support, which strengthens their interdependence without binding them to any untenable homogeneity. Whereas authoritarians may seek to direct action in the third sector towards insulating geographical communities with an impenetrable sheet of dogmatic rules and commands, communitarians would look to community action as a key instrument for breaking down such oppressive dogmas. Attempts to protect power structures – within nations, neighbourhoods, or families – from the participatory deliberations of all of those affected by the structures would be challenged directly until they give way to the development of inclusive community relationships.

The effectiveness of community action would be measured by the extent that it enhances citizens' capacities to develop themselves and care for others as equal members in every sphere of shared living. Beginning with the family, all parents are to be supported by their community in carrying out their duties to their children. Education for parenthood should not stop with a new-born child leaving the hospital, it should continue in the community, with advice provided on an on-going basis by people who know the parents. Parents should be encouraged to meet and share experiences, both concerning the joys of having children, and the problems that arise. When problems occur, these should be dealt with swiftly, with medical advice being sought, or techniques on handling disobedient children being introduced. It is vital that, instead of allowing parents to ignore the disruptive behaviour of their children, or to resort to violent forms of discipline which only instil a disposition to violence in the children, parents must be able to learn from people they trust how to set down firm guidelines to develop their children's behaviour.

Community networks of parental advice would enable families to access support and advice without any authoritarian conception of parental dictatorship gaining a foothold as some kind of state-imposed approach. Citizens should not be constrained to any single way of bringing up children, since the fulfilling interplay between parents and children is not something which can be predicted or legislated for by other people (for communitarian views on the notion of 'family sovereignty', see Galindo and Perez-Adan, 1996). What other people in a community can, and should, do is to offer assistance when it is needed. This includes community-run facilities for parents who need to have child-care for their young children while the parents earn an income; training for local people who would like to give their time to looking after children; and after-school and holiday activities for older children. Parents making use of such facilities must also volunteer their skills and resources in return to support the operations.

Where there are clear problems, community-based family centres should be available to step in between distressed families and the state. Before the state finds it necessary to take a child away from his or her family, and without leaving a child to extended risks, relatives and neighbours who are already familiar with the family in question through the on-going contact of their local family centre, could work with state agencies to provide temporary care for any child who needs such support. There are occasions when giving parents in such cases a breathing space and firm advice on how to improve their parental behaviour is enough. But parental refusal to respond to help provides a clear signal that drastic measures to relieve certain individuals of their parental responsibilities would be needed after all. Unlike state agencies, community-based centres would have the advantage of working from a base of understanding of the problems and prospects gained from regular and direct interactions with the parents and children in question (for more detailed examples of community-based support for families, see Utting *et al.*, 1993).

In conjunction with family centres, schools should also provide a focal point for community action. Parents and their children should have the opportunity to experience with other families diverse approaches to improving their community's quality of life. Too often the problems of individual families or neighbourhoods are sealed off from the community consciousness. Instead of being helped by the fresh thinking which others in the community can put forward, they are isolated and trapped by 'traditional' values and structures which, contrary to the views of moral authoritarians, provide no way out for the abused children, beaten spouses, neglected under-achievers, harassed neighbours, and households of 'redundant' workers. Problems children bring to school, in the form of depression, apathy or aggressive behaviour, should be taken as signals that their families need help. Community groups should operate through schools to identify and target support towards those who are most in need of their help. School grounds provide a common meeting place for families to give each other support.

Community groups should also actively influence the development of their neighbourhoods. The potential for adaptation of present housing provision to meet the future needs of the ageing population, the availability of amenities for children and young adults, and the accessibility of shops, communal meeting places and other basic facilities, especially in rural areas, must all be issues around which the community learns to formulate a broadly agreed set of views. It is a key challenge for community groups to work their way through the apathy and, at times, hostility, of different residents in their area to develop a real sense of co-operative working. It takes commitment and an understanding of how citizen participation is to be cultivated in practice. Experiences ranging from the work of the Morningside Gardens Tenant Co-operators Committee, in Harlem in the USA (see D'Antonio, 1996), to the activities of the Meadowell Forum, which grew out of a run-down estate in Tyne and Wear in England (see Gibson, 1993), have shown that sustained results can be achieved by engaging with citizens' readiness to participate in action for their common good.

Rather than accepting the views of planners and housing managers as being definitive, community groups should provide all concerned with democratic mechanisms to study, question, reflect upon and put forward their perspectives on the issues. Experts and professionals should be encouraged to put forward their ideas and explanations so that there are basic reference points for discussions. It does not follow that alternative proposals cannot be formulated, or that these ideas cannot be revised in the course of detailed discussions. Planning assumptions need to be put in touch with people's experience of real problems in their community.

At the same time, citizens should identify issues which neither the state nor the business sector is dealing with effectively. As individual voters or consumers, they have very limited influence on changing the thinking of large organizations but, speaking with a collective voice, their community can get a hearing for their ideas and innovations, challenge thinking on environmental designs, and expose unacceptable behaviour by irresponsible developers, landlords or neighbours. Furthermore, they would be able to draw in the wider public and the media in their campaigns, and provide each other with moral support and legal advice in the face of unsympathetic institutions. In his book, *Building Democracy*, Graham Towers has described vividly how community action in the development of housing projects can contribute to the formation of inclusive communities (Towers, 1995). What stands out is the absence of any centralized system to direct the wide range of community projects. Results have been achieved where active citizens have galvanized their neighbours into co-operative action. By linking housing issues to work opportunities, health and leisure facilities, and care and support networks, local people can make considerable improvements in their quality of life. From the community self-build scheme pioneered by Rod Hackney to save houses which would otherwise have been demolished (Towers, 1995, pp. 77–82), to Walter Segal's approach in applying simplified building techniques to facilitate self-building on a small scale (Towers, 1995, pp. 82–5), the evidence is clear that community action can be initiated effectively by citizens themselves without the involvement of party political organizations. In fact, the absence of party politics is probably a positive factor in enabling fellow citizens to work out common solutions to their problems without being distracted by irrelevant rhetoric.

After key changes have been secured, community groups need to turn their focus to safeguarding the improved conditions. Otherwise, once the high-profile problems that brought people together appear to be solved, people will drift apart and other problems, which might have been prevented, would surface. The difficulty with a protective focus for community action is that it could be hijacked by authoritarians, who would want to impose the protection of their interests on the agenda for the whole community. Community groups should therefore be vigilant against the infiltration of authoritarian tendencies, and should be resolute in their commitment to openness. Those who do participate should be given an equal vote on all the key decisions.

Community groups should establish firm standards for their collective safety. Instead of living in fear of those who threaten constantly to disrupt the lives of others, they should organize themselves into collective forces capable of standing up to such threats. By arriving at standards derived from the co-operative enquiry of the citizens in the area concerned, they can feel confident about enforcing those standards with the assistance of relevant state officials. Disputes which fall outside the established consensus should be resolved with the help of community-based mediation instead of impersonal litigations which only benefit those who have a financial interest in prolonging such disputes. Community-based mediation also has the advantage of helping to identify general tension points in the community that might require special attention. Misunderstandings or psychological pressures might more easily be removed through sympathetic assistance, before they erupt into aggressive conflicts.

For those who violate the security of their fellow citizens, community groups would provide a basis for community service that would make real demands on offenders before they regain the trust and respect of their community. They would be required to carry out duties that are of direct benefit to those in need, particularly those who need regular support to ensure that they remain warm and healthy. It would be a moral test of offenders' character development to see the extent to which they continue on a voluntary basis to carry out such duties when the legal requirement expires. Where appropriate, and with proper supervision, services which involve a degree of restitution should also be carried out for the victims, so that the offenders have an opportunity to make up for the wrongs they have done, and come to understand the pain they have caused others.

Clearly, those who continue to pose a danger to others would have to be kept away from the rest of society to prevent them re-offending. For the majority of offenders, however, their chances of becoming accepted members of the community again would depend on the readiness of the community to work with them in their rehabilitation. Communities which turn their backs on ex-offenders are the ones most likely to push them towards re-offending. Communities with active community groups, concerned with making offenders learn from the pain they have caused their victims, and affording opportunities to repair some of the damages, have a much better chance of reintegrating ex-offenders into them as trusted members.

Beyond local boundaries, the tasks of community action need to cover the development of communities of interests. It is sometimes disputed that such communities cannot constitute a 'community' in any *real* sense, because they lack the physical dimension of a neighbourhood community. However, sharing a locality is not a necessary condition for people to belong to a community. What is important is a common interest. Where this interest is developed with the participation of all concerned as equals, we have an inclusive community. Where some have arbitrary power over what happens to others, we have a power structure which needs to be reformed.

Communities of interests are particularly important when they serve to balance the restricted outlooks of some geographical communities. Small towns and villages where residents' beliefs and attitudes have not been advanced through engagement in co-operative enquiries with the wider community could stifle their members' potential to pursue the values of wisdom, love, justice and fulfilment. The pursuit of such values is enhanced by the depth and breadth of experiences one undergoes directly or shares in communion with others. While the state and business sectors may help to provide the conditions in which such experiences could take place, it is the action of communities of interests which produce them. Through the activities of groups promoting shared interests, citizens (who may live in different geographical communities) would be able to develop social bonds which cut across local and national boundaries. They would also be able to work together to question barriers which businesses or government agencies put in their way. Others sharing their interests would be invited to join on a voluntary basis. The shared interests could be to help people cope with serious illnesses, expose the inhumane practices of repressive political regimes, promote awareness of environmental degradation, or experiment with new art forms. For many people who no longer have strong emotive roots in the areas in which they live, these communities of interest would be where they primarily experience the richness of community life.

The Power and Responsibilities of Community Groups

Since community groups can exert considerable power over the development of their social environment, it follows that they have important responsibilities in relation to all those affected by the use of their power. These interrelated powers and responsibilities can be looked at in terms of their epistemological, economic and political implications.

Epistemologically, the co-operative interactions of community groups provide the basis for discussing diverse knowledge claims about what should be done. Ultimately, our understanding of any problem can expand only as far as the limit of our collective abilities. Community groups can help to facilitate the practical expansion of that understanding as far as possible towards its theoretical limit. The extent to which they succeed in facilitating this expansion reflects their power in formulating the requirements of their community members. This is a very significant power when the alternative is either an authoritarian claim on what is to be done being imposed on the community, or a permanent resignation to the paralysis which results from there being no agreed way forward. However, this power can only be secured if the structure for its delivery is suited to co-operative enquiry. This means that no one who can make a contribution to the deliberations should be excluded from participating in the group. Of course, anyone who joins a group to prevent others from having a free discussions, or seeks to subvert it to goals which conflict with the common values, would no longer be in a position to contribute to the group, and could not expect to be allowed to have a say. Unlike market individualism, communitarianism can and does draw a firm line on not tolerating behaviour that disrupts the common good.

In practice, different groups may develop different criteria for determining when someone is to be excluded from a discussion for attempting to stop others speaking, deny others information with no tenable reason, or subjecting everyone to his or her exposition without allowing a realistic length of time for others to make their contributions. This does not mean that the line can only be drawn arbitrarily. Experience shows that, provided the basic requirements of structured deliberations are made clear, there would be no practical problem in identifying what is or is not acceptable. The 'Planning for Real' process developed by Tony Gibson, for example, has revealed that even in circumstances where some people are suspicious of the motives behind the offer of an open, participative event, and others are angry with the neglect their communities have suffered, once the process has begun with the help of experienced facilitators, participants do gradually develop their input, and learn to consider their own views alongside other views with which they disagree (Gibson, 1993).

What every community group must stand by is the requirement that everyone is to be given all the relevant information and, on that basis, each is to have a say. If on the basis of the discussions concerning more detailed examinations, the participants agreed to assign an advisory role to a sub-group, or to delegate a set of decisions to an agreed team, then the outcomes of these sub-groups and task teams would still be grounded in the support of all those involved in the overall group. The responsibility of facilitators is not to work out an answer which the group must come round to accepting, but to encourage and support all participants in working out what they regard provisionally as being the best answer. To suggest that this might not lead to the right answer would beg the epistemological question of what alternative framework there could be to validate the answer. In practice, only the experience of a community living the consequences of its decisions could point to the correctness of proposed answers, and the need for revisions. Furthermore, it is anticipated that there will be revisions to be discussed and implemented, which provides the best guarantee that community groups would learn from their experiences rather than risk all past practices fossilising into blind dogmas.

Examples of the successful application of grassroots co-operative enquiry to community action can be found in the work of the NAAM movement in Africa and the Working Women's Forum in India (Ekins, 1992, pp. 112–22). The NAAM movement was founded by B. L. Ouedraogo in Burkina Faso. It started as a self-help movement for peasants in 1966, and two decades later there were 2700 NAAM groups with over 160 000 members. Individual peasants were brought together to learn to pool their resources, identify common issues, and articulate their priorities. Participation was promoted on the basis that no one was to be discriminated against on the grounds of social, ethnic, political, religious or any other indefensible factors. NAAM groups have over the years expanded their members' capabilities to grow, manufacture and trade. They have also learnt to draw on skills and resources to engage in the large-scale construction of dams, wells, warehouses, cereal banks, and numerous types of workshop.

The Working Women's Forum was founded by Jaya Arunachalam to enable women, who needed to have paid work but received only a low income, to deliberate together to improve their quality of life in the face of exploitation by employers, prejudice against women, and discrimination against their caste. It began in 1978 with 800 members, and by 1990 the Forum's membership had reached 150 000. Through the Forum, its members can secure reliable credit, organize themselves against those who seek to harass them, and develop projects which they identify as being of key importance to them – such as health care, family welfare, mass inter-caste weddings, and the provision of child-labour rehabilitation centres.

Closely related to the power of expanding citizens' knowledge and understanding issues affecting their lives, is the power to increase the economic strength of organized communities. A vibrant third sector depends on active citizens organizing themselves to generate the income needed to fund their activities (see Hirst, 1994). While donations from caring individuals and corporate citizens are valuable, the goal of community development has to be the enhancement of a community's own capacity to set and achieve its goals, without being dependent on the charitable inclinations of donors persisting through the years into succeeding generations. Community groups should therefore aim to generate their income using methods consistent with the aims of inclusive communities. One such method is to market goods and services which support the realization of common values.

Communitarian marketing techniques are already exemplified by the activities of a wide range of consumer co-operatives, which position their goods and services to meet people's real needs for healthy eating, fair trade, environmental protection, and community development. There are also charities which develop products that appeal in symbolic terms. Citizens purchase a token, a book or a record to express their support for a cause to help the wider community. Where the symbolism of many goods created by the commercial market are directed at people's sense of vanity, greed or envy, communitarian marketing enables community groups to appeal to people's sense of compassion, fairness and respect for the truth. In the long run, if the appeal to citizens' better senses is to succeed in spite of many other distractions, community groups must recognize the need to strengthen their financial base.

The aim of a community-based enterprise is to achieve a balance with the diverse needs within any given community. People need to have adequate paid work, access to a reasonable range of goods and services, and the opportunity to raise money to invest in large-scale projects for the common good. Instead of dividing citizens into conflicting camps of owners, workers and consumers, any of which might argue that *their* needs should be met, even if those of the others are ignored, the different groups are able to integrate as fellow citizens engaged in a common enterprise. The kind of goods and services to be produced, the pay and working conditions which need to be sustained, the benefits to the community, and the surplus value which is to be reinvested for future development, are issues that must be considered together (Pearce, 1993).

Community groups should ensure that their constitutions, membership selection procedures, decision-making processes and training programmes are developed to enable citizens to apply their co-operative intelligence to maximizing surplus value. This should be monitored in terms of the process of formulating objectives on the socioeconomic values to be generated, the involvement of all concerned in adopting action strategies, and the recording of actual values achieved. The individualist argument that a culture of extensive co-operation would stifle initiative would only have merit in cases where the process of co-operation gets taken over by disorganized meetings with no action points. In practice, effective co-operation demands the clarification of a proposed action, and the task of progress-chasing must be clearly assigned and implemented. Where this basic requirement is adhered to, community groups can initiate a wide range of enterprises capable of generating substantial resources to meet the needs of their community. For example, in Serra do Caldeirao, Southern Portugal, local people came together to carry out a series of local resource audits, which in turn led to the development of children's centres, training facilities, networks for local food products and crafts, and retail outlets. Then they formed their own development agency, IN LOCO, which has no party political or religious allegiance. They can now raise funds to invest in other projects developed locally to tackle unmet needs, and generate an optimum level of income for the citizens and community groups in the area (Melo, 1996).

The economic strengths of such community groups can be further enhanced by collaborating with other community groups in different regions and countries. A readiness to pursue mutually reinforcing economic development, such as technology transfers, flexible credit, and supply-chain relationships, would help co-operating communities improve their quality of life, even when macroeconomic forces are devastating individualistic areas being left to sink or swim on their own. The identification of needs and resources that would lend themselves to co-operative exchange is, of course, not enough when there are other economic pressures that simply do not fit into the framework of a community-based organization. The procurement of supplies, the development of infrastructure and the targeting of new markets would all involve commercial transactions that require access to substantial investment. Community groups need to have the confidence and support of the wider co-operative community to attract investment, both at the local level through credit union development, and at national and international level through co-operative banking networks.

Credit unions are groups of people who save together and lend to each other at rates of interest that are better than those which can be obtained from commercial banks. The movement for the development of credit unions began in Germany in 1849 and they are now found all over the world. In the USA, there are 95 million people belonging to around 71 500 credit unions. In the UK, there are over 500 groups, with one of the biggest being the Licensed Taxi Drivers Association. All profits made are redistributed to members in the form of dividends. At national and international level, the principle of mutual support has been developed successfully through the system of co-operative banking. In 1993, 20 per cent of the European Community's (EC's) savings were deposited with co-operative banks, and five of the top fifty banks in the world are European co-operatives (Johnson, 1993, p. 7). Community groups should make use of such facilities to expand their investment base, so that they can grow in parallel with a vibrant commercial sector. Indeed, from the Grameen Bank in Bangladesh to the Shorebank Corporation in Chicago, communities across the world are learning to apply their savings to producing credit for important developmental work. By 1989, the Shorebank Corporation alone had extended over US$11.4 million of unsubsidized credit to over 7000 local business people and residents, rehabilitated 1142 units of multi-family rental housing, found jobs for 2734 people, and given US$1 million in low interest energy conservation loans (Ekins, 1992, pp. 124–7).

With the help of community development trusts and ethical investment schemes to draw funding into community-based enterprises, community groups should be able to offer their members improvements to their economic power which none of them acting alone could secure. One of the biggest stumbling blocks is the reluctance, still all too commonly found in the third sector, to counter the perception that material well-being can only be attained in the business sector. This is partly connected with deep-seated reservations about material values, which in fact have a legitimate place in our overall values. The third sector should not shy away from the fact that it could bring material as well as other improvements to its members. Underrating and underselling this will only lead to more attempts to dismantle community enterprises in the name of economic necessity. Mutual benefits societies such as building societies in Britain, have in the 1990s suffered from the drive by a minority to hand over what once belonged to all users of the enterprise to shareholders who are only willing to support these new companies so long as they yield a satisfactory level of dividends. It is essential that community groups, which have built up a strong economic base through the support of their members, stand firmly by their responsibility to keep that economic strength for those members, and not allow anyone to be deceived into thinking that some inherent limitation of community enterprise requires their collective assets to be surrendered to people who do not remotely share their community concerns.

It is the possession of economic power which in turn adds to the potential of community groups to exert political power at three levels. First, it can be used to expose proposals by government bodies or businesses to communal deliberations. Attempts to introduce new policies and practices, regardless of what those who are putting them forward may say, should be subjected to critical examination by those who will be affected by their introduction. It is crucial that the process of citizens' discussion is of a deliberative nature, so that participants can engage in open and co-operative enquiry. Any attempt to use simplistic polling or referendums must be avoided, unless the issues concerned are already well explained, and the capacity of any group to use emotive distortion techniques is strictly regulated, to maintain a fair debate.

Second, once a community group has been able to identify its position after deliberation among concerned citizens, it can act as a platform to rally support for that position, and request those in charge to respond appropriately. This may concern, for example, a proposal to close a factory when the option of employee buy-out has not even been considered; to define levels for the use of non-renewable resources far below what those who study these problems impartially would recommend; or to allow the continued supply of arms to an oppressive regime abroad when awareness of the activities of that regime has led to widespread opposition to further arms trade with the regime. The group can utilize every opportunity to make it clear that the position it has adopted must be taken into account.

Third, the political power of community groups can be used to organize opposition to decisions that go against the wishes of affected citizens. The opposition may take the form of a petition, a protest march, the withdrawal of co-operation from joint tasks, the refusal to comply with disputed policies or orders, the boycott of targeted goods and services, or, in extreme cases, armed struggle. Clearly, such power is liable to be abused, especially by those who seek to exploit community action to impose their own personal agenda. Community groups must therefore ensure that the exercise of their political power conforms to communitarian principles. The power to articulate a community-based viewpoint can only be legitimized by the involvement of members of the community concerned, in deliberating over any given proposal and its implications. The power to rally support for an agreed position should be used on the basis that the promotion of the common cause does not distort what is being put forward by others, or surreptitiously bring in claims and demands which have not been supported during the process of co-operative enquiry.

The difficulty with any insistence on subjecting confrontational tactics to extensive community deliberations is that the very nature of confrontation does not lend itself to prolonged reflection. Having learnt that the strong reservations a group has expressed about a proposal are to be completely ignored by those responsible for the proposal, there may be little time to organize an effective response. However, depending on the likely consequences of different responses, and the effects they might have on other people, any misjudged response could harm the well-being of citizens as much as any badly-thought-out proposal. If, in both cases, citizens were marginalized and prevented from having any real say in the outcomes, then the community activists concerned would be as authoritarian as the organization they oppose. To argue that community involvement would only delay implementation of the 'correct' response, or risk it being displaced by some less appropriate response, would be to suppose that there is a community elite capable of validating knowledge claims about appropriate responses, in isolation from any form of co-operative enquiry. Since such epistemological validation is impossible, the only real issue to be addressed is how to develop the quickest process for formulating a collective response, which can maximize citizen participation. In practice, this must involve long-term communicative relationships being developed well in advance of any crisis situation.

However, if a community is deeply divided on an issue, and there is no prospect of a consensus emerging, then it would not be possible to establish a collective view on the best response to make. Yet this is precisely why in such circumstances any move to take drastic action must be questioned. Responsible community groups would have to learn to weigh up competing claims and decide which should have the benefit of the doubt. One can contrast the proposal to open a nuclear power station, and the corresponding disputed response of occupying the site to prevent construction, with the proposal to extend the operational period of an existing nuclear power station, and the corresponding disputed response of occupying the station to prevent its continued operation. While the benefit of the doubt may go appropriately to confrontational action to prevent the construction of something a significant section of society has major doubts about, in the latter case, the benefit of the doubt would probably go against a response that could cause more danger than it might remove. This example illustrates not how decisions are always to be taken in such cases, but the caution which must be brought to bear when the available information does not enable the community to give its unanimous backing to one judgement and one course of action.

Although many radicals may feel that communitarian caution is a weakness that should not be allowed to infect swift confrontational action, it is in fact a vital checkpoint for people who are feeling so frustrated and angry that they could easily get drawn into action which, on reflection, they might view quite differently. Instead of excluding those who have reservations, and cutting off links with everyone associated with the 'enemy', community groups must allow for the possibility of revising their strategies for direct action. One of the most tragic episodes to emerge from the failed attempt by Chinese activists to secure political democratization in 1989, for example, was the hijacking of the movement by a small group of extremists who refused to co-operate with the moderate reformist elements within the Chinese Communist Party. The extremists were more interested in provoking a bloody confrontation than in the real possibility of securing reforms. Consequently, China's political masters survived the global democratic wave which swept away most other totalitarian regimes, and the reformists were totally displaced by the authoritarian hardliners.

Of course, sometimes it is necessary to resort to drastic action. In such cases, knowing that one is not heading dogmatically into confrontation, but taking what, given the evidence, is recognized to be the most effective course of action, must strengthen one's resolve to act. In response to employers who insist on wage cuts for workers who must also work longer hours or face redundancies, while the employers themselves increase their own pay, dividends and pension packages out of the profits generated by the workforce, the only option may well be to take strike action to force the employers to rethink their approach. Similarly, governments which refuse to tolerate criticisms of their policies, arrest anyone who dares to speak out, and shoot at protestors, may leave their citizens with no choice but to attempt to overthrow them with force. Deliberative caution in these circumstances does not stand in the way of action, but serves to remind us that, in pursuit of common values, it cannot be justifiable to act in any way that betrays those values.

If it is impossible to engage in co-operative enquiry under a regime, then it must be included in any plan to construct a new regime. All too often the self-styled vanguard of revolutionary action has claimed that it had to make all the decisions because it was too dangerous to open up discussions. Yet, when the old regime is overthrown, the new leadership turns out to be just as authoritarian. Community groups aspiring to develop and apply their political power should never forget that they have the responsibility to ensure that whatever replaces the authoritarian power structures they challenge must secure citizen participation in the future.

The Challenges for Active Citizens

The idea that the revival of community life needs a surge of volunteers willing to give their time to help their fellow citizens barely scratches the surface of the matter (see *Economist Report*, 1997). The third sector can only deliver its contributions to the comprehensive development of inclusive communities if the volunteers who come forward are prepared and able to meet the communitarian demands made of active citizens. Active citizens need to recognize the connection between the specific activities in which they are engaged, and the wider strategies that affect their communities. No one can abdicate responsibility to the community as a whole simply because a pledge of support for one particular voluntary group has been made. If what one group demands is incompatible with the overall good of the community, then the good of the community should override the demands of the group.

For example, the growth of residential community associations in the USA has led observers such as Daniel Bell to warn that, far from enabling citizens to come together to work for the good of their community, these bodies are encouraging their residents to 'act as privatized individuals who participate in public affairs only for the most narrow of self-interested reasons, with profoundly detrimental consequences for the public at large' (Bell, 1995, p. 32). By developing residential enclaves which disengage from the problems of the wider community, those involved only think about getting the best bargain for their own association and leave people outside their electronic gates with even fewer collective resources to enhance their common safety. From a communitarian point of view, just as the poor cannot turn their backs on social expectations, the rich cannot be allowed to opt out of their responsibilities to society. Instead of letting them hide behind the mask of community action, they must be challenged to demonstrate that their actions are at least compatible with the good of the wider community.

The challenge to work with others also applies to formulating input into policy proposals. If every group only presses for what it wants, the total demands either contradict each other or are likely to be too great to be met. The more powerful ones would then squeeze out the small and newly-established ones. On the other hand, by working together, all groups can integrate their requirements to produce a united front, and it is more likely that proponents of policy changes would take on board their demands. Even the more powerful groups, which might have on their own gained some short-term advantages, would benefit from the co-operative spirit engendered from the process, and be able to achieve more in the future with the support of others in the community.

Related to the readiness to displace zero-sum negotiations by co-operative working is the need to acknowledge the epistemological deficiency of challenging the views of others without an objective basis for one's own. Active citizens need to understand how to arrive at validated claims so that they will be in a position to question and revise ideas raised in public policy debates (Butcher *et al.*, 1993, chs 5 to 10; also European Foundation for the Improvement of Living and Working Conditions, 1993). Citizens in general are having to rely increasingly on specialist groups to alert them to issues of concern to them. When these issues involve disputes over experts' rival claims on the social, economic and environmental implications of major initiatives, the specialist groups have a duty to ensure that their contributions are derived from co-operative enquiries, and not from their own prejudices.

The main task ahead is therefore not so much to arrest the decline of traditional community groups, but rather to stimulate the growth of inclusive ones (Knight and Stokes, 1996). Church groups and other charities which reinforced the view that the poor were a permanent class to be pitied should give way to ecumenical groups devoted to ending poverty by empowering those afflicted with poverty to work as members of those groups. Trade unions which allowed a few individuals to dictate policies to the majority of members, should give way to new workers' associations in which the demands for democratic power structures are made consistently in relation to both management at the workplace and management within the associations themselves. The same applies to the proliferating single-issue groups, which all too often demand unquestioning support for the decisions of the activist vanguard. Citizens involved with them should press for the opening up of their decision-making processes. No one should rally to their call for action unless they are prepared to have the reasons for their proposed actions examined. The emergence of authoritarian community groups – in the form of neo-Fascists, paramilitary platoons or extremist campaigners – is undoubtedly one of the most serious threats to common values.

If internal reforms of some single-issue groups prove difficult to achieve, a parallel strategy would involve the development of community groups which aim to tackle similar issues, but which are organized on communitarian principles. However, even for groups which are started on the basis that all those affected by their activities would be able to play a part in their deliberations, there is always the possibility that power could become stuck with a self-proclaimed elite who, in return for promised efficiency in the running of the group, persuade others to make an apathetic retreat from the decision-making process altogether.

Active citizens need to be vigilant to sustain communitarian power structures. One method of maintaining the required level of vigilance is to set up community audit teams which report to a standing conference of community groups, but operate independently of any particular group. After giving their initial support to the setting up of such audit teams, community groups can rely on ongoing assessment to check any drift towards authoritarian tendencies. The audit teams can be staffed by volunteers from different community groups on a rotation basis, and none of them is allowed to audit their own group. The community audit teams would be responsible for drawing active citizens' attention to three key sets of issues concerning their respective community groups: organizational development; communications; and external partnerships.

The voluntary nature of much of third-sector activities tends to obscure the need for effective organizational development. Unpaid as well as paid members of community groups should be given training and support to run their organization efficiently. Management techniques tried and tested in other sectors should be adapted and applied to 'social entrepreneurship' (Leadbeater, 1997). They should learn to appreciate how democratic power relations can be an asset in setting targets, allocating tasks and resources, and monitoring performance. Group objectives should be developed with real members' involvement and, once formulated, should be pursued systematically. Continuous training is a vital element, because the process of learning to develop and apply one's skills and understanding to changing conditions simply does not have a cut-off point.

The community audit on communications would serve to remind citizens in charge of community groups that they must not only strive to develop communication with all those affected by their groups' activities, but must also apply the wide range of techniques available to improve their communication. A community group could be run well as an organization, but fail to deliver what it sets out to do because it fixes its targets in the absence of any substantial input from other citizens in the community. Superficial surveys, unattractive notices, and poorly-attended public meetings can all contribute to the lack of dialogue. What community group leaders should be prompted to do by the periodic audit is the application of the best communications techniques to break down barriers. Outreach work through local facilities, neighbourhood newspapers, community radio broadcasts, regular deliberative forums, collaborative projects with local and national media, and high profile campaigns can all help to engage more citizens in shaping the goals and strategies of groups which operate in their community.

Finally, the audit should cover external partnerships. Collaboration between community groups is not an optional extra to be left to the personal preferences of individual community leaders. All community leaders have a duty to work for the common good of their community. What that common good entails can only be legitimately determined through the involvement of all citizens as equal and responsible members in a shared deliberative process. Partnerships are therefore essential to combat any attempt by proponents of identity politics, who threaten to fragment overlapping communities into antagonistic and insular groups under the headings of religion, ethnicity, sexual orientation or any other factor.

The community audit process can also help to promote best practice in partnership development. Organizations such as the Citizen Organizing Foundation in Britain have developed broad-based community organizations in all parts of the country, bringing together different racial and religious groups to address common issues and increase participation in civic life. In America, there are examples such as the Shelby County Interfaith in Memphis, Tennessee, which brought fifty congregations, half of them black and half white, together in a wide range of job creation, adult education, housing and crime prevention initiatives. Another notable project is the Common Ground initiative which brought pro-choice and pro-life sides of the abortion issue together, and enabled them to recognize that, in spite of the points that divided them, they could work together on issues on which they could agree, such as adoption procedures, the quality of foster care, and the securing of adequate prenatal services for all mothers (Boyte *et al.*, 1994, pp. 14–15). Beyond local and national levels, partnerships must also be explored across continental regions (McConnell, 1991) and on a global basis. All communities, be they based on geographical, historical or other common interest, are ultimately all part of a single overarching global community. Third-sector action can therefore only succeed in the context of effective global co-operation between communities.

9

Criticisms of Communitarian Ideas

The Ideal of Inclusive Community

Social commentators and politicians who invoke the notion of 'community' are often criticized for expressing vague, nostalgic yearnings for small, close-knit communities which are neither possible to recreate, nor indeed desirable, as they could be highly oppressive. Philosophical discussions of the relationships between individuals and communities have not been of much help in clarifying this matter as they have remained at generally an abstract level. In this book, however, we have specified the model of 'inclusive community' as the ideal form of community to be developed, and spelt out the three principles that support it. On this basis, we have considered a range of reforms that should take place to provide the education, work opportunities and protective arrangements citizens need to build inclusive communities. Such communities are not restricted to interactions within neighbourhood areas, but are to be established at all levels across the state, business and third sectors to enable everyone to pursue the identified common values. We may now turn our attention to the criticisms that may be directed at the ideal of inclusive community which informs our reform agenda.

Attacks on the ideal of inclusive community may include challenges to what the ideal implies, and criticisms of the communitarian principles of co-operative enquiry, mutual responsibility and citizen participation, which support that ideal. Let us begin with the concept of inclusive community itself. It is a common fallacy to suppose that communitarians are in favour of whatever is associated with community life. On this supposition, it is not at all difficult to accuse communitarians of recommending all kinds of oppressive

219

practices to be found in a range of communities, past and present. But it would be no less absurd to suggest that environmentalists approve of everything, such as contaminated land or polluted rivers, which is now part of our environment. Environmentalists advocate change so that future generations can inherit an environment closer to the ideal of what the environment should be like. Similarly, communitarians want to transform communities so that they move closer to the ideal of community life (Walzer, 1994; Etzioni, 1995; and Bellah, 1995/6). What this ideal is cannot be derived simply from what social commentators at any time take to be the most attractive (or unattractive, for that matter) features of communities that have caught their attention. At the most basic level, a community is no more than a group of people who have something in common which brings them (and keeps them) together. What is in common could be a geographical location, a historical identity, the fear of a common enemy, a place of worship, a shared interest, a common employer, or a bond which grows out of solidarity against similar prejudices and discrimination.

Without being part of some form of community life, human beings cannot develop linguistically, culturally or morally. All that is distinctly human is only realized when human beings interact with each other as members of shared communities (Miller, 1990; Taylor, 1990; and Bell, 1993). There is no sharp demarcation, except perhaps in pathological cases where the normal pattern of development is disrupted at an early age, between what matters to us because it affects us on an individual basis, and what matters to us because it affects others about whom we care. Through community life, we learn the value of integrating what we seek individually with the needs and aspirations of other people. Neither individualist nor authoritarian attempts to bypass this issue can be sustained. Without a harmonious integration of diverse interests, we could not evolve an understanding of common values, and destructive tensions would permeate the relationships between those powerful enough to get their own way, and those who are neglected or suppressed.

Communitarian writers, such as Durkheim and Hobhouse, have always maintained that while a community, at a primitive stage of its development, may only be capable of achieving a 'mechanical' form of solidarity, wherein individuals 'could only operate in harmony in so far as they do not operate independently', with technological development and productive specialization, it would become 'more capable of operating in harmony, in so far as each of its elements operates more independently' (Durkheim, 1984, pp. 130, 131). Durkheim stressed that this 'organic' form of solidarity, made possible by the socioeconomic advancement of communities, can only be realized and sustained if those in authority learn to let go of what they should no longer control, and those who have more freedom to act independently learn to respect the common values and practices that underpin their activities. If they do, then both social cohesion and individual autonomy could be enhanced at the same time. However, just because socioeconomic conditions have evolved to make it possible for organic solidarity to emerge, there is no guarantee that the possibility would be realized. Hobhouse warned that without effective co-ordination, the opposite could occur, and social disintegration would be followed by the reduction of all too many people into being servile subordinates:

> there may be a development of collective unity and achievement with no corresponding development of harmony. But such development tends to reduce social life to a mechanism, while a more harmonious system giving larger play to human faculty would have a greater sum of co-operative intelligence behind it, and therefore a greater elasticity and vitality. (Hobhouse, 1966, p. 72)

The key to securing greater organic solidarity, which offers social cohesion through the integrated realization of community members' distinctive potential, thus lies with the development of co-operative intelligence. Only those communities which, culturally and structurally, support this development can be said to embody the ideal of inclusive community. Instead of invoking some indisputable text, or drawing up a comprehensive technocratic blueprint for society, the onus is placed on the ability of human beings to assess problems and opportunities and come up with tentative solutions to be tested and revised by successive generations. Accordingly, John Dewey defined the criterion by which 'we judge the worth of any sort of institutional arrangements' in terms of the extent to which they approximate the 'maximum opportunity for free exchange and communication' (Dewey, 1973, p. 92). This criterion is to be applied to the distribution of power within and across communities because among fundamental obstacles to the development of co-operative intelligence are the unequal power relations that prevent many people from developing their own ideas, let alone having the opportunity to express them.

Dewey's targets are indicative of the changes needed to approximate the ideal of inclusive community. These include the 'strong paternalistic family system, in which communication of thought and sharing of feeling are all but impossible between the head of the family on the one hand, and the other members who owe him respect and obedience on the other', the authoritarian state in which 'the government decides what is best for the inhabitants, who are to accept the decisions', the clergy which in many countries 'constitute a special class, [and] . . . become so preoccupied with the offices and rituals of their profession that they lose effective contact with the laity', and management systems which do not allow workers 'any share in determining the purposes of the factory where they work' (Dewey, 1973, pp. 90–1, 95).

In short, the building of inclusive communities must involve the displacement of 'any system of relationship which effectively places one person in subjugation to another – children to their parents, wives to their husbands, subjects to their rulers, laborers to their employers', by new forms of power relations which enable equal citizen participation to take place (Dewey, 1973, p. 92). Far from invoking some vague, romanticized notion of 'community' before which its members should surrender their individuality, Dewey pressed for the democratization of prevailing structures and processes to develop the kind of community in which individuality can be fulfilled harmoniously. This distinction, according to Tony Skillen, is of fundamental significance:

> Against the idea of 'community' as transcendent entity through which I have my identity, Deweyan communitarianism denotes patterns of co-operation, reciprocity and fellowship. It is a characteristic among individuals rather than an object transcending those individuals. (Skillen, 1996, p. 146)

It is this ideal of inclusive community that is consistently championed by communitarian writers (for example, Marquand, 1988; Boswell, 1994; Tam, 1996b; and Bellah, 1995/6; see also, Ryan, 1995, pp. 357–9). It cannot be confused with the nostalgic yearning for past communities which only 'inhibits, rather than serves, serious social criticism' (Bellah, 1995/6, p. 49). On the basis of this ideal, we can now look at criticisms of communitarianism which focus on the acceptability of what is involved in the proposed ideal for community life.

First, there is the criticism that communitarian ideas rely on traditional structures of community life and therefore offer no basis for social and political reforms. Amy Gutmann, for example, argued that communitarians such as Alasdair MacIntyre and Michael Sandel are either too complacent about traditional societies, or too optimistic about those societies' inclinations to change oppressive practices. 'A great deal of intolerance', she noted, 'has come from societies of selves so 'confidently situated' that they were sure repression would serve a higher course' (Gutmann, 1992, p. 132). However, Gutmann also recognized that while some communitarian writers have not sufficiently considered the need to change traditional social arrangements, the 'constructive potential of communitarian values' is there to be developed. She acknowledged that this is a task which is taken up by other communitarian thinkers such as Benjamin Barber and Michael Walzer, who have put forward significant political and economic reforms (Gutmann, 1992, p. 135). In the case of Barber, his work in reorientating democracy towards 'civic engagement and political community' is directly influenced by Dewey's communitarian thinking which, as we have seen, is far from complacent about traditional communities (Barber, 1984, 1995).

Second, communitarians have been accused of demanding homogeneity as a precondition for effective community life. It is claimed that they want to secure social cohesion at the expense of cultural pluralism because they believe that the rejection of a common set of values and practices would lead to instability and conflicts. Derek L. Phillips writes:

> MacIntyre, Sandel, and Taylor all argue that we derive our identity from our community and that this in itself gives rise to valid obligations . . . The danger of communitarian thinking here is obvious. It obliterates individual autonomy entirely and dissolves the self into whatever roles are imposed by one's position in society . . . the obligations stemming from membership in Nazi Germany or South Africa [before the end of Apartheid], for example, far from being mandatory, ought to be vehemently rejected because of these societies' violations of basic human rights. (Phillips, 1993, pp. 182, 183, 184)

What Phillips has overlooked is that the emphasis on the importance of common values and practices is not inherently incompatible with individual autonomy. The distinction Durkheim and

Hobhouse drew between mechanical and organic solidarity helps to explain that whereas the common values underlying mechanical solidarity demand total homogeneity, organic solidarity offers the opportunity for individuals to develop themselves and attain a stronger sense of social cohesion at the same time. This is the culture Durkheim referred to as 'moral individualism', in which individuals are encouraged to fulfil their potential while recognizing that being able to contribute to the fulfilment of others is an integral (and *not* an instrumental) part of their own fulfilment. Hobhouse, committed to build on rather than reject Mill's ideas on intellectual pluralism, wanted to see that commitment shared by all, so that individuals might develop their own feelings and ideas within a common framework which allows all to develop, and not just some who happen to be powerful and who might otherwise deprive others of their developmental opportunities (Hobhouse, 1994).

MacIntyre, Sandel and Charles Taylor have concentrated more on defending the need for such a common framework because individualism has been in the ascendancy in the latter half of the twentieth century. From the communitarian perspective of earlier thinkers such as Hobhouse and Dewey, there is no question that a critique of any prevailing framework should be carried out with reference to its effectiveness in realizing the potential to enhance both social cohesion *and* individual autonomy. More importantly, such a critique would be formulated through the application of co-operative intelligence to concrete social problems rather than by checking off some abstractly constituted list of human rights.

The third type of criticism concerns the lack of awareness among some communitarian writers regarding the issues of power and dominance in established communities. Marilyn Friedman cited three features of communitarian thinking which are 'troubling from a feminist standpoint'. These are:

First . . . the communitarian's metaphysical conception of an inherently social self has little usefulness for normative analysis . . . Second, communitarian theory fails to acknowledge that many communities make illegitimate moral claims on their members, linked to hierarchies of domination and subordination. Third, the specific communities of family, neighbourhood, and nation so commonly invoked by communitarians are troubling paradigms of social relationship and communal life. (Friedman, 1989, p. 279)

Friedman is right to criticize metaphysical conceptions which offer little normative substance. By contrast, the sociological starting point we have adopted suggests that there are different forms of community life, and that to develop those which are most likely to promote the widest opportunities for individual growth without fragmenting communal links into a state of indifference or even conflicts, we need to break down barriers to equal power distribution so that through open communications and co-operation we can identify appropriate reform strategies. This position takes into account Friedman's other two concerns. Existing communities of family, neighbourhood and nation should be evaluated in relation to the ideal of inclusive community which has been put forward. The more they contain oppressive hierarchies which demand the unquestioned obedience of those in subordinate positions, the more they need to be exposed as authoritarian and subject to radical redistribution of power.

The fourth and final area of criticism concerns the exclusivity of communities. In his exposition of communitarian ideas, David Miller considered two particular objections (Miller, 1990, pp. 229–51). One of these concerns communities not leaving 'adequate space for the development of individuality', and raises the issues of homogeneity that were dealt with above. The other objection concerns the compatibility between strong community identity and the inclusive ideal of a community of communities. Miller claimed that the two are incompatible because, for him, communities must have a high degree of exclusivity if they are to provide their members with a real sense of belonging:

> If a community is to make a claim on my allegiance, it must represent a distinct way of life; there must be something about the community and its members that makes it *my* community . . . What goes by the board, however, is the idea of a community of communities, of inter-communal relations as merely a less intense version of intra-communal relations. Communities which make strong claims on their members' allegiances need to be linked together by a framework of a different, non-communitarian kind. (Miller, 1990, pp. 231–2)

Miller further suggested that 'communal identification must occur at the level at which most major decisions affecting the shape of a society are made – meaning, in practice, at the level of the nation state.' (Miller, 1990, p. 236). Miller is mistaken in three respects, however. First, community identity does not rest on exclusive allegiance. We can, and many of us do, feel a real sense of belonging towards a multiplicity of communities: our neighbourhoods, towns, counties, regions, nations, clubs, unions, professional bodies, work teams, interest-based societies, lobbying groups and so on. Many of these enable their members to be involved in major decisions that affect their lives. Second, these communities do associate with each other, horizontally and vertically. For example, the voluntary groups of a town coming together to form an umbrella group for the town; clubs across Europe forming a continental association; local businesses joining with regional businesses to set up a business support organization; and national and regional politicians working together on issues of common interest. Some of these links are not strong, but others create their own communities where the sense of identity and belonging is as important as that within one of the constituent communities. Finally, the nation-state, is just one of these communities. In terms of opportunities for influence and participation, it is far less significant than local authority areas – and more power should for this reason alone be devolved to more local units of government. In terms of macroeconomic issues, it is not just the nation-state, but also transnational political institutions and multinational corporations that affect societies – and more involvement by citizens in the deliberations of such bodies needs to be promoted.

No communitarian theory can be sustained on the basis of a single overriding community which commands the exclusive allegiance of its members. The need for association and interaction with others simply cannot be satisfied in this arbitrary manner. Furthermore, the task of developing communal association among the multiplicity of communities is becoming more urgent as the process of globalization takes out the option of communities existing in splendid isolation from one another. As different communities have more and more interaction with each other, they will only be able to flourish if they learn to relate to each other by working out a set of common values and practices to which they will give their support. The alternative is a collision course between rival communities that will undermine the well-being of all. Etzioni has argued that not only is there no sociological evidence to suggest that commitment to one's own culture is incompatible with knowing and respecting those of others, there is, in fact, a growing need for an equilibrium of 'layered loyalties' to be developed between particular constitutent communities and the overarching framing community (Etzioni, 1997, pp. 189–205).

Having established that the ideal of inclusive community offers a normative model for social and political action, we now turn to considering the criticisms that may be directed at the three communitarian principles to be applied in identifying the gap to be bridged between the proposed model and prevailing structures and practices.

The Principle of Co-operative Enquiry

Both individualists and authoritarians might argue that the communitarian principle of co-operative enquiry is an unacceptable basis for attaining political knowledge, and reject it as a guide for decision-making. Although questions concerning the foundation for knowledge claims involve intricate epistemological issues not usually discussed in political theory, unless these questions are addressed, the acceptance or dismissal of communitarian political thinking would remain at the level of rhetoric. From a communitarian point of view, what can rightly be declared as a valid claim in society is not a matter that can be left to *ad hoc* preferences or self-proclaimed authorities. A conception of what gives knowledge claims their validity must inform the way power structures for decision-making are organized. The crucial question is whether we are to consider the source of validity as a factor external to a particular claimant which makes the claim acceptable, or a factor that is external to *all* possible claimants.

If the source of validity needs only to be external to a particular claimant, then I can claim to know, for example, that a military mission ordered by a political leader has led to the deaths of hundreds of children, provided that there is something to validate that claim other than what I claim myself. This could be a combination of reports by journalists, testimony of witnesses who survived the attack, revelations from official documents and so on. However, if the source of validity must be external to all possible claimants, then even if there were reports by journalists, testimony, documentation and so on, put forward by others in support of my claim, I would still not have a valid foundation for my claim, because what other people claim (for example, that they saw the attack, that they filmed the event, that they read the official report of the mission) would in turn require further external validation. But since nothing can ultimately enter our discourse on validation except the propositions of claimants, the quest for a foundation could never end. Even the most incontrovertible fact – for example, that the killings were witnessed by a reporter – cannot escape from being a claim which could be dismissed for a variety of reasons (the troops responsible were mistakenly identified, the reporter was deceived, suffered from delusions, was a deliberate liar and so on). Any attempt to back the reporter's claim would involve further claims which would need to be validated, and so on, for ever (see Vesey, 1976; Dancy, 1985).

Anyone who insists on the latter conception of epistemological foundation would therefore automatically fall into an infinite regress. On such a conception, no claim can ever be validated, and total scepticism is the only response. However, there is no reason why we should not adopt the former as the appropriate conception for epistemological foundation. In fact, where human communities have succeeded in making significant progress with specific processes of validating knowledge-claims, it is the former conception that has been used. For example, in the development of medical treatment, criminal trial procedures, or manufacturing techniques, it is not the quest for some transcendental factor that has enabled various knowledge-claims to be validated. In all cases, it has been the formulation of claims by some individuals, subject to the scrutiny and evaluation by others whose claims are in turn weighed for their support, which have eventually led to new practices being adopted.

New medical treatments were never established by a single proof, but by claims of successful treatment tried and tested, and reported through further claims before some gained wider acceptance and others were rejected as unreliable. Criminal procedures have been adjusted in the light of suggestions and criticisms which linked certain practices to more reliable convictions than others. Manufacturing techniques would never have altered if producers' decisions had been dependent on the discovery of an indubitable claim; instead, they considered the views of different groups of people when aspects of new techniques were proposed. If these examples seem commonplace, they none the less illustrate why the development and validation of knowledge-claims must be rooted in the free exchange of a community of enquirers (Dewey, 1930; Cohen, 1977, Habermas, 1984; and Tam, 1993b).

We would not know what we should or should not believe, or what might be better alternatives to the way we do things (which was, in fact, the situation for centuries when primitive beliefs and practices were shielded from criticisms) unless we give new knowledge-claims the opportunity to develop and offer themselves for appraisal by others through observation, investigation and experimentation. However, when some claims are heavily backed by others who have tested them vigorously, this should still only accord those claims provisional validation. In opening up current ideas and practices to the challenges of new knowledge-claims, we cannot arbitrarily pronounce some claims as being absolutely unrevisable, and shut the door to future challenges. At any one time those claims that have the strongest validation from others who have carried out independent tests and investigations would be adopted as reliable for a time, but the process of further revision and improvement is ongoing. Indeed, one of the reasons why some people object to capital punishment is precisely because they feel that as the emergence of new evidence is always possible, no single trial process could produce a degree of reliability so high that one could confidently approve the termination of another human being's life. The alternative is not to let all those found guilty of murder go free, but to keep them imprisoned in case new evidence might be put forward to challenge the 'guilty' verdict. This also illustrates the importance of considering the evaluation of claims in conjunction with the practices that will be influenced by the outcome of any evaluation. It must never be pretended that people can stand back from the consequences of their epistemological judgements.

Three possible lines of attack remain for the critics of communitarianism. They could try to show that the principle of co-operative enquiry does not, in fact, succeed in escaping from the arguments of scepticism (which, as we argued in Chapter 2, underpins individualism and anarchic power distribution); that its merits are only relative to some cultures and not applicable universally (and could thus be ignored by culturally 'distinct' authoritarian regimes); or that its implicit reliance on the paradigm of experimental science is untenable, because that paradigm has no place in a 'post-everything' world.

Let us tackle scepticism first. The sceptic extends the doubt concerning the ability to know what is to be done politically, to become an all-inclusive doubt. No one could know anything, because every claim which could logically be true could also logically be false, and there is nothing that can be invoked (without falling into an infinite regress) to rule out the possibility of any claim being true or false (Unger, 1975). Examples such as the fact that one cannot even know that one is not now dreaming, or that one is but a disembodied brain stimulated by electrodes to 'experience' all the things one thinks one is experiencing, are commonly used by philosophical sceptics, who would be no less sceptical about the epistemological soundness of co-operative enquiry.

Yet the sceptical position is one that undermines itself. It simply cannot be maintained consistently. If we suspended all our beliefs, we could not long survive. Nor, for that matter, could we survive by insisting that certain beliefs are absolutely indubitable, and persist in acting on them even if they lead visibly to perils. Habits are formed in the light of our experiences and, except where dogmatic practices are forced upon us, they are further adjusted as their impact on our experiences is felt. Human beings can discuss the dubiousness and reliability of particular claims only in the light of their common experiences. Abstracted from all possible exchanges of ideas and their implications for our shared experiences, the concept of doubt itself becomes untenable (Hume, 1975, 1978; Wittgenstein, 1978, 1979). The problem with scepticism is that it supposes that we are each to question the validity of knowledge claims as isolated individuals without reference to our shared experiences with other human beings. On such a supposition, knowledge would indeed be impossible. In fact, such a supposition is misconceived. Human beings do not formulate critical thoughts as isolated individuals – if they were not social beings by nature, they would not even have evolved common languages without which critical thoughts, including the concept of doubt, could not even be formulated.

Unless one believes that everything one 'experiences' is one long arbitrary dream sequence – and on sceptical grounds, there would be no basis at all for allowing such a premise – then clearly the reliability of any knowledge claim is in direct proportion to the extent to which it stands up to examination by others, provided, of course that the examination is an open and honest one, and the participants are not tempted or threatened to disrupt the process of enquiry in order to benefit or protect themselves in any way. Decision-making by a jury exemplifies this approach. To the extent that individuals have a shared form of life within which they can compare notes on ideas and experiences, they can evaluate specific knowledge-claims without doubting all knowledge-claims (Hanfling, 1976; Strawson, 1985; Bell and McGinn, 1990).

According to the second line of attack, co-operative enquiry is only one mode of knowledge validation that happened to develop in parts of Western societies, and it should not be regarded as being superior to other modes of understanding the world. The findings of co-operative enquiry are themselves merely based on the thoughts and feelings of a particular group of people at a particular time, and should not be granted any higher degree of reliability than the findings that emerge from other cultures at other times. Unlike philosophical sceptics, cultural relativists accept that discourse is rooted in the exchanges between members of a community. However, in lifting the communicative barrier that sceptics put up between individuals, they erect it instead between communities (Winch, 1958; Bloor, 1976). They then seek to argue that the ideas of different cultures are incommensurable, and therefore cannot be compared. But while there are matters of customs and traditions that are not appropriate for ranking in any critical sense – for example, in the way different cultures dress, or dance, or their use of colours in art and decoration, there are clearly numerous issues which can be compared directly in terms of the validity of rival knowledge claims.

If one community claims that it can preserve the lives of its members from various disasters and diseases by ordering them to bow before their spiritual leaders, and another community claims that it can protect its members by means of emergency planning and medical practices, unless both sides remain totally ignorant of each other, it would not be too difficult for them to see which community is more successful in achieving its stated goals. If awareness of each other's practices leads to open communication, there should be no reason why a wider understanding of which claims are more reliable would not emerge. The same applies to the ideas of past communities which some may seek to retain. They cannot pretend that those ideas can be cut off from critical examination alongside ideas developed by contemporary communities. Once the arbitrary barriers to comparisons are removed, any relativist attempt to shield the knowledge claims of particular cultures from critical evaluation collapses. As Charles Taylor pointed out:

> What we have here is not an antecedently accepted common criterion, but a facet of our activity . . . which remains implicit or

unrecognized in earlier views, but which cannot be ignored once realized in practice. The very existence of technological advance forces the issue. In this way, one set of practices can pose a challenge for an incommensurable interlocutor, not indeed in the language of this interlocutor, but in terms which the interlocutor cannot ignore. And out of this can arise valid transcultural judgements of superiority. (Taylor, 1983, pp. 103)

This does not mean that communities may proclaim their superiority arbitrarily. Cultural relativists are right to react against arrogant assumptions of superiority when there is no evidence or analysis that remotely supports that claim. However, far from accepting that such claims cannot be evaluated, they should be put to the test when enquirers from different communities co-operate to ascertain the validity of rival claims. The case of alternative medicine illustrates the difference between those who want to ignore it dogmatically as being inferior to Western medicine, and those who set up research forums to bring together proponents of both sides to determine what they each can learn from the other.

The advancement of science illustrates why the Baconian model of co-operative enquiry is one that can usefully guide our practices for evaluating political knowledge claims. Yet the final challenge to co-operative enquiry is based on the allegation that science itself is no less relativistic in the light of criticisms by theorists such as Thomas Kuhn and Paul Feyerabend (Kuhn, 1970; Feyerabend, 1977). In this view, scientists are no more able than anyone else to come up with validated knowledge claims. For a variety of reasons, one scientific theory will gain wide acceptance, and another will be marginalized, but in time a further theory will be developed, and in the course of such continuous theory-displacement, there is no basis to say that one theory is more valid than another. They are simply incommensurable.

Those who seek to invoke Kuhn and Feyerabend to undermine co-operative enquiry must, however, understand that they do not, in fact, reject such enquiry as being unreliable. What they do reject is the interpretation of such a process as revealing more and more of an independent reality. Since the Baconian basis of co-operative enquiry does not subscribe to any such interpretation (Pérez-Ramos, 1988), it is important to identify just how Kuhn's and Feyerabend's ideas have an impact on our understanding of the validation of knowledge claims. In *The Structure of Scientific Revolutions*, Kuhn compares the development of science with Darwinian evolution. Theories are not displaced in accordance with some pre-established goal. New theories displace old ones in so far as they are more adaptable to solving the problems encountered. Far from dismissing the advancement in science, he characterizes the outcome of such co-operative enquiry as 'the wonderfully adapted set of instruments we call modern scientific knowledge', and maintains that 'Successive stages in that developmental process are marked by an increase in articulation and specialization' (Kuhn, 1970, p. 172). Increases in articulation and specialization are important because where broad principles are established, it is the resolution of differences over details that makes improved understanding possible.

Similarly, Feyerabend is concerned with mistaken conceptions of science getting in the way of the *correct* selection of scientific theories. He attacked those who suppose that there can be a single methodology for deciding on the validity of scientific claims. He endorsed Mill's approach, which allows for standards and proce-dures to evolve so long as their adaptations are based on the open exchange of views and criticisms by enquirers co-operating to solve a common set of problems (Feyerabend, 1975, pp. 4–8; see also Hacking, 1981; and Lakatos and Musgrave, 1979). The criticisms that Kuhn and Feyerabend level at misconceptions of the develop-ment of science in fact help to clarify why co-operative enquiry should be used to evaluate knowledge claims. Science, like all forms of knowledge, progresses through active engagement with problems encountered. Its effectiveness as an instrument in overcoming these problems is ultimately the only criterion with which to judge its advancement in relation to, not some 'reality' beyond all possible experience, but rather past attempts at tackling those problems. Since this criterion is firmly located in the experiential realm, anyone capable of experiencing the problems, and understanding past attempts at solving them, would be in a position to contribute to the evaluation of new attempts to solve those problems. To exclude anyone who shares the relevant experiences from the process of co-operative enquiry would therefore undermine the likelihood of all relevant factors being considered – for example, if someone who has discovered new experimental findings is not allowed to present his or her findings, or if a forensic expert is not allowed to testify in a case that raises issues about which he or she has made extensive studies. This does not imply that every process of enquiry must involve every person who has a contribution to make, participating without any kind of distortion or hindrance. What is required is that the circumstances under which the enquiry is carried out warrant the assumption that had the ideal conditions for unhindered co-operative deliberations been fully met, its finding would have been endorsed (see Habermas's concept of the ideal speech situation: Habermas, 1984 and 1992, pp. 170–3). While different methodologies need to be developed for different subjects in different circumstances, the basic structure of co-operative enquiry remains the one that is necessary in all cases for communities to consider and decide on the merits of rival knowledge claims.

The Principle of Mutual Responsibility

By applying the principle of co-operative enquiry to social and political practices, communities would not accept that everything traditionally valued by previous generations must continue to be valued, or that all values are to be rejected as being without foundations. Instead, a community of co-operative enquirers would review and revise their common understanding of values in the context of changing circumstances. This does not imply that communitarian values lack objective validity. In fact, they would be no less objectively valid than medical judgements regarding suitable treatment, which also have to be adjusted to deal with different illnesses at different times.

On the basis of values such as love, wisdom, justice and fulfilment, which have stood the test of time and across diverse cultures, citizens must accept that they have responsibilities to each other in maximising the opportunities to pursue those values, and minimizing barriers that may stand in the way. The existence of these common values means that no one can deny having a responsibility to contribute to their attainment (see Beehler, 1978). However, the principle of mutual responsibility could be attacked from three directions: it cannot be sustained by linking what people do value to what people *should* value; people do not, in fact, value the same kinds of thing; and broad agreements on what people do value are inadequate for defining the responsibilities of citizens.

First, let us take the charge that what people happen to value cannot be legitimately linked to what should be valued. Authoritarians rely on the claim that they alone know what people should value, even if that conflicts with what people do value. They use it as their platform to counter prevailing attitudes and practices, and to launch 'moral' crusades to dismantle 'liberal' reforms. However, once the link between what people value and what are to be adopted as appropriate values is severed, then anything goes. Rival fundamentalists would preach opposing views on what should be done to save society from moral decay, and there would be no means of evaluating their claims. Yet, there is no reason to deny the link. Even the most sophisticated argument that might be deployed to block this link – namely, the Humean distinction between 'is' and 'ought' – does not so much rule it out as clarify the conditions under which it can be established (Hume, 1978, bk 3, pt I, s. I; see also Hudson, 1969). The essence of Hume's argument is that statements about what ought to be the case cannot be deduced from statements about what *is* the case, *in the manner of logical deduction*. What is to be rejected is the kind of sleight of hand used by authoritarians in proclaiming various moral obligations, which they have been able to deduce from principles that they alone know to be indubitably true. Hume's position is clear:

> Men are now cured of their passion for hypotheses and systems in natural philosophy, and will hearken to no argument but those derived from experience. It is full time they should attempt a like reformation in all moral disquisitions and reject every system of ethics, however subtle or ingenious, which is not founded on fact and observation. (Hume, 1975, s. I)

In reality, human beings generalize over time their experiences of what is found to be agreeable to them and what is repugnant. As there are sufficient continuities throughout history, people come to view certain traits and qualities as morally desirable in that they should be recommended to all, while other characteristics would become widely regarded as contemptible, and society would seek to oppose them. It would therefore be in line with the Humean analysis of the community-based evolution of values to suggest that values such as love, wisdom, justice and fulfilment are validated through communities' shared reflections on their realization in experience (Livingston, 1984; Hudson, 1986). Correspondingly, the manifestations of hatred, callousness, negligence, ignorance, prejudice, irrationality, injustice, alienation and deprivation are detected gradually and traced back to causes which are then condemned.

Turning to the second criticism, we need to deal with the fact that people *do* continue to have conflicting values. The communitarian position could, therefore, be attacked for relying too much on shared moral outlooks which are simply not there. Judith Lichtenberg, for example, has used the example of trying to change the mind of someone who is a defender of slavery, to illustrate how at a certain point there appears to be nothing further to invoke to criticize the opposing view (Lichtenberg, 1994, p. 203). However, what she overlooked is that values are not validated merely through their possessors, but rather through their impact on the interactions within and between communities. While values have to be open and inclusive to be the common values for all, the values of those blinded by prejudices are closed and exclusive. The latter group can either deny the value of love, wisdom, justice and fulfilment altogether, in which case they would be like solitary predators with no real relationship or any sense of shared values with anyone else, or they would have to restrict the applications of those values arbitrarily, in which case they may live in accordance with them in some respects but – in an ultimate act of bad faith – deny them to others.

Lichtenberg would see this as pointing to an irreducible divergence in how different people approach life: 'What seems certain to one person does not always seem certain to another; what is taken as obvious by the mass of people in a society may be rejected by those living in another society or at another time. Bedrock for one, it appears, may not be bedrock for another' (Lichtenberg, 1994, pp. 193–4). But the two approaches are comparable in a significant sense: the one guided by common values is one which offers a bedrock for all. By contrast, defenders of slavery want to rely on a bedrock of values that is inherently unacceptable to others. Their insistence on the value of 'treating others as slaves' pushes others either to repel the threat of subjugation or to adopt a similar stance and treat the defenders of slavery as slaves. A bedrock of values that enables all who may be affected by the pursuit of those values to share in, develop and realize those values, is therefore quite clearly sustainable, especially when compared with a pseudo-bedrock which is more like a fault line so inherently unstable that no lasting values can be built on it.

What about values that do not demand the subjugation of others? Although the values of authoritarians can be rejected on the grounds that they impinge on others, the values of individualists may not directly interfere with others. Some people may accept that they should not do anything to harm others, but they have no interest in doing anything to help others either. Some prefer ignorance to understanding the complexities of issues on which they enjoy giving their opinions. Some are unmoved by acts of injustice so long as the victims are not in their immediate circle of friends and relatives. Some are content with fulfilment through basic pleasures but scorn those which are developmental. What can be said about these people's pursuit of values? They cannot be accused of making the lives of others intolerable. Yet it can be asked if they have had the support and opportunity to develop their values. The form of co-operative enquiry that Mill proposed for comparing the values of different pleasures is instructive here:

> Of two pleasures, if there be one to which all or almost all who have experienced of both give a decided preference, irrespective of any feeling of moral obligation to prefer it, that is the more desirable pleasure. If one of the two is, by those who are competently acquainted with both, placed so far above the other that they prefer it, even though, knowing it to be attended with a greater amount of discontent, and would not resign it for any quantity of the other pleasure which their nature is capable of, we are justified in ascribing to the preferred enjoyment a superiority in quality. (Mill, 1972, p. 8)

Mill's suggestion points to the need for open discussions in order to develop our understanding of what ought to be valued. The fact that there are individuals who prefer to pursue less demanding values does not mean that the more demanding ones are invalidated. In many cases, those individuals would express their admiration for people who pursue the more demanding values, and thus endorse the worthiness of the latter. They are also likely to agree that society would be better if more and more people aimed for the pursuit of the more demanding values, than if increasing numbers of people gave up the more demanding values for the less demanding ones. It follows that each new generation should be given the support and opportunity to experience the pursuit of those values. Inclusive communities need to ensure that their members understand and apply their shared values to the way they live.

In order to ensure that the interpretations of common values do not become rigid and outmoded, there must be ongoing opportunities to discuss their place in the lives of citizens. Durkheim has for this very reason stressed the importance of both the state in providing an overarching view of how the values of different groups relate to each other, and representative groups within society in providing a counterbalance to the state lest its views become detached from the concerns of real communities. Society would thus move closer to the ideal of an inclusive community 'the more that deliberation and reflection and a critical spirit play a considerable part in the course of public affairs' (Durkheim, 1957, p. 89).

However, the thrust of the third criticism against the principle of mutual responsibility is that the values which survive cross-cultural validation are inevitably so broad and vague that they would not be of help when we have to choose between conflicting demands. Life is full of difficult decisions. There are Sartrean choices between rival obligations such as fighting for one's country and looking after one's ailing parent. There are dilemmas about medical priorities that affect different people's life chances differently. There are decisions to be made about those on housing waiting lists. There are demands to switch public funding for services such as the arts – without which life would be impoverished – to services which are needed to save lives.

It would, in fact, be a misconception to suppose that common values are themselves sufficient to resolve every moral dilemma. What they do help to do is to provide a framework – even if it is one subject to possible revision – within which more specific conflict resolution can take place. At its outer boundaries, it uncompromisingly rules out the promotion of hatred, the callous denial of the needs of other human beings, the deception of the public by the state, the silencing of protestors, the torturing of dissenters, the arbitrary interference with other people's attempts to lead a fulfilling life, and many other evils which relativists have found difficult to condemn, let alone oppose, when they are carried out by oppressive regimes abroad and militant bigots at home. At its core it requires all citizens to carry out their responsibilities as parents, contributors to productive enterprises, protectors of their communities' safety, and in relation to state, business and third-sector organizations over which they can exert influence (see Selbourne, 1994, ch. 10).

The framework none the less leaves room for divergent views to arise over ways in which specific moral dilemmas are to be resolved. What the communitarian position is committed to is that conflicting knowledge claims about how such dilemmas are to be resolved should be subjected to critical examination under conditions of co-operative enquiry. As leaving such enquiries to people who are already in a state of desperation would hinder any open, honest and thorough examination, it is essential that the pressures, needs and expectations that give rise to such dilemmas are discussed as far in advance as possible, and with the participation of those whose lives might be affected by them. The emphasis on acknowledging the conflicts as being problematic, and seeking their future resolution through co-operative enquiry, contrasts sharply with the views of relativists such as Richard Rorty, who believe that such conflicts cannot even in principle be rationally resolved. Although some critics have linked Rorty's relativism to communitarian ideas because of the selective influence he drew from Dewey, Levi has put the record straight:

> we should agree with Dewey that the structure of inquiries aimed at realizing ends of diverse kinds should exhibit features to be recognized as rational . . . To suppose, as Rorty suggests, that we should turn to edifying discourses of a hermeneutical character which give priority to 'the way things are said' over 'possession of truths' is to kid ourselves and take a view diametrically opposed to Dewey's. (Levi, 1984, p. 144)

To concede that some conflicts cannot be resolved at present is not to assume that those conflicts cannot be resolved in principle. In the absence of any evidence to the contrary, 'we should not impose any limits in advance of inquiry on the extent in which we may succeed in straightening out conflicts in value which we face' (Levi, 1992, p. 834).

The Principle of Citizen Participation

Linking the requirement to resolve disputes over rival claims by co-operative enquiry, and the assignment of responsibilities on the basis of common values, is the principle of citizen participation. According to this principle, everyone affected by a given power structure must be able to participate as equal citizens in determining how the power in question is to be exercised. Without a structure that makes citizen participation possible, co-operative enquiry would often be restricted, and it would be much more difficult to advance our understanding of the common values we share.

Exhortations to be more responsive and caring towards others would not change our moral culture if individuals were deprived of the ability and opportunity to work for the common good. Ultimately, communities can only become truly democratized if power is shared among their members. However, critics of communitarian ideas may object to the principle of citizen participation for three reasons: that it is too demanding for individuals living in fragmented societies; that it ignores the economic basis for power distribution; and that it diminishes political efficency by seeking to reverse centralization.

Regarding the claim that individuals in fragmented societies would not generally have the time or inclination to participate in political matters, the apathy of the citizen contrasts sharply with the enthusiasm of the consumer who continuously consumes more of the world's non-renewable resources. In *The Public and Its Problems*, Dewey has acknowledged that, as communities grow in complexity, it will become more and more difficult for people to gather relevant information, discuss it in depth, and bring their different views together in a meaningful synthesis (Dewey, 1991). However, rather than assuming that the prevailing apathy is inextricably rooted in human nature, he advocated more innovative experiments in stimulating and supporting the development of public deliberations (Campbell, 1995). In many cases, apathy is linked to a perception of powerlessness, to a view of society as being driven by closed organizations which would carry on regardless of what individual citizens might say. To counter this view, what is needed is an effective exposure of the sensitivity and vulnerability of commercial and public organizations to views expressed by citizens collectively. The growing interest in and support for focused campaigns is testimony to the fact that changes can be made by public discussions and criticisms of such organizations. Citizens do have a real interest in, and are prepared to find the time to take part in, activities that help to change particular neighbourhood, organizational or political communities for the better. What they need is support in identifying the issues to tackle, and organizing themselves in pressing for change. Where this support is forthcoming, as R. Bruce Douglass has observed, citizen participation can 'have much the sort of effect that communitarians say it can. Not only does it empower ordinary citizens and position them better to defend their neighbourhoods against organized special interests, but it brings them together as well . . . Power ends up being redistributed, and the more the effects of this are felt, the more motivation ordinary citizens have to believe in the responsiveness of government' (Douglass, 1994, p. 59).

John Stewart, who has argued for greater innovation in democratic practices to involve more citizens in the deliberation of public matters (Stewart, 1995; Stewart and Tam, 1997), would regard levels of apathy as indications that not enough has been done by those in charge of public authorities. Indeed, if public authorities put as much effort and imagination as do commercial organizations into attracting people towards what they have to offer, the public would become much more disposed to participate in their activities. The experience of local authorities that have applied public awareness techniques imaginatively suggests that there is considerable potential for development in this area (Gyford, 1991).

Another means of overcoming the reluctance to participate is by demonstrating the effectiveness of co-operating in a common enterprise. As societies fragment, isolated individuals may slip into thinking more and more that they should look only to their own interests, with little regard being paid to the implications for others. Through being involved in co-operative ventures, however, they can learn to appreciate having a unity of purpose with others, and experience participating as equals in determining how decisions should be made (Boyte *et al.*, 1994). Such experience in co-operative working would be instructive when applied to new areas where confrontation has become the dominant mode. Even more important, co-operative associations bring together people who would otherwise stand divided before the established power bases in society. Their coming together gives them a combined strength far in excess of the sum of what they could command as individuals (Hirst, 1994, ch. 3). Of course, co-operation could be undermined by those who refuse to co-operate or, worse, by those who profess to co-operate but in fact exploit the trust of others. Instead of looking for some guarantee that would never materialize, we should accept that the organization of co-operation is best developed through experimentation, taking on board the lessons that have emerged from the attempts of others. The history of the Co-operative Movement in Britain, for example, illustrates how the general commitment to co-operation took many years to adapt to practical circumstances. However, in spite of various setbacks, the basic principles of the Rochdale Pioneers have been successfully taken forward in an increasing range of joint enterprises (Bonner, 1961, chs 3–11). It is not the co-operative model that needs to be defended, but its organizational structure, which in practice has become threatened by those who want to dismantle it through the mechanism of hostile takeover so favoured by market individualists as a means of increasing short-term profits.

Overcoming apathy, of course, is not enough on its own. Power relations are often shaped by the distribution of economic resources. It could be argued that citizen participation can at best operate at a superficial level, so long as the economic basis for power distribution remains unaltered. But the principle of citizen participation does not suppose that power relations are to change while the economic basis for power stays the same. On the contrary, the demand for transformation of power relations implies changes to economic structures where these are necessary to democratize power relations between community members. Economic dependency is undeniably a major barrier for citizens to develop and express their own views. It was for this reason that thinkers such as Mill wanted to use the opportunities offered by industrialization to liberate those who had hitherto been at the mercy of others:

> The same reasons which make it no longer necessary that the poor should depend on the rich, make it equally unnecessary that women should depend on men; . . . The ideas and institutions by which the accident of sex is made the groundwork of an inequality of legal rights, and a forced dissimilarity of social functions, must ere long be recognized as the greatest hindrance to moral, social, and even intellectual improvement. (Mill, 1994, pp. 138–9)

What equality as political citizens does not imply is that economic resources are to be redistributed on an equal basis, because attempts at simplistic economic redistribution can perpetuate inequalities in power. After all, in order to equalize the distribution of wealth, a Hobbesian authority has to assume far-reaching powers. It is epistemologically dubious that such an authority can be relied upon to get its economic policies right, and politically dangerous to risk its concentration of powers.

Instead of putting our faith blindly in an authoritarian mechanism for distributing all wealth in society, we should press for particular decision-making processes concerning wealth generation to be opened up to all those affected by those processes to have a say as equal citizens (Boswell, 1994). As work communities are increasingly interconnected, the fairness and rationales of different approaches will be subjected to a process of constant review. While it is most probable that the outcome would, none the less, support different levels of financial benefits for people who make different contributions, it would reflect the considered judgement by all those concerned of what would constitute a reasonable distribution (Semler, 1994; Johnson, 1993).

It is true that there are those who, fearing that their power to control others would be reduced by such a democratized process, would want to block their development. They may concede a few minor changes so as long as they are compatible with their personal wealth-generation strategies, but beyond that they would seek to buy enough influence, directly or indirectly, to steer public decisions in favour of their private agendas. In the face of these entrenched economic powers, whom politicians, voluntary organizations relying on donations, the media, workers and managers alike, must guard against offending, no one can pretend that reforms would be easy to achieve. Communitarians who favour gradual reforms to overcome such barriers have been criticized strongly by those who feel that such an approach ignores the Marxist diagnosis of capitalist power. The underlying economic structures are considered to be immune to the changes driven by the 'blindly pragmatized thought' of theorists such as Dewey (Horkheimer and Adorno, 1972; Macpherson, 1979, chs 3 and 4). However, in practice, it is the gradual, pragmatic reformist approach – and not failed Marxist totalitarian strategies – that brings about lasting changes to power relations (Misgeld, 1987, p. 175).

Gradualist reforms are not limited only to making work communities change through guidance or legislation either. Government institutions also have a role in providing support to all citizens in the manner of 'a great benefit society, or mutual insurance company, for helping . . . that large proportion of its members who cannot help themselves' (Mill, 1980, p. 157). People need to have a basic degree of security before they can reflect on their conditions in life and formulate their views on matters affecting them. The state sector can, and should, assist with enabling citizens to acquire the economic strength to participate fully in decision-making processes that affect them. This is why the basic income for citizens should be set at a level adequate for all to remain dignified members of society.

The danger with projecting the state sector as the source of all solutions is that, instead of helping citizens to develop their abilities to contribute to their communities' well-being, it becomes saddled with the expectation to make all the right decisions for citizens without their involvement at all. The third criticism of the principle of citizen participation, however, seeks to argue that the centralization of political power is necessary to preserve uniformity and enhance efficiency. The fewer people there are with ruling power, the argument goes, the less likely would the swift exercise of power be blocked by excessive checks and balances. In the context of a representative democracy, the more clearly decisive ruling power is vested in a relatively small number of indiviudals, the more the electorate know whom to hold accountable for the consequences of political actions. To allow more and more citizens to have a real share of that power would therefore lead to conflicting decisions being made by different groups of citizens. Much-needed action would be delayed, and political fragmentation would increase in direct proportion to the amount of power being returned to citizens at more local levels.

The centralist argument is misconceived, for three reasons. First, citizen participation does not aim to replace representative democracy, but rather to supplement it. It recognizes the need for swift processes for political decision-making, but disputes the assumption that this can be attained solely by entrusting it completely to a relatively small group of people who, every four or five years, may get the electoral support of barely half the voters. It is not so much a doubt about the integrity of politicians as an epistemological proviso that questions the reliability of a completely closed decision-making system. There are issues on which the daily experiences of citizens need to be brought to bear to clarify what should be done at the local level, issues about which an informed consensus could only emerge if citizens were enabled to deliberate on them together, and issues where it is the centralized decision-making mechanisms themselves that need to be reviewed by citizens not directly involved in state institutions. Unless citizens can become more involved in evaluating policies and practices that affect them, centralized power structures, in the state or any other sector, would continue to make mistakes which could only be corrected by the knowledge possessed by people outside the core of those structures.

Second, centralization ignores the need for citizens to develop civic consciousness through participation in collective policy deliberations. For the sake of apparent short term efficiencies, centralized systems assure citizens that they can leave all the important decisions to the centre. Inevitably, this engenders a sense of detachment in relation to the outcome of those decisions. Citizens no longer feel that they have any responsibility in helping to achieve agreed policy objectives because they do not share in any way in the formulation of those policies. Thus we have the paradox of people demanding that their government do more to protect the environment, and yet resenting any suggestion that they would have to cut down on their use of private motor vehicles, consumption of scarce natural resources, or the purchase of packaged products that exacerbate the global waste disposal problem. Governments which encourage this leave-it-to-those-in-government attitude should not be surprised when the public persist in asking, for example, for more police on patrol, while dismissing requests to be more vigilant in reporting crimes as cynical attempts to save the state money.

The danger of depleting citizens' sense of responsibility for the common good is not confined to the state sector. Businesses and community enterprises can also suffer from their members' neglect of their role in protecting the values that they share. The dismantling of mutual societies and threatened takeovers of co-operative societies are made possible by the failures of those in charge to sustain their members' understanding of the real value of their shared enterprise beyond the attractions of short-term bonus payments. Only by involving their members more in the exercise of power to defend their common values can communities hope to maintain their informed commitment to working together (see Skinner, 1992).

Third, the centralist assumption that it is always the most efficient option to concentrate all decisions in one centre is simply untenable. While some decisions are properly delegated to the institutions of a nation state, there are many that should be passed back to local communities, and an increasing number that can only be handled by organizations that work on behalf of the global community. For the centralized core to insist on dealing with all these matters, would only end in it passing judgements on local issues about which it does not have any real understanding, or pronouncing on international problems it lacks the competence to tackle. The demand for subsidiarity in every sphere of life is a call, not to do away with all nation-state institutions, but to develop a more responsive and flexible structure that would enable those best placed to exercise power for a given set of issues to have that power (Taylor, 1993; Kinsky, 1995).

Dogmas about managerial authority and national sovereignty alike need to give way to practical explorations concerning the location of different decision-making powers. Just as organizations need to learn to decentralize, so societies must learn to entrust more to local bodies, be these local authorities which exemplify Stewart's approach to responsive governance (Ranson and Stewart, 1994), or publicly funded but voluntary and self-governing associations as advocated by Paul Hirst (Hirst, 1994). Except in circumstances where there is a common problem that can only be dealt with effectively by a standard approach across different localities and regions, citizens and local bodies should be allowed to apply their co-operative intelligence and try out their own solutions in tackling the problems they face. This does not preclude their learning from each other, or coming together when it would be suitable to do so. After all, subsidiarity does not point in one direction only. Power could sometimes be concentrated in a number of distinct centres, when in fact it would be much more effectively exercised if a more inclusive association of those centres is given the power. This is why many national associations are formed to add power to what regional groups may not be able to achieve on their own. Equally, when national bodies – and governments are no exception to this – face problems which their national divisions prevent them from tackling effectively, they have to come together to form a new community in which co-operative enquiry can take place without hindrance.

From the local, national level to the global arena, the principle of citizen participation needs to be applied consistently, to reform structures that are only superficially democratic, and democratize those communities that are still dominated by authoritarian rule. Power is to be centralized at a higher level if, and only if, its contributions can be demonstrated to informed citizens openly and regularly. Ultimately, it is not the reversal of centralization, but the refusal to comply with subsidiarity, that requires justification.

10

The Challenge to Build Inclusive Communities

The Communitarian Agenda for Change

Communitarianism holds that our need for community life can only be fully met and sustained through the development of inclusive communities. To ensure that the structures and cultures for human interaction which exist in local neighbourhoods, schools, places of work, towns and cities, government bodies, nations, multinational corporations and global institutions, consistently facilitate rather than obstruct such development, they must all be subject to evaluation in relation to the three communitarian principles set out in this book. These principles have been formulated on the basis of communitarian thinking which has been evolving through the ages. Unlike contemporary reactions against the social disintegration occurring in some American cities, which dwell on the loss of neighbourhood 'community spirit', the application of these principles is directed at establishing the conditions – knowledge, responsibilities, and power structures – necessary for sustainable community life in every sphere of human interaction.

The principle of co-operative enquiry challenges the relativistic individualism that has dominated Western thinking since the 1960s. It maintains that the validity of rival claims can be established, provided that the basis of validation rests with the claim's ability to secure the informed consensus of a community of co-operating enquirers. This implies that those who are to be engaged in the process of enquiry must be able to weigh up evidence, follow logical reasoning, suspend judgements when necessary, and reach agreement with others who bring similar capabilities to bear on their discussions.

According to the principle of mutual responsibility, there are common values which can be invoked to define the responsibilities of citizens in the global community of inclusive communities. On the basis of these values, all citizens must refrain from undermining the pursuit of wisdom, love, justice and fulfilment by others, and accept that they have a responsibility to support collective efforts in promoting the well-being of the communities to which they belong. However, detailed interpretations of these values are dependent on citizens being able to share their moral experiences, and discuss them under conditions of co-operative enquiry.

The principle of citizen participation is to be applied to the distribution of power, not just between the state and the governed, but between those who are currently in charge of organizations and those who work for them, between community activists and community members, between men and women, parents and children, and between those who work and live together in neighbourhoods and schools. In all cases, everyone affected by the power in question must have real opportunities to participate in the exercise of that power, understand how they can access those opportunities, and are able to make an informed contribution to reviewing and, where appropriate, reforming existing decision-making processes. Compliance with this principle will serve as the only basis for legitimizing power relations.

By drawing these principles and their practical implications together, this book puts forward a new communitarian agenda for reforms in the state, business and third sectors, from local and regional, to national and global levels. It aims to bring people together – whatever their culture, religion, nationality, or party political affiliation – to combat the influence of individualism, guard against the resurgence of authoritarianism it may provoke, and rally support for those who have to live under existing structures of oppression. Power and responsibility need to be redistributed so that they are neither concentrated in an authoritarian elite, nor left in an anarchic state wherein some can gain increasing power without taking on additional responsibilities, while others are required to shoulder more responsibilities even as their power to influence events radically diminishes. Communitarian reforms aim to secure the support needed by citizens in their moral and intellectual development, and the power structures under which they have to live and work together (compare the reform focus of what has been termed 'dialogic communitarianism': Frazer and Lacey, 1993; and the radical agenda of 'dialogic democracy'; set out in Giddens, 1994).

It is clear that attempts to make citizens behave more responsibly cannot succeed if the prevailing power structures in society remain oppressive. Similarly, efforts to make power structures more open and participatory cannot renew community life if people do not take up the available opportunities in an informed or responsible manner. The two approaches must be carried out together, and organizations which provide the frameworks for most forms of human interaction – from schools and community associations, to businesses and state institutions – have a crucial role in implementing the necessary reforms.

We saw in Chapters 3 to 5 that communitarian citizenship is not just about the relationship between the state and those who fall under its jurisdiction, but about the support which all those with power and influence over the education, employment and protection of others should give. In terms of education, support must be given to develop students' abilities to assess the validity of knowledge claims; teach them to reflect on the nature of their common values, and acquire a habit of acting responsibly; and introduce them to sharing and exercising power with others for the common good. With work opportunities, support is to be given to develop workers' abilities to understand claims concerning the performance of their enterprise and how it can be improved, ensure that their needs and concerns are fully incorporated in defining the corporate objectives, and involve them as equal partners in shaping their organizations' decision-making processes. As for protection, support should be given to enable everyone to deliberate on what really constitutes a threat and what action can be taken to counter it, instil a strong sense of civic duty to oppose the threats to our common values, and ensure that no one is denied the opportunity to participate in determining how the power for collective protection is to be exercised.

The responsibility to bring about these changes must be carried out by every type of organization in the state, business and third sectors. As we saw in Chapters 6 to 8, in all sectors there are encouraging examples of where communitarian structures and policies are established extensively. The communitarian approach is helping to initiate reforms at local, national and global levels. People are turning away from contrived programmes under the banners of the Left or the Right, and looking for changes which can transform their lives for the better without resorting to more individualism, or risking the dangers of authoritarianism.

From Local to Global Reforms

Starting at the local level, we witness inclusive communities being built through the growing co-operation among state, business and community agencies which, until the late 1980s, have generally kept to their own activities. Now pioneering local authorities are assuming the role of community facilitators, developing their democratic basis to provide an inclusive framework for everyone in their locality to contribute to their common good. The approach of community politics, once confined to a small number of local councillors who sought to engage their constituents in ongoing discussions beyond superficial contact at canvassing time, is now recognized as good practice, not just for councillors, but for everyone acting on behalf of local authorities. Consequently, on the agenda for change considered by local authorities across the world, a prominent issue is how to promote genuine community involvement. In response to this, initiatives are being developed to decentralize power, establish neighbourhood and issue forums, and encourage as many people as possible – especially among those who are most disadvantaged and marginalized – to participate in shaping policies and practices that affect their lives. The commitment by world leaders at the Earth Summit in 1992 to promote the development of Local Agenda 21 has given this approach even greater impetus. Localities in every country are now monitored for progress on informing and involving local people in formulating a common agenda to enhance their quality of life in a global context in the twenty-first century. International networks of local authorities are helping to exchange practical experiences in the development of these mutually supportive local agendas.

In parallel with the work of local authorities, voluntary and community groups are becoming increasingly aware that they must not only give help to those in need, or campaign for their demands, but they must also engage those they set out to help in the very process of changing the conditions that have been so unfavourable to them. National associations in support of third-sector activities, as well as a new breed of advisers on social entrepreneurship, are advising local groups to act in accordance with the requirements of inclusive communities. The same applies to working with other groups and agencies in the locality. Instead of regarding their role as pushing their group's interests forward at the expense of others, they are learning to appreciate how, by identifying the common values they share and the common threats they face, they can work together to improve their local communities. In practice, this involves participation in local networks which help to formulate community-based strategies such as Local Agenda 21, subjecting their proposals to wider community scrutiny, and working with local authorities and businesses to develop long-term policies which all partners will take responsibility for implementing. This is shifting the focus from just providing services to people who cannot otherwise access those services, to building their capacity to secure those services for themselves in the future.

There is a clear communitarian trend towards wider inclusion. Increasing numbers of community centres, tenant forums and youth associations are looking to build on the relationships they have established with their own members to develop interaction with, not only other groups in neighbouring areas, but also groups in other countries. In Europe, for example, the European Commission (EC) has consistently supported exchange initiatives that nurture the growth of membership groups which cross national boundaries. Contrary to philosophical concerns raised about the exclusivity of group membership, what has been happening is that citizens are being offered opportunities to participate in a variety of groups which, because they cut across geographical and hierarchical boundaries, help them to develop their sense of belonging to a multiplicity of communities within the framework of an inclusive global community.

Against both authoritarian practices and individualist indifference, an increasing number of local groups are being formed to tackle problems which market forces have singularly failed to solve. Without conceding to blind nostalgia which yearns for the return of unchallengeable authority figures to dictate what is to be done, these groups are operating in an open and participatory manner to provide mediation between conflicting neighbours; advice and support for parents who are finding it difficult to cope on their own; care and a sense of security for children whose parents are failing to carry out their responsibilities; and community activities to help those young people who need to enhance their self-esteem.

Local partnerships between organizations from different sectors are also helping to improve education, work opportunities and protection for everyone. Schools and the wider community are learning to support each other more. The more schools engage in voluntary projects with local residents, councils and businesses, the more their students gain experience of working for common values that go beyond personal interests. Businesses are themselves being encouraged by business-led associations to reach out to local communities, not simply because of the impact this may have on their own economic interests, but also because they have a responsibility to contribute to the well-being of any area in which they operate. Through giving financial support and staff time to assist with community projects, providing mentoring opportunities for young people, and sharing expertise with local groups seeking to establish their own community enterprise, they are making a significant contribution to the economic development of local communities. In relation to the strengthening of collective protection, businesses, along with schools and local residents, are responding to the proposals of statutory agencies to participate in schemes which involve them in identifying and reducing health risks, criminal offences and environmental damage more thoroughly than ever before.

Moving beyond the local level, organizations are also looking increasingly towards building up regional structures that will serve to bridge local concerns and deliberations at the national level. Despite theoretical claims that the development of inclusive communities cannot take place on a large scale at the national level, the movement towards greater democratic involvement of local groups in the establishment of regional bodies makes it practically viable for local communities to deliberate on values and political priorities with other communities. This also requires those who hold power at the national level to take action to ensure that local communities can participate in a meaningful way in shaping new policies and practices. As was noted in Chapter 1, communitarian ideas are becoming widely discussed among influential politicians in the leading parties of most Western countries. Commentators are impressed by the emergence of communitarian themes on responsibility, democratic participation, vitality of community life, and respect for common values in the pronouncements of political figures in charge of government institutions in the UK, USA, France and Germany (Barnes, 1991; Phillips, 1993; Joas, 1994/5;

and Grant, 1995). This does not mean that politicians who make communitarian speeches would necessarily translate them into practical reforms. What is significant is the extent to which communitarian measures are advanced on the national political agenda. There are five areas in particular where communitarian influence on government action can be assessed. These are: commitment to inform and involve citizens in state activities; emphasis on the teaching of common values and corresponding responsibilities in schools; ending the exploitation of abstract rights by those who threaten the well-being of others; priority of addressing the insufficient opportunities for obtaining paid work by those in need; and moving from an individualist to a communitarian approach in working with other countries.

First, the communitarian model differentiates sharply between reforms which merely encourage citizens to complain about the lack of state responsiveness to their individual demands, and reforms which aim to develop citizens' rational, moral and political capacities by involving them in public affairs. It is therefore encouraging that, instead of superficial service 'charters' which confine citizens to the role of individualist consumers, there are now good prospects of power being decentralized to local and regional groups. More information pertinent to the formulation of government policies could be made widely accessible, enabling informed feedback to be developed by citizens. Decisions by non-elected government agencies could be subjected to greater public scrutiny, and perhaps to controls by locally elected representatives. The ability to experiment with local variations and innovations, within an explicit national framework, will in turn stimulate greater interest among the public as to the way that political power is being exercised.

Second, the debate about whether schools are better run privately or as part of the state system is rightly becoming as irrelevant as outmoded arguments about the inherent merits or defects of nationalizing/privatizing industries. The emphasis now is on how the government of the day is to carry out its duty in ensuring that common values and corresponding responsibilities are taught effectively in every school. There is a danger that a focus on teaching methods, especially in relation to basic literacy and numeracy skills, could overshadow the challenge to make character development central to the education of children. The latter requires a commitment to enable young people to learn through constructive team work, performing valuable community service of their choice, and questioning authority in a rational and responsible manner. It has to involve reforming the organization culture of schools, which concerns not just how teachers approach their jobs, but also how governors view their role in developing their schools as good models of inclusive communities.

Third, the fact that even in individualist countries such as the UK and USA, the government is taking firm action to restrain the influence of the tobacco industry is a positive sign that attempts to exploit abstract rights by those who threaten the well-being of others will increasingly not be tolerated. The invocation of rights to justify activities which threaten the well-being of others is a tool that has been left for too long in the hands of those who do not care about the harm they cause. A stand should be taken by the state on behalf of all citizens against corporations and individuals who think that their business strategies or personal lifestyle preferences should be immune from public intervention, even if they expose others to greater health risks or environmental degradation (see Donaldson and Werhane, 1983; Andre *et al.*, 1994). Whatever is found by independent research institutions under conditions of co-operative enquiry to endanger the well-being of others should be subjected to effective sanctions. This would be reflected by a distinct shift from concentrating public resources on curing problems when it is often already too late, to deploying preventative measures which may well restrict what individuals or companies might otherwise wish to do.

Some businesses may try to slide from a defence on the grounds of rights to one based on the economic contributions they make. After all, they maintain, the sale of destructive weapons, environmentally hostile products and disease-causing substances all help to generate revenue to pay taxes and keep many people employed. However, this line of argument can no more shield these industries from tighter legal restrictions than it can help to lift existing restrictions on the trade in cocaine and other harmful materials, regardless of how many people derive their income from it. What is important is not how much money people can make out of a particular trade, but whether that trade is morally as well as economically sustainable in providing employment opportunities. This takes us to the fourth area of national policies to be considered – namely, the urgent need to enable everyone who needs paid work to access it in a manner compatible with meeting the demands of parental responsibility. Both European and US governments now view unemployment, not as a by-product of the market system to be managed through welfare, but as a priority problem that seriously undermines community life for all. Increasing productivity must not be allowed to be used to make increasing numbers of people redundant. The state must work with economic partners in the business sector to integrate training and job-seeking support with the development of employees' abilities to meet changing market needs. This requires co-operation from the business community, and from other countries in formulating global economic policies.

This takes us to the final key area where the national government should be applying communitarian thinking. A move away from the highly counter-productive individualist approach in working with other countries is long overdue. Individualist zero-sum bargaining has hindered the development of transnational institutions. When most problems can be tackled within the framework of a nation-state, this may be a tolerable drawback, but in the face of rapid globalization, it must be superseded by communitarian co-operation. There are signs that all European governments may at last be ready to ensure that the common good of Europeans is not to be made subordinate to the exclusive interests of any single nation. The Fascist mentality of always defining one's national interest in terms of advantages gained over other nations has already led to two world wars, and must be eradicated for good. This needs to be reflected by greater democratization of institutions such as the European Parliament, and the development of intra-European projects with more extensive community participation. Similar considerations should be given to other continental political networks and, ultimately, to the United Nations, where radical reforms to strengthen its democratic accountabilities seem at last to be firmly on the international agenda.

National governments must take the lead in establishing a better global system for implementing communitarian reforms. They must not delay the implementation of the action points set out in the Copenhagen Declaration, which were agreed by 117 heads of state at the World Summit for Social Development in 1995. Since the 1970s the integration of Third World countries into the global economy has meant that established economic powers can increasingly undermine structures crucial to communitarian development. Instead of moving closer to what communitarian citizenship requires, the supportive conditions for education, work and protection have been eroded, on the basis that individuals should not look to state or society for these conditions, but rather to the marketplace to meet their needs. Meanwhile, the global marketplace ensures that, for the economically weak, employment goes to those who will take the lowest wages and work in the most unsafe conditions; military support through the arms trade is given to those regimes prepared to keep their citizens politically weak in compliance with the wishes of the market ideologues; and growing job insecurity among workers in general undermines their readiness to campaign for changes that would displease their paymasters.

The top priority for the future is international support for those in the weakest economic positions across the world. National debts to rich countries should be written off if the debtor countries agree to drastic reductions in their governments' military spending. Resources must be channelled instead into the social and economic infrastructure to enable the development of genuine forms of citizen participation in state, business and third-sector institutions. Authoritarian regimes, regardless of their willingness to work with the global economic establishment, must abandon the use of torture and intimidation to make their citizens submissive to external demands, or face economic sanctions.

So long as the economically most vulnerable are there for powerful businesses to exploit, all attempts to improve economic management and environmentally sensitive production will be subverted by businesses shifting their resources to places where there will be neither state control nor social pressure to make improvements. It is clear, for example, that if only a handful of employers in nineteenth-century Britain had adopted more humane employment practices when all others continued to undercut them, those few would have been forced out of business, and all workers would have gone on suffering. It was only because the enlightened practices of the few were linked to wider actions which led to regulations applied to all employers, that everyone gained. The gain of the employees meant that, in the longer term, employers also gained from their workers' increase in skills, confidence and purchasing power. Yet without co-ordinated action across the whole country, short-term greed would have presented everyone from gaining access to such a virtuous circle.

Globalization has meant that we are facing a re-run of the nineteenth-century experience. What Britain and other countries gained during that century is now at risk of being wiped away by business powers which might evade the controls established for the common good. These powers are determined to prevent such controls from being established on a global level, and they do so by invoking individualist arguments to suppose that the world's quality of life could only be improved by the competitiveness borne of an increasingly deregulated market system. In reality, the obsession with maintaining a low-waged, 'flexible' labour market has only forced the most disadvantaged in society to suffer even more in countries such as the UK, USA and New Zealand, and is putting pressure on France, Germany, and other European countries to do the same. But a descent in that direction is not inevitable. National governments can secure international agreements on working conditions to reverse the slide, and bring everyone up to a better standard.

In an interesting parallel with Britain's situation in the nineteenth century, national governments in the late 1990s are finding that they are not without support from enlightened business leaders in meeting the challenge of building inclusive communities in place of individualist competition (Cooke and Morgan, 1991; Kay, 1993; and Moore, 1996). The business sector has provided many fine examples of how community life can thrive in the midst of commercial pressures and organizational demands. The key is to develop inclusive power structures and enable all those affected – often termed the 'stakeholders' – to participate fully in those structures. As was seen in Chapter 7, the RSA report demonstrated that many companies steeped in the Anglo-American business culture regard the communitarian approach as being vital to the future success of their enterprise (RSA Inquiry, 1995).

The communitarian model exposes the weaknesses of arguments against the likelihood of the business sector playing a key part in developing inclusive communities. These arguments seek to suggest that turning the workplace into a 'cosy' community is neither feasible, nor indeed desirable. But the essence of inclusive community life has nothing to do with turning business relationships into idealized forms of neighbourliness. It has to do with the distribution of power and responsibility so that all those who work in a business understand that it is their duty to work for the good of all, whatever their personal feelings about one another individually. It is this approach, as we have seen, that has sustained the growth of companies such as the John Lewis Partnership and the Co-operative Bank, and which can be adopted by others to secure greater competitiveness. It is not by preaching the virtues of compassion that such a business culture is developed, but by explicating why and how the conditions of inclusive community should be secured for social *and* economic reasons that business leaders, worker representatives and government departments can be persuaded of the importance of establishing new working conditions and decision-making procedures.

From small businesses such as the Dorset-based food and drinks distribution company, DPP, where authoritarian management has been replaced gradually by communitarian practices, to large corporations such as the Body Shop, which places mutual responsibility and open participation at the heart of its management philosophy, the number of companies actively supporting government initiatives to build a global framework for inclusive communities is increasing. As David Wheeler and Maria Sillanpaa observed in their wide-ranging study of this emerging management approach, it can be traced back directly to the ideas and practices of reformists such as Robert Owen and his communitarian followers (Wheeler and Sillanpaa, 1997, ch. 7).

What is adding to the momentum of communitarian reforms as the twenty-first century approaches is the realization of the strength that interdependence can bring. Reforms of state institutions, businesses, and voluntary and community groups are no longer pigeonholed into distinct compartments labelled politics, management, and community issues, but are seen as being interrelated strands which should be co-ordinated in accordance with an overall vision. Where politicians and business leaders are not doing enough to move the necessary reforms forward, the challenge for the third sector is not to retreat towards a self-sufficient enclave, but to play its part in engaging the others in revitalizing the reform movement.

One of the key tasks is to apply the lesson of communitarian co-operation to bringing fragmented groups together. The proliferation of single-issue pressure groups is not in itself a sign that community life is being restored. On the contrary, unless groups learn to appreciate the common values they share with others, their determination to pursue their objectives whatever others in society might think could seriously damage the prospects of inclusive communities being realized. The informal networks which exist among communitarian-minded groups need to be strengthened into effective decision-making structures. Attempts to influence educative organizations, to train their trainers and teachers, and to co-ordinate progress across traditionally compartmentalized sectors, need to be planned and implemented carefully.

Community groups should focus on developing their capacity to cultivate long-term alliances, establish coalition opportunities, and target common barriers which diverse groups can contribute towards overthrowing. There are all too many institutional interests, traditional prejudices and selfish desires that stand in the way of the redistribution of power and responsibility. In recognition of the magnitude of these obstacles, different groups must work on a united front. While particular groups should concentrate on delivering what they are set up to do, where they cannot achieve the greater impact that only an organized alliance can achieve, they must give their support to a broader organization. There are signs that this approach is becoming more widespread. For example, the UK witnessed in the mid-1990s a series of coalition-building exercises by voluntary and campaigning organizations, such as the launch of *The Real World Coalition* (Jacobs, 1996), and *The Citizens' Agenda* (Tam, 1995a). At the global level, we have seen the publication of *Our Global Neighbourhood* (Commission on Global Governance, 1995). What they have in common is not just their appreciation of communitarian thinking as an alternative to individualism and authoritarianism, but also their commitment to bring a wide range of individuals and organizations to work together on a permanent basis to press for changes in attitudes and practices.

Unity is particularly important in breaking down the barriers to communicating the need for communitarian reforms. Communitarians have not succeeded in the past in articulating their alternative vision very effectively, and this has meant that the ideas of one or two well-known academics have been taken as representing the whole of the communitarian tradition, therefore distorting public understanding of communitarianism itself. The situation has not been helped by a media culture that adores simplistic soundbites and polarizes debates into misconceived dichotomies. It is not surprising that the many examples of communitarian practices discussed in earlier chapters of this book are rarely covered. Instead, we are surrounded by the same old stale debates about 'traditional' (that is, authoritarian) versus 'progressive' (that is, individualist) teaching; individualist market processes versus authoritarian union interventions; or the threat of an expanded authoritarian state sector versus the dangers of the individualist call for a reduced state sector. The problem is compounded by the fact that many in the media are so immersed in relativist thinking that they simply cannot appreciate any social philosophy wishing to counter threats against vulnerable people by invoking common values that make such threats morally intolerable. Some developments in the third sector, however, are helping to open up new channels to explain the need for communitarian reforms. Community-based networks are starting to take greater advantage of cable television and Internet facilities to draw people's attention to reform opportunities the established media consider uninteresting. Community newspapers and local radio networks are also being developed to enable citizens who do not have easy access to computer terminals to learn about public issues affecting them, and how they can participate to make a difference to their communities. Past suspicions about the utilization of communications techniques are giving way to a realistic appraisal of how such techniques can help to raise awareness and understanding of issues that might otherwise be neglected. After all, social marketers have successfully applied communications techniques to achieve socially desirable objectives. These have ranged from alerting the public to the dangers of alcohol consumption, unsafe sex and smoking, to publicize training and employment opportunities; give healthy eating advice; and advise about complaints procedures for public services (Tam, 1994b, pt D).

Ultimately, however, the third sector cannot rely on its own communications channels alone to counter the weight of what the established media produce. Opinion formers in the media need to be briefed on the objective of building inclusive communities and how this contrasts with other kinds of social and political thinking. Apart from distinguishing it from individualist and authoritarian ideas, it is very important to ensure that communitarianism is not projected as sitting somewhere between the two. There is simply no middle ground where a mixture of watered-down individualism and authoritarianism can give rise to communitarian ideas. Communitarianism should be seen as the true opposite of authoritarianism, with individualism being a sceptical middle ground that leaves individuals to find solutions to their problems.

Furthermore, the media themselves should be assisted in learning to apply communitarian ideas to their own practices. In most Western countries, the media already play a key role in checking authoritarian tendencies in society. However, they have on the whole become stuck in the individualist position, and have a long way to go if they are to progress into exemplifying co-operative enquiry in their work. Instead of maintaining the stultifying approach of presenting every major issue in society by inviting two people to express uncompromisingly opposite viewpoints, the media should consider how they can contribute to a new culture of deliberative discussion. Readers, listeners and viewers should all be encouraged to participate, not in putting forward their unreflective views, but rather in learning about the relevant facts and ideas connected with an issue, reviewing their own beliefs, discussing their opinions with each other openly, and coming to a consensus conclusion about the position they are to adopt (Fishkin, 1991).

Communitarian Faith

As can be seen from the interrelated reforms which apply from the local to the global level, the success of communitarianism is dependent not so much on its adoption by any single political party, but on its serving as a common framework for people who would not otherwise have a unifying agenda under which to work for reform. Among conservatives, socialists, liberals, feminists, environmentalists, anti-racists, Christians, Muslims, Buddhists, and numerous other faiths and groups, there are those who reject the view that they must either be authoritarian or individualist in their approach to social and political reforms. For them, the communitarian agenda offers a way to co-operate with others and develop policies to improve community life for all. Of course, they may still have differences that are significant to them, but in spite of those differences they can work together to support their common values.

This does not mean that, in place of all the oppressive structures and fragmented communities, inclusive communities will within a few years be built in every sphere and at every level of human existence. There is no guarantee that the spread of communitarian thinking and practices will continue with sufficient speed or extensiveness. History has taught us that every form of human progress can be reversed by folly or the determined opposition of those who want to maintain their domination over others. What communitarians have to rely on to overcome the hurdles in front of them is the effective use of reform instruments ranging from the teaching and disseminating of best practice examples, through the use of publicity, lobbying, and peer group pressure, to using legislative power to bring about changes directly. Only when political power is concentrated in the hands of a dictatorial regime should reform tactics give way to revolutionary measures. However, it should be remembered that inclusive communities do not simply emerge from the demolition of oppressive power structures; they have to rely on the development of inclusive power relations and responsible citizenship. Revolutionaries, who call for the overthrow of existing structures and practices, may claim to offer the imminent prospect of a brave new dawn. In reality, unless they acknowledge common values, and anticipate how they would be supported after the revolution, a new breed of oppressors would inevitably rise from the ashes of the old regime. It could be argued that all too often there is just not enough time to work out how a new regime would function, and drastic action has to be taken if there is to be any hope for a change. For the people across the world who are suffering from the tightening squeeze of authoritarian power domination, on the one hand, and the free fall of health and education spending in the individualist global market championed by the likes of the IMF, on the other, the waiting has gone on for far too long already. If the squeeze is relatively less painful in Western market democracies, it does not in any way make the plight of people in other parts of the global community any more tolerable.

It is precisely because this situation has to be taken seriously that people need an approach in which they can place their faith. After centuries of struggle against oppression and injustice, it is at least clear what they *cannot* put their faith in. It cannot be put in the 'invisible hand' of the market individualists, or in any form of authoritarian guarantee, whether it is couched in terms of a pseudo-scientific interpretation of the historical dialectic, or in the pronouncement of some self-styled interpreter of divine messages. And it certainly cannot be put in any movement that is keen to destroy what now exists insisting that what will take its place will be dealt with by the few who constitute the revolutionary elite.

From a communitarian point of view, the validation of what should be valued and pursued rests with the ongoing reviews conducted under conditions of co-operative enquiry. This presents people with a set of common values, and to accept these values is to believe in their realization as the overriding objective of life. To remove the barriers to people attaining love, wisdom, justice and fulfilment, and promote practices developed with citizen participation to increase opportunities for their realization, would provide common aims in the action to be taken. To embrace this as the pointer for moral direction is to have faith in the ideal of inclusive community. It is faith in the meaning of life which human existence has the potential to generate, and in the power human beings can bring together to achieve it.

This faith is not to be confused with what is sometimes described as the 'positivistic' faith in progress. According to the latter, people's common values will be realized progressively through the enlightened actions of individuals and organizations. Communitarians, by contrast, are deeply concerned that there is no such natural progression in life. The ascendancy of free market individualism has shown most disturbingly that efforts to build communities of mutually caring citizens can be undermined radically by those who are determined to break down communitarian structures and provisions. What communitarians do have faith in is the possibility of building inclusive communities through the combined efforts of individuals. For some, this faith may need to be underpinned further by membership of some form of organized religion, and provided this is not interpreted by those concerned as the only correct way to have faith, it would not be incompatible with communitarianism. For others, what makes it possible for them to maintain their faith might be their particular world views, which may be shaped by, for example, a Buddhist interpretation of the nature of experiences, a Confucian cultural background, or a humanist commitment to moral development. The only obstruction to the sharing of a common faith would be the dogmatic insistence that co-operation is not to be extended to people who partake in that faith for different cultural or theological reasons.

On the above understanding, it is not the loss of faith in any particular religion, but the inability to sustain one's faith in pursuing the ideal of inclusive communities, which contributes to the deterioration of community life. If people's beliefs in the doctrines of a particular religion help them to strengthen their resolve to promote the realization of common values, then those beliefs are to be welcomed. However, if a religion commands its adherents to reject the principles of co-operative enquiry, mutual responsibility and citizen participation, because they are not specifically derived from the central texts on which it is based, it would be better if that religion had little influence.

What is important is a sense of deep commitment to the cause of building inclusive communities. It can be described as a spiritual or religious impulse, but it does not have to be connected to any particular organized religion. Philosophers such as John Macmurray, Emmanuel Mounier and Martin Buber have drawn on different religious traditions to describe the faith which supports their work on strengthening community life (Macmurray, 1932, 1941; Mounier, 1952; and Buber, 1970). On the other hand, thinkers as diverse as John Dewey and Albert Camus have observed how people can have a very strong faith and devote themselves to common values, without subscribing to any organized religion or theological doctrine (Dewey, 1962; Camus, 1960 and 1971). This is not to suggest that a belief in the divine is not necessary for reforming the world. For some people it is necessary to conceptualize their understanding of what gives their lives meaning in terms of a divine entity. For others, even if 'divine' is the term used to describe the highest order of moral perfection, it is still a term best expressed through discourse that does not invoke the existence of any supernatural being.

It could be argued that here lies a weakness of communitarian faith, because it does not have the backing of a divine guarantee affirming that the Kingdom of God will be realized. Whereas the followers of an organized religion can act on the assumption that the project they support will be completed by the most supreme Being, communitarianism in itself offers no such guarantee. This means that, however strong their faith, communitarians must acknowledge that their attempts at reform may not ever lead to a fully communitarian global community of inclusive communities. Yet this is a faith grounded on what is experienced, rather than on beliefs about what will definitely happen in the future. It is not unknown for people who lose their religious faith to slip into a moral crisis about how they should live, since up to the point of their loss they had judged themselves with reference to a divine plan that would be realized at some time in the future. For communitarians, however, actions for reform are not pursued because there is some absolute guarantee that they will lead to the complete transformation of the world; they are adopted only because they are the options validated by co-operative enquiries on the basis of the experiences people have already had up to that time.

Having faith in communitarian reforms could be dismissed as complacent were it not for two factors. First, there is the recognition that no individual or group can legislate for all time, thus it is always possible to revise action plans in the light of experiences in the future. After all, communitarianism places considerable emphasis on the importance of continuous learning through community deliberations. Second, reflections on historical experience suggest that actions flowing from communitarian ideas do help to secure improvements and break down barriers.

Following the initial phase of the development of communitarian ideas by Aristotle and his students, each of the successive key phases (see Chapter 1) has witnessed the application of communitarian thinking to effective social and political actions. During the seventeenth and eighteenth centuries, the Baconian model of co-operative research communities inspired a growing number of demands to subject more and more types of knowledge claims to the test of co-operative enquiry (Gay, 1970). At first, these focused on establishing open channels of enquiry for people who had previously carried out their scientific studies in isolation from each other. Then they put pressures on institutional barriers which prevented interested citizens from participating in moral and political discussions that affected their lives. At one level the French Revolution represented the culmination of the pressures to remove the then prevailing barriers to the development of inclusive communities (Schama, 1989). However, its authoritarian turn under the Jacobins not only destroyed its potential for greater achievements, it also gave enemies of the movement the ammunition to mount their campaigns to block its non-authoritarian development across Europe.

During the nineteenth century, a new generation of thinkers who were all too aware of the authoritarian failings of the French Revolution, put forward practical reform models that explicitly ruled out the concentration of power in the hands of a few individuals. Under the influence of communitarian advocates such as Robert Owen and Charles Fourier, and J. S. Mill, who injected a strong communitarian dimension to the liberal reform agenda, the nineteenth century witnessed pressures to give better protection to workers and children; the development of local self-help groups; the launch of national co-operative enterprises; a growing interest in providing a moral education for all; recognition of the oppressive subjection of women to those with the power to abuse them; and the introduction of decentralized, democratically-elected and community-based local authorities (Bowle, 1954).

Towards the end of the nineteenth century, however, political opinion became increasingly polarized between Spencerian individualism and Marxist authoritarianism. The former's obsession with the ideal of the free market encouraged powerful individuals to ignore the plight of weak individuals and exploit their feeble bargaining positions. Marxism devoted itself to attacking gradualist community-based reforms, and fuelled passion for another revolutionary dictatorship, which not only brought lasting oppression to the people of Russia, but also deliberately provoked the rise of Fascist authoritarianism in Italy and Germany. In reaction against these trends, communitarian thinkers such as Hobhouse, Dewey and Durkheim, advocated reforms throughout the early twentieth century, and helped to develop the role of the state in promoting equal citizenship, the role of educational institutions in improving citizenship skills of the young, and the role of organizations in providing new forms of community interaction (Lukes, 1973; Freeden, 1986; Kloppenberg, 1986; and Ryan, 1995).

The advocacy of communitarian reforms therefore has a long history of achievements which supports our faith in their ability to secure a better community life for all in the years to come. Only those who write about communitarian ideas as if they had just been invented could seriously doubt whether they would have any long-term impact, but it is their historically misguided perspective which should be questioned. However, this does not mean that people sympathetic to communitarian thinking can wait complacently for progress to take place without themselves acting on reform opportunities. We only have to look at the powerful resurgence of individualism in the second half of the twentieth century. Now as the twenty-first century approaches, we must combine our faith in communitarian ideas that have inspired progressive changes in the past with a renewed commitment to act for the sake of our common future.

The embrace by politicians of the language of community and responsibility must in future be cross-checked with any action they take in support of the building of inclusive communities. In the UK, USA and other English-speaking countries which have been particularly immersed in the politics of market individualism, priority should be given to removing the grip of marketization on policy-making in governments. This means that social policies should no longer be made to serve the economy under misleadingly narrow indicators, but economic policies should be directed towards meeting social objectives which give central importance to the responsible upbringing of children, citizenship education, and meaningful access to paid work and protection. It also means that governments in these countries should seek to end the spreading of the market individualist culture to other countries through the global network of financial institutions and management advisers. In the poorer countries in particular, enough damage has already been done to destroy social protection and stable community life for the sake of generating trade to meet the demands of the rich nations. Among continental European countries, the challenge is to stand firm against the untenable (but none the less ideologically powerful) view that Anglo-American-style individualism generates better social and economic results. The governments in these countries should apply themselves to developing communitarian practices more extensively, and demonstrate their commitment to promoting the greater involvement of citizens in improving their state, business and third sectors, through reforms of their own structures, and by strengthening the educative, employment and protective support for all their citizens. There is scope to cut down authoritarian tendencies which still prevent citizens from having an understanding of, let alone the opportunity to deliberate with others, and influence decisions that affect their lives. The shortcomings of the market system do not imply that politicians and state officials should be allowed to concentrate power in themselves at the national or European level.

As for non-Western countries, the myth that authoritarian leadership is required to guard against the corrupting influences of Western individualism must be exposed once and for all. It is true that the individualist culture can be highly corrosive of community life, but authoritarianism does not provide a viable alternative either. Among countries with a democratic electoral system, such as Japan and India, corruptive influences are more likely to be found where power structures are still inherently authoritarian, as in the organization of their established political parties. The best hope for building inclusive communities would be by reforming the systems through which the ruling elite secure their power. And for those countries which are still fundamentally authoritarian in their social and political systems, the communitarian agenda offers reformists a rallying point that cannot be dismissed as individualist in orientation. Furthermore, just as communitarians in Europe and America draw on different backgrounds and traditions to sustain their faith in the ideal of inclusive community, people in Asia, the Middle East and Africa have no reason to feel that such an ideal is an exclusively Western notion that cannot be expressed in terms of their own culture. Furthermore, the common values identified as underlying the inclusive community ideal are by no means values that feature only in the lives of Western people.

One of the most enduring legacies of the 1989 revolutions may turn out to be the final resolution of the dilemma left us by Friedrich Nietzsche in the late nineteenth century: he claimed that we must either follow some unquestionable authority and live the life we are told to live, or throw authority aside completely and each of us decide the way we want to live (Nietzsche, 1972, 1988). There can be no doubt that the rejection of authoritarian rule by the people of Eastern Europe and the former Soviet Union should be repeated with all other political regimes and fundamentalist groups which still strive to force others to comply with their demands, when these have no co-operative validation. But this should not lead to the embrace of the free market utopia of individualists, which in practice brings with it the relentless division of communities into the economically powerful and those who live in perpetual insecurity. The key to overcoming this dilemma rests with all citizens, with our commitment to live authentically by the faith we place in our common values, and thus to play our part in the building of inclusive communities.

Bibliography

Almond, B. (ed.) (1995) *Introducing Applied Ethics*, Oxford, Blackwell.

Anderson, V. (1991) *Alternative Economic Indicators*, London, Routledge.

Andre, C., M. Velasquez and T. Mazur (1994) 'Voluntary Health Risks: Who Should Pay?', *The Responsive Community*, vol. 4, no. 2, Spring.

Aristotle (1966) *Ethics*, Harmondsworth, Penguin.

Aristotle (1987) *Politics*, Harmondsworth, Penguin.

Avineri, S. and A. de-Shalit (eds) (1992) *Communitarianism and Individualism*, Oxford University Press.

Bacon, F. (1905) *The Philosophical Works* (edited J. M. Robertson from the texts, trans. Ellis and Spedding), London, George Routledge & Sons.

Ball, J. (1995) 'Agenda for a Political Discussion', *Management Today*, London, Management Publications, November.

Barber, B. (1975) 'Justifying Justice: Problems of Psychology, Politics and Measurement in Rawls', in N. Daniels (1975).

Barber, B. (1984) *Strong Democracy: Participatory Politics for a New Age*, University of California Press.

Barber, B. (1992) 'Opinion Polls: Public Judgement or Private Prejudice', *The Responsive Community*, vol. 2, no. 2, Spring.

Barber, B. (1995) *Jihad versus McWorld*, New York, Times Books.

Barker, E. (1906) *The Political Thought of Plato and Aristotle*, London, Methuen.

Barnes, J. A. (1991) 'The New Guru of Communitarianism', *National Journal*, 30 November.

Baxter, S. (1995) 'I Am the Way, I Am the Truth', *Sunday Times*, 19 March.

Bayer, R. (1995) 'AIDS Prevention vs. Cultural Sensitivity', *The Responsive Community*, vol. 6, no. 1, Winter.

Beehler, R. (1978) *Moral Life*, Oxford, Basil Blackwell.

Beetham, D. (1993) 'Liberal Democracy and the Limits of Democratization', in D. Held (1993).

Bell, D. (1993) *Communitarianism and Its Critics*, Oxford University Press.

Bell, D. (1995) 'Residential Community Associations: Community or Disunity?', *The Responsive Community*, vol. 5, no. 4, Fall.

Bell, M. and M. McGinn (1990) 'Naturalism and Scepticism', *Philosophy*, October.

Bellah, R. N. (1995/96) 'Community Properly Understood', *The Responsive Community*, vol. 6, no. 1, Winter.

Benn, S. I. (1979) 'Problematic Rationality of Political Participation', in P. Laslet and J. Fishkin (eds), *Philosophy, Politics and Society*, (5th series), Oxford, Basil Blackwell.

Berkley, J. B. (1996) 'Involuntary Manslaughter', in *The Whistle*, vol. IV, no. 10, April.

Berlin, I. (1969) *Four Essays on Liberty*, Oxford University Press.

Bestor, A. E. (1950) *Backwoods Utopias, the Sectarian and Owenite Phases of Communitarian Socialism in America, 1663–1829*, Pennsylvania Press.

Bloor, D. (1976) *Knowledge and Social Imagery*, London, Routledge and Kegan Paul.

Bonner, A. (1961) *British Co-operation*, Manchester, Co-operative Union.

Bosanquet, N. (1989) *After the New Right*, Aldershot, Dartmouth.

Boswell, J. (1994) *Community and the Economy: The Theory of Public Co-operation*, London, Routledge.

Bowle, J. (1954) *Politics and Opinion in the 19th Century*, London, Jonathan Cape.

Boyte, H., B. Barber and W. Marshall (1994) *Civic Declaration: A Call for a New Citizenship*, Dayton, Ohio, Kettering Foundation.

Bracher, K. D. (1978) *The German Dictatorship*, Harmondsworth, Penguin.

Braybrooke, D. (1987) *Meeting Needs*, Princeton, NJ., Princeton University Press.

Brigley, S. (1994) *Walking the Tightrope: A Survey of Ethics in Management*, Corby, Northants, The Institute of Management.

Browne, C. (1996) 'Reclaiming the Streets: Transatlantic Partners Against Crime', *Crime Prevention News*, Home Office Communication Directorate, April–June.

Buber, M. (1970) *I and Thou*, New York, Charles Scribner and Sons.

Bulmer, M. and A. M. Rees (eds) (1996) *Citizenship Today*, London, UCL Press.

Butcher, H., A. Glen, P. Henderson and J. Smith (eds) (1993) *Community and Public Policy*, London, Pluto Press.

Campbell, J. (1995) *Understanding John Dewey*, La Salle, Illinois, Open Court Publishing.

Camus, A. (1960) *The Plague*, Harmondsworth, Penguin.

Camus, A. (1971) *The Rebel*, Harmondsworth, Penguin.

Carr, A. (1968) in 'Is Business Bluffing Ethical?', in T. Donaldson and P. H. Werhane (1983).

Chaplin, J. (1996) 'Subsidiarity: The Concept and the Connections', Paper presented at a conference, *Subsidiarity and Communitarianism: Concrete Implications*, Cambridge, 13–14 December.

Chomsky, N. 1994) *World Order, Old and New*, London, Pluto Press.

Cladis, M. S. (1992) *A Communitarian Defense of Liberalism: Emile Durkheim and Contemporary Social Theory*, Stanford, Calif., Stanford University Press.

Clarke, R. (ed.) (1990) *Enterprising Neighbours: The Development of the Community Association Movement in Britain*, London, NFCO.

Close, F. P. (1993/94) 'The Case for Moral Education', *Responsive Community*, vol. 4, no. 1, Winter.

Coenen, H. and P. Leisink (1993) *Work and Citizenship in the New Europe*, Aldershot, Edward Elgar.

Cohen, J. and J. Rogers (1995) 'Secondary Associations and Democratic Governance', in E. O. Wright (ed.) (1995).

Cohen, L. J. (1954) *The Principles of World Citizenship*, Oxford, Basil Blackwell.

Cohen, L. J. (1977) *The Probable and the Provable*, Oxford, Clarendon Press.

Cohen, N. (1995) 'Communitarianism: A Quick Guide', *Independent on Sunday*, 5 February.

Collini, S. (1979) *Liberalism and Sociology: L. T. Hobhouse and Political Argument in England 1880–1914*, Cambridge University Press.

Commission on Global Governance (1995) *Our Global Neighbourhood*, Oxford University Press.

Conradi, P. 'State Sell-offs: One Bright Spot in Troubled Russian Economy', *The European*, 5–11 August.

Cooke, P. and K. Morgan (1991) *The Network Paradigm: New Departures in Corporate and Regional Development*, Cardiff, Regional Industrial Research.

Cooper, J. M. (1986) *Reason and Human Good in Aristotle*, Indianapolis, Ind., Hackett.

Cooperative Bank (1996) *Ethical Policy*, Manchester, Cooperative Bank.

Coquillette, D. R. (1992) *Francis Bacon*, Edinburgh University Press.

Crewe, I. (1997) 'Presentation of Research Findings', in P. Phillips (ed.), *Citizenship and Civic Education*, London, The Citizenship Foundation.

Crouch, C. and D. Marquand (1995) *Reinventing Collective Action*, Oxford, Basil Blackwell.

Culpitt, I. (1992) *Welfare and Citizenship*, London, Sage.

Dahrendorf, R. (1995) 'A Precarious Balance: Economic Opportunity, Civil Society, and Political Liberty', *The Responsive Community*, vol. 5, no. 3, Summer.

Dalton, R. J. (1988) *Citizen Politics in Western Democracies*, Chatham, NJ., Chatham House.

Dancy, J. (1985) *Introduction to Contemporary Epistemology*, Oxford, Basil Blackwell.

Daniels, N. (ed.) (1975) *Reading Rawls*, Oxford, Basil Blackwell.

D'Antonio, M. (1996) 'A High-Rise Village', *The Responsive Community*, vol. 6, no. 4, Fall.

Davies, H. (1994) 'The City and the Manufacturing Industry', *Business Ethics: A European Review*, vol. 3, no. 2, April.

De George, R. T. (1993) *Competing with Integrity in International Business*, Oxford University Press.

Dehn, G. (1994) 'Public Concern at Work', *Business Ethics: A European Review*, vol. 3, no. 4, October.

Demaine, J. and H. Entwistle (eds) (1996) *Beyond Communitarianism: Citizenship, Politics and Education*, London, Macmillan.

Dennis, N. and A. H. Halsey (1988) *English Ethical Socialism*, Oxford, Clarendon Press.

Derber, C. (1994) 'Communitarian Economics', *The Responsive Community*, vol. 4, no. 4, Fall.

Dewey, J. (1930) *The Quest for Certainty*, London, George Allen & Unwin.

Dewey, J. (1939) *Liberalism and Social Action*, reprinted in J. Ratner (ed.) *Intelligence in the Modern World: John Dewey's Philosophy*, New York, Random House.

Dewey, J. (1958) *Experience and Nature*, New York, Dover Publications.
Dewey, J. (1962) *A Common Faith*, New Haven, Conn., Yale University Press.
Dewey, J. (1963) *Experience and Education*, New York, Collier Books.
Dewey, J. (1966) *Democracy and Education*, New York, Free Press.
Dewey, J. (1973) *Lectures in China 1919–1920*, trans. and ed. by R. W. Clopton and Tsuin-Chen, Ou, Honolulu, University Press of Hawaii.
Dewey, J. (1991) *The Public and Its Problems*, Athens, Ohio, Ohio University Press.
Donaldson, T. and P. H. Werhane (ed.) (1983) *Ethical Issues in Business*, Englewood Cliffs, NJ., Prentice-Hall.
Donnison, D. (1991) *A Radical Agenda: After the New Right and the Old Left*, London, Rivers Oram Press.
Douglass, R. B. (1994) 'The Renewal of Democracy and the Communitarian Prospect', *The Responsive Community*, vol. 4, issue 3, Summer.
Doyal, L. and I. Gough (1991) *A Theory of Human Need*, London, Macmillan.
Dreyfus, H. L. and P. Rabinow (1982) *Michel Focault: Beyond Structuralism and Hermeneutics*, Brighton, Harvester Press.
Drucker, P. F. (1988) *The Effective Executive*, Oxford, Butterworth–Heinemann.
Drucker, P. F. (1993) *Post-capitalist Society*, Oxford, Butterworth–Heinemann.
Duff, A. (1996) 'Punishment, Citizenship and Responsibility', in H. Tam (ed.) (1996a).
Durkheim, E. (1957) *Professional Ethics and Civic Morals*, London, Routledge & Kegan Paul.
Durkheim, E. (1961) *Moral Education*, trans. E. K. Wilson and H. Schnurer, New York, Free Press of Glencoe.
Durkheim, E. (1984) *The Division of Labour in Society*, London, Macmillan.
Eco, U. (1995) 'Pointing a Finger at the Fascists', *Guardian*, 19 August.
Economist Report (1995) 'The Politics of Restoration', *The Economist*, 24 December – 6 January.
Economist Report (1997) 'The Worker and the Volunteer', *The Economist*, 26 April.
Ekins, P. (1992) *A New World Order: Grassroots Movements for Global Changes*, London, Routledge.
Entwistle, H. (1996) 'Knowledge of Most Worth to Citizens', in Demaine and Entwistle (1996).
Etzioni, A. (1995a) 'Common Values', *New Statesman and Society*, 12 May.
Etzioni, A. (1995b) *The Spirit of Community*, London, Fontana.
Etzioni, A. (1997) *The New Golden Rule: Community and Morality in a Democratic Society*, New York, Basic Books.
European Foundation for the Improvement of Living and Working Conditions (1993) *Local Community Action and Social Policy, Luxembourg*, Office for Official Publications of the European Communities.
Feyerabend, P. (1975) 'How to Defend Society Against Science', *Radical Philosophy*, vol. 2 Summer.

Feyerabend, P. (1977) *Against Method*, London, New Left Books.
Fishkin, J. (1991) *Democracy and Deliberation*, New Haven, Conn., Yale University Press.
Fogelin, R. (1976) *Wittgenstein*, London, Routledge & Kegan Paul.
Fogelman, K. (1996) 'Education for Citizenship and the National Curriculum', in Demaine and Entwistle (1996).
Foucault, M. (1979) *Discipline and Punish: The Birth of the Prison*, New York, Vintage/Random House.
Frazer, E. and N. Lacey (1993) *The Politics of Community: A Feminist Critique of the Liberal–Communitarian Debate*, Hemel Hempstead, Harvester Wheatsheaf.
Freeden, M. (1986) *The New Liberalism: An Ideology of Social Reform*, Oxford, Clarendon Press.
Friedan, B. (1996) 'To Transcend Identity Politics', *The Responsive Community*, vol. 6, no. 2, Spring.
Friedman, Milton (1962) *Capitalism and Freedom*, University of Chicago Press.
Friedman, Marilyn (1989) 'Feminism and Modern Friendship: Dislocating the Community', *Ethics*, vol. 99, no. 2 January.
Fukuyama, F. (1992) *The End of History and the Last Man*, London, Hamish Hamilton.
Fullinwider, R. K. (1995) 'Citizenship, Individualism, and Democratic Politics', *Ethics*, vol. 105, no. 3.
Galindo, M. A. and J. Perez-Adan (1996) *The Spanish Communitarian Agenda*, Paper presented at the Communitarian Summit, Geneva, July 12–14.
Galston, W. (1990/91) 'A Liberal-Democratic Case for the Two-Parent Family', *The Responsive Community*, vol. 1, no. 1, Winter.
Galston, W. (1991) *Liberal Purposes: Goods, Virtues, and Diversity in the Liberal State*, Cambridge University Press.
Garforth, F. W. (1980) *Educative Democracy: John Stuart Mill on Education in Society*, Oxford University Press.
Gaster, L. (1996) 'Quality Services in Local Government: A Bottom-up Approach', *Journal of Management Development*, vol. 15, no. 2, pp. 80–96.
Gay, P. (1970) *The Enlightenment: An Interpretation*, 2 vols, London, Wildwood House.
Gellner, E. (1983) 'Relativism and Universals', in M. Hollis and S. Lukes (1983).
Gellner, E. (1995) 'On Isiah Berlin', *Prospect*, November.
Gellner, E. (1996) *Conditions of Liberty: Civil Society and Its Rivals*, Harmondsworth, Penguin.
Gibson, S. (1995) 'Reasons for Having Children: Ends, Means and "Family Values"', *Journal of Applied Philosophy*, vol. 12, no. 3.
Gibson, T. (1993) *Danger: Opportunity*, Telford, Neighbourhood Initiatives Foundation.
Giddens, A. (1994) *Beyond Left and Right: The Future of Radical Politics*, Cambridge, Polity Press.

Glover, J. (1977) *Causing Death and Saving Lives*, Harmondsworth, Penguin.
Gomex, M. and J. Schneider (1992) 'Euro Works Council', *Die Mitbestimmung* (Special English edition of the Journal of the Hans-Bockler Foundation).
Goodhart, D. (1994) *The Reshaping of the German Social Market*, London, IPPR.
Gorbachev, M. (1993) 'Man in Changing World', *First*, vol. 7, no. 4,.
Gran, G. (1983) *Development by People: Citizen Construction of a Just World*, New York, Praeger.
Grant, C. (1995) 'Delors: After Power', *Prospect*, October.
Gray, J. (1993) *Beyond the New Right*, London, Routledge.
Gray, J. (1995a) 'Beggering Our Own Neighbours', *Guardian*, 17 February.
Gray, J. (1995b) *Issiah Berlin*, London, HarperCollins.
Guthrie, W. K. C. (1990) *Aristotle: An Encounter*, Cambridge University Press.
Gutmann, A. (1987) *Democratic Education*, Princeton, NJ., Princeton University Press.
Gutmann, A. (1992) 'Communitarian Critics of Liberalism', in Avineri and de-Shalit (eds) (1992).
Gutmann, A. (1995) 'Civic Education and Social Diversity', *Ethics*, vol. 105, no. 3, Apri.
Gyford, J. (1991) *Citizens, Consumers & Councils*, London, Macmillan.
Habermas, J. (1984) *The Theory of Communicative Action*, vol. 1, trans. T. McCarthy, Boston, Mass., Beacon.
Habermas, J. (1992) *Autonomy and Solidarity*, ed. P. Dews, London, Verso.
Hacking, I. (ed.) (1981) *Scientific Revolutions*, Oxford University Press.
Haigh, G. (1995) 'Europe in the Frame', *Times Educational Supplement*, 28 July .
Hall J. A. (ed.) (1995) *Civil Society*, Cambridge, Polity Press.
Hamner, C. J. (1995) 'Community-building Strategies in Smaller Cities: Longview and Tyler, Texas', *The Responsive Community*, vol. 5, no. 3, Summer.
Handy, C. (1994) *The Empty Raincoat*, London, Hutchinson.
Handy, C. (1996) 'Let's Be Citizens, Not Mercenaries', *Management Today*, October.
Hanfling, O. (1976) 'Hume and Wittgenstein', in G. Vesey (ed.) (1976).
Harris, A. (1996) 'Wanted: Insiders', *Management Today*, July.
Haste, H. (1993) 'Moral Creativity and Education for Citizenship', *Creativity Research Journal*, vol. 6, (nos 1 and 2).
Hayek, F. (1944) *The Road to Serfdom*, London, Routledge and Kegan Paul.
Healy, K. (1996) 'Peirce, Community and Belief', *Prospero*, vol. 2, no. 2.
Heater, D. (1990) *Citizenship: The Civic Ideal in World History, Politics and Education*, Harlow, Longman.
Hegel, G. W. F. (1942) *Philosophy of Right*, trans. T. M. Knox, Oxford, Clarendon.
Held, D. (ed.) (1993) *Prospects for Democracy*, Cambridge, Polity Press.
Heller, R. (1994) 'The Manager's Dilemma', *Management Today*, January.

Heller, R. (1995) 'Unlocking Business's Potential', *Management Today*, May.

Hewitt, P. (1993) *About Time: The Revolution in Work and Family Life*, London, Rivers Oram Press.

Hickman, L. A. (1990) *John Dewey's Pragmatic Technology*, Bloomington and Indianapolis, Ind., Indiana University Press.

Hill, C. (1991) *The Intellectual Origins of the English Revolution*, Oxford University Press.

Hirst, P. (1993) 'Associational Democracy', in D. Held (ed.), *Prospects for Democracy*, Cambridge, Polity Press.

Hirst, P. (1994) *Associative Democracy: New Forms of Social and Economic Governance*, Cambridge, Polity Press.

Hirszowicz, M. (1977) 'Industrial Democracy, Self-management and Social Control of Production', in L. Kolakowski and S. Hampshire (ed.) (1977).

Hobbes T. (1968) *Leviathan*, Harmondsworth, Penguin.

Hobhouse, L. T. (1921) *The Rational Good*, London, George Allen & Unwin.

Hobhouse, L. T. (1966) *Social Development*, London, George Allen & Unwin.

Hobhouse, L. T. (1994) *Liberalism and Other Writings*, ed. J. Meadowcroft, Cambridge University Press.

Hockey, L. (1997) *Partners in Learning: Ten Community Based Case Studies*, London, LGMB.

Hogg, C. (1994) 'The POW in Empowerment', *Human Resources*, no. 70, Winter.

Hollenbach, D. (1994/95) 'Beyond the Public–Private Dichotomy', *The Responsive Community*, vol. 5, no. 1, Winter.

Hollis, M. and S. Lukes (eds) (1983) *Rationality and Relativism*, Oxford, Basil Blackwell.

Holloway, D. (1972) 'Scientific Truth and Political Authority in the Soviet Union', in L. Schapiro (ed.), *Political Opposition in One-Party States*, London, Macmillan.

Horkheimer, M. and T. Adorno (1972) *The Dialectic of Enlightenment*, New York, Herder and Herder.

Howard League (1997) 'Join the Howard League Today', leaflet, London, Howard League.

Howe, S. (1991) 'Citizenship in the New Europe', in G. Andrews (ed.), *Citizenship*, London, Lawrence & Wishart.

Hsu, I. C. Y. (1983) *The Rise of Modern China*, Oxford University Press.

Hudson, S. D. (1986) *Human Character and Morality*, London, Routledge & Kegan Paul.

Hudson, W. D. (ed.) (1969) *The Is/Ought Question*, London, Macmillan.

Hume, D. (1975) *Enquiries Concerning Human Understanding and Concerning the Principles of Morals*, L. A. Selby-Brigge and P. H. Nidditch (eds), Oxford University Press.

Hume, D. (1978) *A Treatise of Human Nature*, L. A. Selby-Brigge and P. H. Nidditch (eds), Oxford University Press.

Hunt, G. M. K. (1990) *Philosophy and Politics*, Cambridge University Press.

Hutton, W. (1995) *The State We're In*, London, Jonathan Cape.

Iannone, A. P. (ed.) (1989) *Contemporary Moral Controversies in Business,* Oxford University Press.

Institute for Citizenship Studies Report (1994) *Learning for Citizenship,* London, Institute for Citizenship Studies.

Jacobs, M. (1996) *The Politics of the Real World,* London, Earthscan.

Joas, H. (1994/5) 'Communitarianism in Germany', *The Responsive Community,* vol. 5, no. 1, Winter.

John Lewis Partnership Report and Accounts (1995) London, John Lewis Partnership.

Johnson, T. (1993) *Strategies for Democratic Employee Ownership,* Leeds, Industrial Common Ownership Movement Ltd.

Journal of the Japan Local Government Centre (1997) 'A Welfare System for a Rapidly Ageing Population', *Journal of the Japan Local Government Centre,* no. 22, Spring.

Kainz, H. P. (1988) *Ethics in Context,* London, Macmillan Press.

Kanter, R. M. (1992) *The Change Masters,* London, Routledge.

Kay, J. (1993) *Foundations of Corporate Success,* Oxford University Press.

Kean, D. (1996) 'A New Community Explodes Into Life', *Municipal Journal,* 12 July.

Kidder, R. M. (1994) *Shared Values for a Troubled World,* San Francisco: Jossey-Bass.

King, D. (1987) *The New Right: Politics, Markets, and Citizenship,* London, Macmillan.

Kinsky, F. (1995) *Federalism: A Global Theory,* Nice, Centre International de Formation Européenne.

Kitson, M. (1995) *Seedcorn or Chaff? Unemployment and Small Firm Performance,* Cambridge, ESRC Centre for Business Research.

Kloppenberg, J. T. (1986) *Uncertain Victory: Social Democracy and Progressivism in European and American Thought, 1870–1920,* Oxford University Press.

Knight, B. and P. Stokes (1996) *The Deficit in Civil Society,* Birmingham, Foundation for Civil Society.

Kolakowski, L. and S. Hampshire (ed.) (1977) *The Socialist Idea: A Reappraisal,* London, Quartet Books.

Kooiman, J. (1993) *Modern Governance: New Government–Society Interactions,* London, Sage.

Kozol, J. (1993) 'The Sharks Move In', *New Internationalist,* no. 248, October.

Kuhn, T. (1970) *The Structure of Scientific Revolutions,* University of Chicago Press.

Kymlicka, W. and W. Norman (1994) 'Return of the Citizen: A Survey of Recent Work on Citizenship Theory', *Ethics,* vol. 104, no. 2, January.

Lakatos, I. and A. Musgrave (eds) (1979) *Criticism and the Growth of Knowledge,* Cambridge University Press.

Laslet, P. and J. Fishkin (eds) (1979) *Philosophy, Politics and Society* (5th series), Oxford, Basil Blackwell.

Leadbeater, C. (1997) *The Rise of the Social Entrepreneur,* London, Demos.

Lemming, J. (1994) 'Character Education and the Creation of Community', *The Responsive Community,* vol. 4, no. 4, Fall.

Lester T. (1993) 'The Gores' Happy Family', *Management Today*, February.
Levi, I. (1984) *Decisions and Revisions*, Cambridge University Press.
Levi, I. (1992) 'Conflict and Inquiry', *Ethics*, vol. 102, no. 4 July.
Lippmann, W. (1972) *The Phantom Public*, New York, Macmillan.
Lichtenberg, J. (1994) 'Moral Certainty', *Philosophy*, vol. 69, no. 268 April.
Lightfoot, J. (1990) *Involving Young People in their Communities*, London, Community Development Foundation.
Livingston, D. W. (1984) *Hume's Philosophy of Common Life*, University of Chicago Press.
Loney, M., R. Bocock, J. Clarke, A. Cochrane, P. Graham and M. Wilson (1991) *The State or the Market*, London, Sage.
Lukes, S. (1973) *Emile Durkheim: His Life and Work*, Harmondsworth, Penguin.
Lyotard, J.-F. (1988) 'The Postmodern Condition', in K. Baynes, J. Bohman and T. McCarthy (eds), *After Philosophy*, Cambridge, Mass., MIT Press.
Macedo, S. (1995) 'Liberal Civic Education and Religious Fundamentalism', *Ethics*, vol. 105, no. 3, April.
Machan, T. (1989) *Individuals and Their Rights*, La Salle, Open Court.
MacIntyre, A. (1967) *A Short History of Ethics*, London, Routledge & Kegan Paul.
MacIntyre, A. (1981) *After Virtue*, London, Duckworth.
MacIntyre, A. (1988) *Whose Justice? Which Rationality?*, London, Duckworth.
Macmurray, J. (1932) *Freedom in the Modern World*, London, Faber.
Macmurray, J. (1935) *Reason and Emotion*, London, Faber.
Macmurray, J. (1941) *Challenge to the Churches: Religion and Democracy*, London, Kegan Paul.
Macpherson, C. B. (1962) *The Political Theory of Possessive Individualism*, Oxford University Press.
Macpherson, C. B. (1979) *The Life and Times of Liberal Democracy*, Oxford University Press.
Macpherson, C. B. (1985) *The Rise and Fall of Economic Justice*, Oxford University Press.
Management Today Report on NFC (1993) *Management Today*, March.
Mandeville, B. (1989) *The Fable of the Bees*, Harmondsworth, Penguin.
Marquand, D. (1988) *The Unprincipled Society*, London, Fontana.
Marquand, D. (1995) 'The Political Lowlands' Flood of Fears', *Guardian*, 3 February.
Martin, B. (1993) *In the Public Interest? Privatisation and Public Sector Reform*, London, Zed Books.
Marx, K. and F. Engels (1977) *The Communist Manifesto*, trans. S. Moore, Harmondsworth, Penguin.
McConnell, C. (1991) *Promoting Community Development in Europe*, London, Community Development Foundation.
McCormick, J. (1994) *Citizens' Service*, London, IPPR.
McLaughlin, T. H. (1992) 'Citizenship, Diversity and Education: A Philosophical Perspective', *Journal of Moral Education*, vol. 21, no. 3.

McLaughlin, T. H. (1996) 'Educating Responsible Citizens', in H. Tam (ed.) (1996a).

Melo, A. (1996) 'The Voice of the People', *Leda*, no. 11, Spring.

Meyer-Bisch, P. (ed.) (1995) *Culture of Democracy: A Challenge for Schools*, Paris, UNESCO.

Midgley, M. and J. Hughes (1995) 'Trouble with Families', in B. Almond (ed.) (1995).

Mill, J. S. (1972) *Utilitarianism, On Liberty and Considerations on Representative Government*, (ed.) H. B. Acton, London, J. M. Dent.

Mill, J. S. (1987) *On Socialism*, Buffalo, NY., Prometheus Books.

Mill, J. S. (1980) *On Bentham and Coleridge*, Cambridge University Press.

Mill, J. S. (1994) *Principles of Political Economy*, Oxford University Press.

Miller, D. (1990) *Market, State and Community*, Oxford, Clarendon Press.

Miller, D. (1993) 'Deliberative Democracy and Social Choice', in D. Held (ed.) (1993).

Misgeld, D. (1987) 'The Limits of a Theory of Practice', in E. Simpson (ed.) *Anti-Foundationalism and Practical Reasoning*, Edmonton, Alberta, Academic Printing & Publishing.

Molander, E. A. (1980) *Responsive Capitalism*, New York, McGraw-Hill.

Moore, J. F. (1996) *The Death of Competition*, Chichester, John Wiley.

Mouffe, C. (ed.) (1992) *Dimensions of Radical Democracy: Pluralism, Citizenship and Community*, London, Verso.

Mounier, E. (1952) *Personalism*, London, Routledge.

Mudd, P. (1997) *Lifetime Learning*, London, LGMB.

Mulhal, S. and A. Swift (1992) *Liberals and Communitarians*, Oxford, Basil Blackwell.

Muller, J. Z. (1993) *Adam Smith In His Time and Ours*, New York, Free Press.

Mulligan, J. (1995) *Take Part! Service Learning in Schools*, London, Community Service Volunteers.

Murphy, J. G. (1995) 'Crime and Punishment: Where does Repentance Fit?', *The Responsive Community*, vol. 5, no. 4, Fall.

Murphy, P. E. (1994) 'European Managers' Views on Corporate Ethics', *Business Ethics: A European Review*, vol. 3, no. 3, July.

New Internationalist (1993) *New Internationalist*, August.

Newman, M. (1996) *Democracy, Sovereignty and the European Union*, London, Hurst & Co.

Nietzsche, F. (1972) *Beyond Good and Evil*, Harmondsworth, Penguin.

Nietzsche, F. (1988) *Thus Spoke Zarathustra*, Harmondsworth, Penguin.

Norman, E. (1979) *Christianity and the World Order*, Oxford University Press.

Nozick, R. (1974) *Anarchy, State and Utopia*, New York, Basic Books.

Oldfield A. (1990) *Citizenship and Community: Civic Republicanism and the Modern World*, London, Routledge.

Ormell, C. (1996) 'Individual versus social values', in H. Tam (ed.) (1996a).

Ormerod, P. (1994) *The Death of Economics*, London, Faber & Faber.

Osborn, S. and H. Shaftoe (1997) *Crime – the Local Solution*, London, LGMB.

Osborne, D. (1992) 'Beyond Left and Right: A New Political Paradigm', *The Responsive Community*, vol. 2, no. 2, Spring.

Panitch, L. (1986) 'The Impasse of Social Democratic Politics', in *The Socialist Register*, London, Merlin, 1985/6.

Parekh, B. (1995) 'Oakeshott's Theory of Association', *Ethics*, vol. 106, no. 1 October.

Parker, D. and S. Martin (1993) 'Testing Time for Privatisation', *Management Today*, August.

Pateman, C. (1970) *Participation and Democratic Theory*, Cambridge University Press.

Paul, J. (ed.) (1983) *Reading Nozick*, Oxford, Basil Blackwell.

Pearce, J. (1993) *At the Heart of the Community Economy*, London, Calouste Gulbenkian Foundation.

Pérez-Ramos, A. (1988) *Francis Bacon's Idea of Science and the Maker's Knowledge Tradition*, Oxford, Clarendon Press.

Peters, R. S. (ed.) (1973) *The Philosophy of Education*, Oxford University Press.

Peters, T. (1992) *Liberation Management: Necessary Disorganization for the Nanosecond Nineties*, New York, Alfred A. Knopf.

Phillips, D. L. (1993) *Looking Backward: A Critical Appraisal of Communitarian Thought*, Princeton, NJ., Princeton University Press.

Phillips, M. (1993) 'Plain-speaking Founder of New Moral Order', *Observer*, 24 October.

Pickard, J. (1993) 'The Real Meaning of Empowerment', *Personnel Management*, November.

Plato (1975) *The Republic*, Harmondsworth, Penguin.

Popper, K. (1973) *The Open Society and Its Enemies*, London, Routledge & Kegan Paul.

Prior, D., J. Stewart and K. Walsh (1995) *Citizenship: Rights, Community & Participation*, London, Pitman.

Purver, M. (1967) *The Royal Society*, Cambridge, Mass., MIT Press.

Putnam, R. D. (1995) 'Bowling Alone, Revisited', *The Responsive Community*, vol. 5, no. 2, Spring.

Pybus, E. and T. H. McLaughlin (1995) *Values, Education and Responsibility*, St Andrews, Centre for Philosophy and Public Affairs.

Ranson, S. and J. Stewart (1994) *Management for the Public Domain*, London, Macmillan.

Rasmussen, D. (1989) 'Individual Rights and Human Flourishing', *Public Affairs Quarterly*, vol. 5.

Rassam, C. (1993) 'Science in Crisis', *Management Today*, June.

Ratner, J. (ed.) (1939) *Intelligence in the Modern World: John Dewey's Philosophy*, New York, Random House.

Rawls, J.(1973) *A Theory of Justice*, Oxford University Press.

Regan, D. H. (1980) *Utilitarianism and Co-operation*, Oxford, Clarendon Press.

Reischauer, E. O. (1964) *Japan: Past and Present*, Tokyo, Charles E. Tuttle.

Report of the Wetenschappelijk Instituut voor het CDA (1996) *Dignity and Truth: Civil Society and European Cooperation*, The Hague, Wetenschappelijk Instituut voor het CDA.

Responsive Community (1991/2) 'The First Communitarian Teach-in', *Responsive Community*, vol. 2, no. 1, Winter.

Ridley, M. (1996) *The Origins of Virtue*, London, Viking.

Robson, J. M. (1968) *The Improvement of Mankind: The Social and Political Thought of John Stuart Mill*, London, Routledge & Kegan Paul.

Roche, M. (1992) *Rethinking Citizenship: Welfare, Ideology and Change in Modern Society*, Cambridge, Polity Press.

Rorty, R. (1989) *Contingency, Irony and Solidarity*, Cambridge University Press.

Rousseau, J. J. (1968) *The Social Contract*, trans. M. Cranston, Harmondsworth, Penguin.

RSA Inquiry (1995) *Tomorrow's Company*, London, RSA.

Ryan, A. (1995) *John Dewey and the High Tide of American Liberalism*, New York, W. W. Norton.

Saffran, D. (1996) 'Public Housing Safety versus Tenants' Rights', *The Responsive Community*, vol. 6, no. 4, Fall.

Sandel, M. (1982) *Liberalism and the Limits of Justice*, Cambridge University Press.

Schama, S. (1989) *Citizens: A Chronicle of the French Revolution*, Harmondsworth, Penguin.

Schapiro, L. (1972) *Totalitarianism*, London, Macmillan.

Scharping, R. (1996) 'Freedom, Solidarity, Individual Responsibility' *The Responsive Community*, vol. 6, no. 4, Fall.

Schumpeter, J. A. (1976) *Capitalism, Socialism and Democracy*, London, George Allen & Unwin.

Selbourne, D. (1994) *The Principle of Duty*, London, Sinclair-Stevenson.

Selznick, P. (1992) *The Moral Commonwealth: Social Theory and the Promise of Community*, Berkeley and Los Angeles: University of California Press.

Semler, R. (1994) *Maverick*, London, Arrow.

Simpson, E. (ed.) (1987) *Anti-Foundationalism and Practical Reasoning*, Edmonton, Alberta, Academic Printing & Publishing.

Skillen, T. (1996) 'Community, Communities and the Education of Citizens', in H. Tam (ed.) (1996a).

Skinner Q. (1992) 'On Justice, the Common Good, and the Priority of Liberty', in C. Mouffe (ed.) (1992).

Sleeper, R. W. (1986) *The Necessity of Pragmatism*, New Haven, Conn., Yale University Press.

Smith, A. (1979) *An Inquiry into the Nature and Causes of the Wealth of Nations*, Glasgow, Oxford University Press.

Smith, C. (1997) 'Intranets for Citizens', *Electronic Public Information*, London, SPIN.

Snowdon, R. (1996) 'Mood of the Nation', *Marketing*, 4 January.

Solomon, R. C. (1993) *Ethics and Excellence: Co-operation and Integrity in Business*, New York, Oxford University Press.

Sorel, G. (1915) *Reflections on Violence*, trans. T. E. Hulme, London, Allen & Unwin.

Sorensen, G. (1993) *Democracy and Democratization*, Boulder, Col., Westview Press.

Soskice, D. (1996) 'The Stake We're In', *Prospect*, April.
Spencer, H. (1884) *The Man versus the State*, London, F. H. Collins.
Steele, J. (1995) 'Suppression of Protest', *Guardian*, 11 November.
Steinfels, P. (1992) 'Ideas and Trends', *New York Times*, 24 May.
Sterba, J. P. (1994) 'From Liberty to Welfare', *Ethics*, vol. 105, no. 1.
Stewart, J., E. Kendall and A. Coote (1994) *Citizens' Juries*, London, IPPR.
Stewart, J. (1995) *Innovation in Democratic Practice*, Birmingham, INLOGOV.
Stewart, J. and H. Tam (1997) *Putting Citizens First*, London, MJ/ SOLACE.
Stone, N. (1994) 'There Can Never Be a Middle Way', *Sunday Times*, 9 October.
Strawson, P. F. (1987) *Skepticism and Naturalism*, London, Methuen.
Sutcliffe, R. (1995) 'Philosophy for Children: A Community of Enquiry', *Prospero*, vol. 1, no. 2.
Swift, R. (1990) 'Fundamentalism: Reaching for Certainty', *New Internationalist*, no. 210, August.
Tam, H. (1981) 'Sources and Perspectives of Social Democracy', *Samizdat*, Trinity 1981, Oxford University Social Studies Centre.
Tam, H. (1990) *Responsibility and Personal Interactions: A Philosophical Study of the Criteria for Responsibility Ascriptions*, Lampeter, Edwin Mellen Press.
Tam, H. (1993a) *Serving the Public*, Harlow, Longman.
Tam, H. (1993b) 'How We Should Live', *The Philosopher*, October.
Tam, H. (1994a) *Citizenship Development: Towards an Organizational Model*, Luton, Local Government Management Board.
Tam, H. (ed.) (1994b) *Marketing, Competition and the Public Sector*, Harlow, Longman.
Tam, H. (1994c) 'Empowerment: Too Big a Task?' *Professional Manager*, March.
Tam, H. (ed.) (1995a) *The Citizens' Agenda*, Cambridge, White Horse Press.
Tam, H. (1995b) 'Crime and Responsibility', in B. Almond (ed.) (1995).
Tam, H. (1995c) 'Enabling Structures', in D. Atkinson (ed.) *Cities of Pride*, London, Cassell.
Tam, H. (ed.) (1996a) *Punishment, Excuses and Moral Development*, Aldershot, Avebury.
Tam, H. (1996b) 'Education and the Communitarian Movement', *Journal for Pastoral Care in Education*, September.
Tam, H. (1996c) *Haverhill Regeneration*, Bury St Edmunds, St Edmundsbury Borough Council.
Tarrant, J. M. (1989) *Democracy and Education*, Aldershot, Avebury.
Tarrow, S. (1994) *Power in Movement*, Cambridge University Press.
Tassin, E. (1992) 'Europe: A Political Community', in C. Mouffe (ed.).
Taverner, P. (1996) 'Will They Work?', *Children's Services News*, August.
Tawney, R. H. (1927) *The Acquisitive Society*, London, G. Bell and Sons.
Tawney, R. H. (1964) *The Radical Tradition*, Harmondsworth, Penguin.
Taylor, C. (1971) *Philosophical Papers*, vols 1 and 2, Cambridge University Press.
Taylor, C. (1983) 'Rationality', in M. Hollis and S. Lukes (1983).

Taylor, C. (1990) *Sources of the Self*, Cambridge University Press.
Taylor, C. (1993) 'The Dangers of Soft Despotism', *The Responsive Community*, vol. 3, no. 4, Fall.
Thomson, G. (1987) *Needs*, London, Routledge & Kegan Paul.
Towers, G. (1995) *Building Democracy*, London, UCL Press.
Thomas, R. (1989) *The British Philosophy of Administration*, Cambridge, Centre for Business and Public Sector Ethics.
Treitschke, H. von, (1916) *Politics*, trans. B. Dugdale and T. de Bille, London, Constable.
Turner, B. (ed.) (1993) *Citizenship and Social Theory*, London, Sage.
Twine, F. (1994) *Citizenship and Social Rights*, London, Sage.
Unger, P. (1975) *Ignorance: A Case for Scepticism*, Oxford, Clarendon Press.
Urbach, P. (1987) *Francis Bacon's Philosophy of Science*, La Salle, Illinois, Open Court.
Urquhart, B. and E. Childers (1990) *A World in Need of Leadership: Tomorrow's United Nations*, Uppsala, Dag Hammarskjold Foundation.
Utting, D., J. Bright and C. Henricson (1993) *Crime and the Family*, London, Family Policy Studies Centre.
Van der Gaag, N. (1996) 'Field of Dreams', *New Internationalist*, no. 283, September.
Veatch, R. M. (1976) *Death, Dying, and the Biological Revolution*, New Haven, Conn., and London, Yale University Press.
Vesey, G. (ed.) (1976) *Impressions of Empiricism*, London, Macmillan.
Vidal, J. and A. Harvey (1996) *One Thousand Days*, London, *Guardian* and WWF-UK.
Walker, M. (1995) 'Community Spirit', *Guardian*, 13 March.
Walsh, K. (1994) 'The Impact of Competition', in H. Tam (ed.) (1994b).
Walzer, M. (1983) *Spheres of Justice*, New York, Basic Books.
Walzer, M. (1987) *Interpretation and Social Criticism*, Cambridge, Mass., Harvard University Press.
Walzer, M. (1989) *The Company of Critics*, London, Peter Halban.
Walzer, M. (1992) 'The Civil Society Argument', in C. Mouffe (ed.) (1992).
Walzer, M. (1994) *Thick and Thin*, Notre Dame, Ind., University of Notre Dame Press.
Warnock, M. (1973) 'Towards a Definition of Quality in Education', in R. S. Peters (ed.) (1973).
Wellington, P. (1996) 'Shifting Fundamental Values in Customer Care', *Professional Manager*, May.
Wesolowski, W. (1995) 'The Nature of Social Ties and the Future of Postcommunist Society', in J. A. Hall (ed.) (1995).
Wheeler, D. and M. Sillanpaa (1997) *The Stakeholder Corporation*, London, Pitman.
Wilkinson, R. (1991) 'Inequality is Bad for Your Health', *Guardian*, 12 June.
Willetts, D. (1994) *Civic Conservatism*, London, The Social Market Foundation.
Wilson, J. (1987) *A Preface to Morality*, London, Macmillan.

Winch, P. (1958) *The Idea of a Social Science and its Relation to Philosophy*, London, Routledge & Kegan Paul.

Winkler, A. (1994) 'Centre of Attention', *Times Higher Education Supplement*, 15 April.

Wittgenstein, L. (1978) *Philosophical Investigations*, Oxford, Basil Blackwell.

Wittgenstein, L. (1979) *On Certainty*, Oxford, Basil Blackwell.

Wolff, R. P. (1983) 'Robert Nozick's Derivation of the Minimal State', in J. Paul (ed.) (1983).

World Summit for Social Development Report (1995) *The Copenhagen Declaration and Programme for Action*, New York, United Nations Department of Public Information.

Wragg, T. (ed.) (1993) *Education: A Different Vision*, London, IPPR.

Wright, E. O. (ed.) (1995) *Associations and Democracy*, London, Verso.

Young, M. and A. H. Halsey (1995) *Family and Community Socialism*, London, IPPR.

Index